HOW TO
PRAY

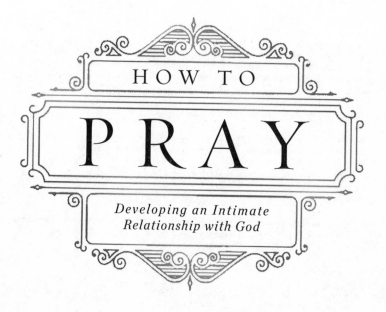

HOW TO

PRAY

*Developing an Intimate
Relationship with God*

RONNIE
FLOYD

W PUBLISHING GROUP

An Imprint of Thomas Nelson

Published in Nashville, Tennessee, by W Publishing, an imprint of Thomas Nelson.

Thomas Nelson titles may be purchased in bulk for educational, business, fund-raising, or sales promotional use. For information, please e-mail SpecialMarkets@ThomasNelson.com.

Unless otherwise noted, Scripture quotations are taken from New American Standard Bible®. Copyright © 1960, 1962, 1963, 1968, 1971, 1972, 1973, 1975, 1977, 1995 by The Lockman Foundation. Used by permission. (www.Lockman.org)

Scripture quotations marked CSB are from the Christian Standard Bible®. Copyright © 2017 by Holman Bible Publishers. Used by permission. Christian Standard Bible®, and CSB® are federally registered trademarks of Holman Bible Publishers.

Scripture quotations marked KJV are from the King James Version. Public domain.

Scripture quotations marked NKJV are from the New King James Version®. © 1982 by Thomas Nelson. Used by permission. All rights reserved.

Any Internet addresses, phone numbers, or company or product information printed in this book are offered as a resource and are not intended in any way to be or to imply an endorsement by Thomas Nelson, nor does Thomas Nelson vouch for the existence, content, or services of these sites, phone numbers, companies, or products beyond the life of this book.

ISBN 978-0-7852-2483-9 (TP)
ISBN 978-0-7852-2481-5 (eBook)
ISBN 978-1-4041-1134-9 (custom)

Library of Congress Cataloging-in-Publication Data

Names: Floyd, Ronnie W., 1955- author.
Title: How to pray : developing an intimate relationship with God / Ronnie
  Floyd.
Description: Nashville : W. Publishing Group, 2019. | Originally published:
  Nashville : Word Pub., c1999. | Includes bibliographical references.
Identifiers: LCCN 2018049583 | ISBN 9780785224839 (softcover)
Subjects: LCSH: Prayer--Christianity.
Classification: LCC BV215 .F58 2019 | DDC 248.3/2--dc23
LC record available at https://lccn.loc.gov/2018049583

Printed in the United States of America

19 20 21 22 23   LSC   10 9 8 7 6 5 4 3 2 1

I want to dedicate How to Pray *to my Cross Church family, who has prayed me through all of our years together! One thousand thank-yous!*

CONTENTS

PART FOUR: BARRIERS TO PRAYER

PART FIVE: PRAYING FOR OTHERS

ONE THOUSAND THANK-YOUS

One thousand thank-yous to every person who has helped bring this book about prayer into reality.

I want to say one thousand thank-yous to:

Debbie Wickwire and the entire team from the W Publishing Group of Thomas Nelson, for wanting to provide people with this helpful tool, *How to Pray*.

Brian Dunaway and the Cross Church media team for working with Debbie Wickwire and the W Publishing team on the cover for *How to Pray*.

Gayla Oldham, Melissa Swain, and Dr. Ed Upton for assisting me in this project personally by providing counsel and editing content for *How to Pray*.

Austin Wilson and Robert Wolgemuth of Wolgemuth & Associates, who have coached me and worked with W Publishing to bring about *How to Pray*.

Jonathan Williams and Johnnie Moore of The Kairos Company, for always helping me advance the cause of Christ through writing projects like *How to Pray* and assisting me in sharing its message with America and across the world.

Jeana, my wife, who has sacrificed hours of our time together for the sake of sharing the message of *How to Pray* with others.

To each of you and many others, one thousand thank-yous! Let's tell the world together this message of *How to Pray*.

A DEFINING MOMENT

L ast year when I had the distinct privilege to lead the national observance of the National Day of Prayer in Statuary Hall in the United States Capitol Building, it was truly a great moment in my life. As the president of the National Day of Prayer Task Force, I help mobilize unified public prayer for America. On the first Thursday of May each year, thousands of prayer observances occur across this nation and involve millions of people in prayer for America on the National Day of Prayer.

Being in this historic setting and having this overwhelming responsibility did not occur because of personal charisma or public performance. It was entrusted to me because of my belief in "the secret place." This secret place is not a physical location but a spiritual position. The secret place is wherever you meet God and connect with Him personally.

Jesus said, "But when you pray, go into your private room, shut your door, and pray to your Father who is in secret. And your Father who sees in secret will reward you" (Matthew 6:6 CSB).

Jesus' call to me is to come away with Him in private and connect with Him intimately. In His presence, I develop an intimate relationship with God.

James 4:10 has dominated my life this year, and God has driven it home again and again. This continual call from the Word of God by the Spirit of God to me says, "Humble yourselves before the Lord, and he will exalt you" (CSB).

Humbling myself before the Lord daily in the secret place has defined my life and continues to do so. But I want to be more than clear: it was not on a stage in the dignified Statuary Hall of the United States Capitol Building where God defined me.

What Defines Me Occurred Many Years Ago

There is nothing like a defining moment in your life.

I clearly remember a defining moment that occurred during the closing weeks of my freshman year of college. I was so young. I was open and willing to do the will of God in my life. I came to college not knowing one soul. Yet I was on fire for God. My passion was alive, and His calling was clear to me.

During my first year in college, I met fellow students who were in love with God just like I was. We wanted to please God. We wanted to grow. Our personal passion for God was great. This passion to please God compelled me to accompany a friend to the Dallas/Fort Worth metroplex to attend a Bible conference in which his father was one of the speakers. Little did I know that God had designed this experience to shape my entire life and ministry. It would lead to defining my life even to this day.

This defining moment did not occur inside of a worship center as a response to a biblical message. It occurred late one evening in a restaurant where my friend's father had arranged for us to spend some private time with a godly man. My physical hunger was great, but my spiritual hunger was even greater.

As I listened to this man share his wisdom with us, I was even more encouraged to go deeper with God. Before we left the restaurant, I was eager to ask him how to be a godly minister, so I asked him something like, "Sir, if there is one thing we need to know as young preachers, what is it?" His penetrating eyes looked into mine, and he said, "Ronnie, if you will learn to spend one hour a day with God, there is no telling what God may choose to do with you."

I didn't have any better sense than to take that man at his word. Since that day in 1975, I have honored his challenge to me. His challenge stirred me to prayer. Even though I did not know then what I know today about the subject, I wanted to be a man of prayer.

That night, God began to define who I was to be as a man of God. What appeared to be just a late-night meal in a restaurant became a turning point for me. It was a God moment. Truly, it was one of the most defining moments of my life, perhaps the most defining moment of all.

My lifelong journey toward serious prayer began that evening. I had already taken an introductory prayer course in my college studies. However, on this particular spring evening in Texas, I began my own Prayer 101, a simple introduction to a never-ending call to prayer.

Since that time, I have witnessed God's involvement in my life in many ways. I have seen God heal my wife from cancer. I have seen God move in the lives of both of my children by using them as instruments to win others to Christ. I have seen God interrupt church services with His power. I have seen God bring true revival to His people. I have preached to thousands in convention settings and even a million-plus men on the National Mall in Washington, DC. As the president of the Southern Baptist Convention for two years, I led thousands of spiritual leaders in meaningful, purposeful prayer gatherings.

Additionally, I have also experienced the discipline of God upon my life because of my pride. I have gone through moments of disappointments and periodic moments of discouragement. I have experienced what it is like to walk with God through extended periods of fasting and prayer. I have known what it is like to be overwhelmed with God's presence and absolutely amazed at how He chooses to use me.

Why has this occurred? I am a small-town boy from Texas, raised in a small church with a bi-vocational pastor. I am not someone enabled with great gifts. I do not have the charisma that marks many great leaders, nor the powerful physical presence.

I am confident that it goes back to the defining moment that took place in that restaurant in 1975. I have seen God move in my life because I have been obedient to God's call to prayer. By His grace, I humbly stand amazed at what God does in me and even through my life.

I have not always known, and still do not know today, all the ins and outs of prayer. I am not a prayer guru. I am just like you. I, too, am on a journey of learning what it is like to commune with God through prayer. I come to God each morning with the same request His disciples made of Him: "Lord, teach [me] to pray" (Luke 11:1).

I hope this book will inspire you to pray. I hope it will give you a vision for what God will do in and through you when you pray.

Are you ready to go to a new level in your prayer life? *How to Pray* is a how-to book, not a you-should book. We will let the Bible teach us and the Spirit inspire us to pray.

We cannot let anything stand in the way of learning how to pray. I believe that when these walls come down, our prayers go up. I believe prayer can ignite you to pursue an intimate relationship with God.

I am convinced that if we will deepen our walk with God, He will broaden our influence in the future. This influence does not come because of your ability, but it comes because of prayer.

God can do anything at any time with anyone anywhere. God can do more in a moment than you can do in a lifetime.

The more you enter into the secret place of prayer, the more you will see God operate in your life in this dimension.

This book is a call to action. Now is the time for you to pray.

Twenty Years Ago

Twenty years ago, this book was initially released. On the twentieth anniversary of this book, the publisher wanted to release a newly written and amended anniversary edition. If you read *How to Pray* twenty years ago, you did not read this book.

This book is different, as I have rewritten this book entirely. I have added new chapters:

- How to Pray for the Sick
- How to Pray for Your Family
- How to Pray for Your Pastor and Church
- How to Pray for America

You will discover that this powerful section will lead you to enter into territory that will deepen your love for Christ and enlarge your influence through prayer.

This book is different because I am different. I am not the same man I was twenty years ago. God has taught me so much more about prayer, and I have shared so much of it with you in this book, *How to Pray*.

I want to ask you to get ready to go up in your life. The way up is down. The way up is private. The way up is discovered in learning how to pray more effectively.

Do not underestimate this: *The last thing Satan, your enemy, wants you to do is pray.* He will fight it. He will do whatever it takes to keep you from reading this book in its entirety. He will distract you any time you pray.

Satan knows that he is in trouble if you learn to pray. He knows that prayer initiates the power of God. This is why Satan hates prayer. Do not fear: *God is more powerful than Satan.*

God has used prayer to define my life. I pray that the same kind of God moment I had in a restaurant in my collegiate years will happen for you when you read *How to Pray*. May this be a defining moment in your life.

PART I

AN INTRODUCTION TO PRAYER

CHAPTER 1

WHAT PRAYER IS
ALL ABOUT

The history of God's people is decorated with men and women of prayer. Volumes have been written about men and women of God who knew how to fall before God at the altar of prayer until their prayers were answered. Countless stories have been told about how some of these prayer veterans even gave their lives calling out to the Lord. I know of no greater accolade for any believer on this side of heaven than to be known as a prayer warrior.

As I read about prayer warriors in the Scriptures, I would love to have the boldness of Moses, who represented God's people before the Lord. I am intrigued by the faith of Elijah, who called down the fire of God to consume the false prophets of Baal. I long for the passion of Ezra as he held forth the Word of God and the people fell on their faces before God in repentance, prayer, and fasting. I crave to have the transparency before the Lord that David had in prayer. I know I need to continually practice the brokenness of Nehemiah before God. As well, I have a passion to possess the unwavering nature of Daniel before the Lord in prayer.

When Zacharias prayed about his barren wife, Elizabeth, God gave them a son who became the forerunner of Jesus—John the Baptist. What trust Zacharias and Elizabeth exhibited in their prayer life! Jesus' disciple Peter had a firm grip on prayer after he was filled with the Holy Spirit at pentecost. The epistles of Paul to the churches are testimonies of a man who was obviously a true warrior in prayer. Even as Paul prayed for the church in his day, I want to be able to pray for the church in my day.

I have been to the top of Mount Carmel, where Elijah called down the fire from heaven. I have stood on parts of the wall that Nehemiah built, as well as been in what some say could be the Upper Room where the Spirit of God came down upon disciples. But there has been no place that has impacted me more than the Garden of Gethsemane, where Jesus called out to the Father in prayer during His last hours on earth. Each place has impacted me during the many times I have been to the Holy Land, but each time, the Garden of Gethsemane moves me to get on my face before God and call out to Him for the needs of others.

My life has been further challenged by great prayer warriors who lived after the New Testament days. How I would love to have the courage of John Huss, who was burned at the stake praying to his Master and Lord, Jesus Christ. I am humbled by the faith of George Müller, who was responsible for feeding the children of his orphanage but never asked for one dime from any man. He just prayed in God's supply. I would love to be consumed with such a burden for America that I could pray like John Knox for his nation: "Lord, give me Scotland or I die!"

Each one of these prayer warriors knew what prayer was all about. They were proven veterans of prayer. Time and space will not allow me to mention the countless thousands of other prayer warriors who deserve recognition in a book about prayer.

Whether you are a seasoned veteran of prayer or consider yourself a rookie, this book is for you. Regardless of our experience level in prayer, each of us has much to learn about it. This is why we must learn from the greatest prayer intercessor who ever lived.

Yet, as I thought seriously about who could teach us what prayer is all about, I came to one solid, firm conclusion: The greatest prayer veteran, who modeled what prayer is all about, is someone we know by name—many of us know Him intimately. We have read of His genuine life of prayer, as recorded in the Scriptures. His name is Jesus Christ.

Jesus was a man of prayer. Think about that for a moment. He was the Son of God. He could do anything He wanted to do with His life, but He chose to dedicate His life on this earth to prayer and to service. He personified His deep commitment to prayer before His followers and His enemies. Jesus wanted fellowship with His Father in heaven, and He knew prayer was the only way to experience it.

The greatest prayer veteran, who modeled what prayer is all about, is someone we know by name.... His name is Jesus Christ.

Jesus provided the following insight into His prayer life: "Truly, truly, I say to you, the Son can do nothing of Himself, unless it is something He sees the Father doing; for whatever the Father does, these things the Son also does in like manner" (John 5:19).

In this scripture, Jesus declared His powerlessness. This is stunning since He is the Son of God. However, it was Jesus' personal humility that allowed Him to see what the Father was doing. This humble, suffering Servant was never truly powerless because He was always focused on seeing what the Father was doing in heaven. This is why He did only that which He saw the Father do in heaven.

How did this kind of fellowship exist between Jesus and His Father in heaven? One word: *prayer*! Jesus had an intimate, powerful connection with His Father.

Prayer is the means by which we can know God and His will for our lives. Prayer is our means of communication with God. Prayer is also the way we have spiritual power. All of this is modeled through Jesus Christ.

We can learn so much about prayer from the life of Jesus. Jesus communicated with the Father. But that is not the only element of prayer. The Father also communicated with Jesus. Notice it again: Jesus spoke to the Father. The Father spoke to Jesus. These two realities are what prayer is all about.

A Practical Definition for Prayer

I want to give you a practical definition of prayer that embodies these two truths about prayer modeled through Jesus' life. What is prayer? *Effective prayer occurs when you talk to God and listen to what God is saying to you.*

Prayer involves listening to God as much as it involves talking to God. Prayer is a relationship, a fellowship that occurs between you and God. Prayer is the vehicle that takes you into the privilege of experiencing fellowship with God.

Jeana and I have been married for more than forty years. Through our marriage journey, we have both learned a great deal about what it means to have a relationship with each other. We have learned that our fellowship is not driven by our *commitment* alone to each other; our fellowship is driven mainly by our *communication* with each other. This communication is marked by each of us talking to and listening to the other. Each of these skills—talking and listening—is valuable and essential in our fellowship as husband and wife.

I can also tell you this about marriage: listening is even more important than talking to your spouse. Even though this is true about marriage, it is even more true in your relationship with God. Effective communication with God begins with listening to God, not just talking to God. Do you want to communicate with God? Do you want to be a prayer warrior and intercessor who is known for praying effectively? If you do, then practice what Jesus modeled in prayer.

Notice the two components of the practical definition of effective prayer that I gave to you: *talking* to God and *listening* to what God is saying to you. This is what prayer is all about. I want to share with you the talking principles and the listening principles of prayer.

The Talking Principles of Prayer

Many of you will be familiar with the talking principles of prayer. A real student of prayer is willing to be teachable because he or she is aware that God can always give fresh insights. Take time to think through these talking principles. Do not let your possible familiarity with them move you to skip this section.

Since prayer involves talking to God in a genuine and transparent way, let us investigate the five talking principles of prayer. Although you may have learned these principles in a different order, in this section I will discuss how I incorporate them into my own prayer life. In my prayer time, I usually begin with the first talking principle of confession.

Principle #1: Confession

As I write this, the topic of confession has been getting a lot of media attention. Last year, the #MeToo movement exposed many individuals who had engaged in abusive behavior toward others. The movement was so successful that many of those involved put out statements of confession for past instances of abhorrent behavior against others. Talk shows on television, radio, and even blogs were inundated with discussions concerning confessions in the #MeToo movement.

While this movement received much attention and confession for wrongs toward others, as it should have, it is even more important that we understand the need for confession of our own sin before God each day. Additionally, we have a dire need to simply confess our own personal weaknesses to God daily.

This is why I like to begin with a time of confession in my personal prayer time. This confession travels along two avenues.

The first area of confession that I like to make in my daily prayers is the confession that I am nothing without the Lord. I cry out to God, confessing my helpless state before Him. I declare that I am inadequate and need this time of fellowship with Him in prayer. I often quote the words our Lord spoke to His disciples: "Apart from Me you can do nothing" (John 15:5). I confess daily to the Lord that without Him I am nothing.

> *Talking to God and listening to what God is saying to you . . . is what prayer is all about.*

The other area of confession that I practice in my daily prayer time is the confession of sin. There is a daily need to confess our sins before the Lord. Let me explain further.

It is quite obvious to me that Jesus instructed us to say to the Father in prayer, "Forgive us our sins" (Luke 11:4). This statement indicates that Christ's followers are to confess their sins to God. Many Christians are also familiar with the promise of 1 John 1:9: "If we confess our sins, He is faithful and righteous to forgive us our sins and to cleanse us from all unrighteousness." These words of encouragement notify believers of their need for personal forgiveness of sins.

The word *confess* used in the Scriptures is the Greek word *homologeo*, which means "to say the same as God says." Therefore, when we confess our sins, we are saying the same as God says about our sins. As Bible teacher John MacArthur wrote: "To 'confess' our sins in the truest sense involves despising the sin, being grieved by it, and judging it. That is what it means to say the same as God concerning our sin."[1]

Confession is more than admitting to God that you have sinned; it is seeing your sin in view of God's holiness and being as offended by and grieved by your sin as God is. Confession does not involve hiding the truth or shading the truth. True confession is coming clean before God and others about what you have done that is sinful.

For years, when I have confessed my sins, I have attempted to gain God's attitude about my sins. I am grieved that I have violated the privileges given to me by a loving and holy God. I pray, *Lord, my sin deserves death, hell, and the grave. Thank You for judging my sin at the cross. Thank You for forgiving me of my sins.* I take the time to ask the Spirit of God to reveal sins that I have committed before others and God. At that point, I ask God to give me His attitude about these sins. I believe God is more concerned about my attitude toward my sin than He is about the sin itself.

I have a deep respect and awe for God. Since I am aware of His holy nature, I pray more effectively once I confess my sinfulness before Him and receive His forgiveness. I thank God for the cross, which positions me before Him as a forgiven man.

We can never forget that we stand in the finished work of Jesus Christ on the cross. He has placed upon us His righteousness, and we are clothed in His righteousness. When the Father looks at us, He sees His Son's righteousness; therefore, He looks at us as if we have never sinned before.

Principle #2: Praise

Once I have spent time before God, confessing to Him my great need for Him and confessing to Him about my sins, my heart is bursting with joy because I am granted His compassion. I am now ready to move into a period of time when I offer praise to God.

Praise is expressing your love and adoration for who God is. The attention in praise is not on the hands of God for what He has done for you but on the face of God for who He is.

I love to be around people who accept me for who I am as a person. This is refreshing in comparison to the vast majority who may want to associate with me because of my title or position.

Since we are made in the image of God, I believe that God wants to be praised for who He is, not just for what He has done for us. I find it helpful to focus each day on three attributes of God's character. For example, attributes such as His holiness, His mercy, and His love. Each day they can be different or the same, but praise is about getting your eyes on God and adoring Him for who He is.

Principle #3: Thanksgiving

Thanksgiving is different from praise. Do not confuse these two talking principles of prayer.

While praise is adoring God for who He is, thanksgiving is thanking God for what He has done for you. Thanksgiving is offering God thanks for the way He has moved in your life and for how He has provided for your every need.

When I do something for someone, I like to hear the words "Thank you." I do not do something for someone for the purpose of being thanked, but I do something for them because I love them.

God loves you. He moves in your life regularly. He does many things for you that you do know and some that you do not know. He is always active in your life.

Take time daily to offer thanks to God. Thank Him for a physical blessing He has given you. Thank Him for a provisional blessing He has given you. Thank Him for a person He has brought into your life who has blessed you. Thank Him for the spiritual blessings He freely bestows upon you as you walk with Him and trust Him with the details of your life. Discipline yourself to have a thankful heart before God.

Principle #4: Petition

Once my heart is overflowing with thankfulness, I am ready to offer my life to the Lord. I do not think of my personal petitions in prayer as being selfish. When I pray, I am showing my dependence upon the Lord. Since God is interested in me personally and in my life, I believe He wants me to petition Him about whatever is on my heart.

I begin this time of petitioning the Lord by surrendering my entire life to God. I offer Him my mind, my will, my emotions, my spirit, my body, my attitude, my tongue, my motives, my dreams, my goals, my past, my present, my future, my family, and my career. I ask Him to control me with the Holy Spirit. I want to be a Spirit-intoxicated man who is controlled and consumed by the leadership of the Holy Spirit.

I petition the Lord daily to make me an anointed man of God. I do not want to be known as Dr. Floyd, but I want to be known as a man of God who has a mighty and special touch of God upon his life. I ask the Lord to anoint me with the authority of Jesus Christ so that I might see what He sees, hear what He hears, feel what He feels, and say what He wants said in all situations of life.

In this time of petition, I offer God several personal requests that may be on my heart about my life, my needs, and the ministry the Lord has entrusted to me. These might be various problems that I turn over to God. These may be various concerns I want to share with God. God already knows everything about me. God can meet all my needs.

Therefore, I discipline myself to have a transparent and open heart before God in prayer. I believe God is attracted to my transparency before Him.

Through the principles of confession, praise, thanksgiving, and petition, I am now prepared to enter into one of the most important talking principles in prayer.

Principle #5: Intercession

When I think of intercession, I imagine myself standing in the gap between the God of heaven and the person I am praying for at the time. I want my prayer to be used as the link between the two. I believe if God puts a person and his or her need upon my heart, He wants to move in that person's life.

I begin my time of intercession praying for my family. I present each member of my family and any personal needs I am aware of before the Lord.

I petition the Lord to make me an anointed man of God. I do not want to be known as Dr. Floyd, but I want to be known as a man of God who has a mighty and special touch of God upon his life.

For example, my oldest son, Josh, is the head football coach at Hewitt-Trussville High School in Trussville, Alabama, located in metro Birmingham. I pray about his future and influence over so many young lives every day.

My younger son, Nick, is the teaching pastor and the staff leader for Cross Church. I pray for him daily as he preaches week in and week out and as he leads the entire staff team of our church.

Both of my sons are now married with families of their own. I lift up Josh's wife, Kate, and Nick's wife, Meredith. I pray for each of my grandchildren by name: Peyton, Reese, Parker, Beckham, Jack, Norah, and Maya.

Then of course, I pray daily for my wife, Jeana. Each night we pray together before we go to sleep. At this time we pray once again for our children and grandchildren as well as any people we are aware of who need prayer.

One of the most important things I pray for my family each day is for the armor of God to be upon us. I place the teaching of Ephesians 6:10–18 upon us in prayer. This is critical! In the times in which we live, we need God's spiritual armor upon our lives. (I will discuss this in more detail in chapter 10.)

Once I have interceded for my family, I move on to interceding for the needs of my church. As a pastor, I feel God has given me three priorities for my ministry: leading God's people, feeding God's people, and interceding for God's people. I present the needs of God's people before Him in prayer.

In this time of intercession, I have developed a real burden to pray for people who do not know Jesus Christ in a personal way. I pray by name for people I know who do not know Christ. I pray for God to engineer circumstances in their lives through which they will see their need for Him. I pray for God to give me opportunities to build my relationship with them so I might be able to share with them the good news of Christ. I also spend time praying for people I do not know personally who do not know the Lord. God has a heart for people who are lost. I believe I need to pray for their eternal salvation.

I usually conclude this time of intercession by praying for people who have asked me to pray for them or for people whom God puts on my heart on a particular day.

Sometimes it feels like prayer is not enough. And at times, we must take other actions for our friends and family. However, Oswald Chambers reminds us, "Prayer does not equip us for greater works— prayer is the greater work. . . . Prayer is the battle, and it makes no difference where you are."[2]

Effective prayer occurs when you talk to God. The five talking principles of prayer are confession, praise, thanksgiving, petition, and intercession.

Practice them. Grow in them. Learn from others about them. However, do not forget that effective prayer also involves listening to God.

The Listening Principles of Prayer

As I said earlier, effective prayer occurs when you talk to God and listen to what God is saying to you. Prayer is not a one-way means of communication that only allows you to talk to God. Prayer is a two-way means of communication in which you talk to God and then listen to what He is saying to you.

Personally, I believe deeply that listening to God is more important than talking to God. When I listen to God effectively, it will affect the way I talk to God personally.

Let me share with you the three listening principles of prayer. I hope you will consider them and begin to practice them in your prayer life if you are not presently doing so.

Principle #1: Be Still and Quiet Before God

Since I believe that the Bible is God's primary way of speaking to me, I always attempt to have a Bible near me when I pray. If I want to hear Him, then I must read, know, study, and understand His Word. An open Bible should always accompany a bended knee.

In our fast-paced and noisy society, it is difficult to be still and quiet before the Lord. Our minds are usually racing a thousand directions, our smartphones beckoning to us with the sounds of emails, text messages, calendar reminders, and social media notifications, so much so that focus is usually a challenge. Discipline is the only way we can learn to be still and quiet before the Lord.

One thing I really attempt to do is meditate upon the Scriptures, to think deeply upon His Word. Each day I ask myself, "What is God saying to me?"

I need to know what God is saying to me through His Word and through the circumstances in my life. I know that God is committed to His relationship with me. He wants me to know what He thinks. He wants me to know His will. My challenge is to be still and quiet before Him long enough to hear Him speak to me.

At times, it might be healthy for me to have a change of scenery when I am trying to listen to God. Sometimes I get into my car and drive, without any particular destination, for the purpose of discerning what God may be saying to me. Maybe we need to put down our phones, turn off the television, shut down social media for a while, and just be still before the Lord. Do whatever it takes to be quiet and still before the Lord. When this occurs, God will say something to you about your life. Therefore, be still and quiet before the Lord.

Principle #2: Do Not Be in a Hurry in Your Time with God

We live in a world today that is running faster than ever. Almost everything you want can be delivered at lightning speed. Entire movies can be downloaded in a matter of minutes. Books can be uploaded to your device in seconds. Often in our lives, the easier things get, the faster we move. You can rush here and rush there and become a victim of the hurry disease.

But there is something you must never forget: *do not be in a hurry in your time with God.* You cannot grab a Bible verse like you grab a doughnut or a cup of coffee on your way to work or school. God does not work like that. God works in His own time. God works in His own way.

God wants us to learn to wait before Him. He wants to still our spirits. He wants to silence our hearts. He wants us to learn not to be in a hurry with Him. You will not experience meaningful times with God if you are trying to rush God into your schedule.

"Jesus first" does not simply mean that Jesus is first in your long list of priorities; rather, "Jesus first" begins mostly with you understanding it is *only* Jesus. Then, after He has met with you in a meaningful way, you are prepared to move forward.

On numerous occasions I have had the opportunity to lead worship in various settings, including my own church. Sometimes I feel the schedules have not permitted us to encounter God in such a way that true spiritual freedom exists. Whenever I have the responsibility to lead God's people into spiritual renewal within the context of a rigid, compact, or limited schedule, I always come away unsatisfied with the results. You cannot rush God.

This does not mean that God needs time. It means that we need time to be with God. Nor does it mean that God cannot meet with us when schedules are set. He can and He will. But when the schedules are so complex, at times we become the problem because our focus moves to the next thing before God has met with us powerfully and personally.

Learn not to be in a hurry in your time with God. God does not speak on your timetable. He has His own timetable. In His time, He will make Himself known to you. Therefore, learn the power of waiting before Him.

Principle #3: Spend Various Seasons of Your Life with God

I have discovered the power of setting aside specific periods of time to be alone with God. In these personal retreats away from the distraction of family, business, and life, I have grown by quantum leaps. God is attracted to someone who will set aside everything else just to be with Him.

A season can be defined in several ways. It can be a period of days in which you devote a select number of hours a day to wait before the Lord. It can be an entire day that you draw aside to be with God. A season can be a time of retreat during which you exit the affairs of this life to be with God for a while. It can be an extended time when you are away from your job or ministry for the purpose of being with God and listening to Him.

I have been on some two- and three-day retreats with God that have profoundly impacted my life. At times, when a preaching assignment feels more significant compared to the norm, I will spend time away in a nearby hotel just to be with God and hear Him speak to me. At times, these retreats are joined together with days of fasting or even times when fasts have been concluded.

Remember: effective prayer involves listening to what God is saying to you. Consider these three listening principles. I promise you, they have the power to change your life. Let God do something new in your life today. This new and fresh work will occur when you learn to listen to what God is saying.

Perspective and Balance

I want to be more than clear: *effective prayer occurs when you talk to God and listen to what God is saying to you.* I hope you will personally consider the truth of this principle in your life.

When you listen to God as well as talk to Him, you gain a whole new perspective on God. You also gain a new perspective on yourself. By God's grace, you even gain a new perspective on the circumstances of your life. If all you ever do is rattle your mouth in prayer, you will never operate with God's perspective in your life.

> Remember: effective prayer involves listening to what God is saying to you.

When you listen to God as well as talk to God, you are able to maintain balance in your life. Which is more important: what you say to God or what God says to you? The answer is obvious: it is much more important what God says to you than what you say to God. What you say to God will be greatly affected by what God says to you in your life. This is what prayer is all about.

An old adage says, "God gave you two ears and one mouth. Therefore, you should listen twice as much as you talk." This is good counsel for your life. It is even better counsel for your prayer life.

CHAPTER 2

WHY CHRISTIANS
DO NOT PRAY

One of the most gut-wrenching races in the sport of track is the four-hundred-meter race. For those who are unfamiliar with this race, four hundred meters is one time around the track. In today's track world, the four-hundred-meter dash is an all-out sprint. Only great, strong athletes can endure the mental and physical challenge of giving it their all for one full lap around the track.

The imperative to being a winning track star on the four-hundred-meter dash is to run the entire race as strong as you began it. The challenge for the athlete is to be so physically fit that the level of exertion is maintained at an optimum level during the entire race. The athlete not physically prepared to run this race cannot keep pace with the conditioned and prepared athletes. He or she may come out of the blocks on that first hundred meters and be in the lead but will be lagging behind in seconds.

One of the greatest challenges in the Christian life is to run the entire race with the same intensity with which we began it. The problem is that we are not running the entire race with great stamina because we are not fit spiritually to expend all we have for God. We come out of the blocks and go like gangbusters at first, but soon we are lagging behind. At times we are not even on our way toward finishing the race.

In my recent book *Living Fit*, I wrote these words about being fit spiritually: "As your spiritual life goes, so goes the rest of your life."[1] Prayer is a conversation with God. Learning how to pray is imperative to living fit spiritually. Your prayer life will influence the rest of your life!

One of the most apparent areas of poor performance in the Christian life is in the area of prayer. How many times have you said you were going to learn how to pray more effectively or become a better prayer warrior? Even though many people have good intentions, they fail to run the race successfully. Initially, they have a great commitment, but in time their intensity wanes. Many times, especially in the area of prayer, their commitment ceases altogether. This is why we must determine to be intentional in our spiritual life!

A frightening paradox is occurring. One of the most vital spiritual disciplines you need in order to run the entire race with great intensity is prayer. Conversely, one of the most difficult challenges you have in your Christian life is to pray.

It is like knowing that your car cannot run without fuel but discovering the fuel is difficult to obtain. Therefore, you might not always have fuel. Consequently, the car cannot run. What is even more disturbing is that you will have to pay the price to obtain the fuel when you really need to be somewhere else.

Does any of this sound familiar? At times, you may not pray because prayer is difficult. The result is that you have little if any spiritual power. Consequently, you live a defeated spiritual life. Yet when things become really difficult, you desperately find a way to pray because you know you cannot make it on your own.

Before we investigate why Christians do not pray, I want you to grasp these two critical statements about prayer:

Statement #1: Prayer occurs when you depend on God.
Statement #2: Prayerlessness occurs when you depend on yourself.

Will you take the time to read these two statements again? In fact, why don't you commit them to memory right now? These statements are critical to understanding prayer. *Prayer occurs when you depend on God. Prayerlessness occurs when you depend on yourself.*

People give thousands of excuses as to why they do not pray. No matter what the excuse, the underlying reason is that they love to depend upon themselves. Prayerlessness is always a result of selfishness.

God is calling you to go to a new level with Him. His Spirit is attempting to inspire you to pray more consistently and effectively. Your greatest need and only hope to make a long-lasting difference for God is to learn how to pray more effectively.

Prayer is not an option; it is essential. If you are going to be serious about your faith, then it is imperative that prayer become a major part of your Christian experience.

Oftentimes, people view prayer as inaction. Listen carefully: *prayer is not inaction; prayer is your greatest action!*

If you are going to learn how to be a consistent prayer warrior, then you must understand your obstacles. Even though your self-dependence is the root cause of prayerlessness, there is more to investigate in this area.

Four Reasons Christians Do Not Pray

I believe there are four major reasons why Christians do not pray. In this chapter I do not want simply to identify these reasons for you, but I also want to tell you why they exist.

Reason #1 Christians Do Not Pray: Pride

It was early on a Sunday morning when God obliterated my pride. I was in the closing days of a forty-day period of fasting and prayer. I could not sleep on Saturday evening, which is a great peril for a preacher. I sensed that God wanted me to interpret my sleeplessness as a call to prayer. Just after midnight, I arose and went into the living room of our home.

Lying prostrate on the floor, I opened my Bible and prayer journal. I asked the Lord what He wanted to tell me. I knew He was up to something. For more than thirty days, I had retreated to be with Him in fasting and prayer. Surely all my sin had been dealt with by now. Little did I know, I was about to experience the awakening of a lifetime.

Your greatest need and only hope to make a long-lasting difference for God is to learn how to pray more effectively. Prayer is not an option; it is essential.

The Lord guided me to the book of Isaiah. Before I knew it, my eyes were fixed upon Isaiah 57:15: "For thus says the high and exalted One who lives forever, whose name is Holy, 'I dwell on a high and holy place, and also with the contrite and lowly of spirit in order to revive the spirit of the lowly and to revive the heart of the contrite.'"

This verse gave me one of the most crushing blows of my entire Christian life. I was filled with fear and shame. It was as if God said, *Ronnie, I dwell in two places: I dwell in heaven and I dwell with the humble. Ronnie, you are not humble but proud. Your pride is the biggest problem in your life. People are not your problem. The church is not your problem. You are your biggest problem. In fact, the biggest problem in your church is you. Repent from your pride immediately. If you really want revival in your church and in your country, you must first repent from your pride.*

This personal message from God was as clear to me that Sunday morning as the day I am writing it to share with you. God meant business. He knew I had a listening ear before Him. He knew I was willing to do anything. It was time for me to understand the real truth about walking with God. God walks with humble people, not proud people. On that early morning, I was embarrassed before God over my pride.

As God's Spirit convicted me, I pleaded guilty. The finger-pointing ceased—I knew that I was the guilty one. If I wanted to be a man of prayer and a true man of God, I needed to be a humble man. I had tried to be all God wanted me to be for a number of years, but on this particular morning, God exposed the real me to me. He informed me in a demonstrative manner what He had known about me for my entire life. I have grown from that experience. I still deal with it today.

It has been almost twenty-five years since that early morning in 1995, but time and again in this season of my life, God has impressed upon me this powerful verse from James 4:10: "Humble yourselves before the Lord, and he will exalt you" (csb).

Why does God keep impressing this verse upon my life and ministry? Let me tell you why.

Pride is the most deceitful sin of all. Pride blinds us. Pride costs us everything. It cost Adam and the entire human race everything. Pride is so dangerous because it masks a multitude of sins. When pride is exposed, the other sins in your life become like countless snakes coming out of a den. You are not aware of those sins until they are uncovered.

Pride is one of the major reasons we do not pray. Why does pride keep us from praying? *Pride keeps us from praying because it overestimates the power of self.*

Remember: prayerlessness occurs because you choose to depend upon yourself.

The closest disciples to Jesus were Peter, James, and John. Just like each one of us, these men struggled with pride. On the evening before Jesus was arrested, Jesus asked them to pray with Him. They began to pray but ended up sleeping. Three times Jesus asked them to watch and pray, and all three times the disciples fell asleep. Their comfort of sleep was more important than denying themselves to do what Jesus asked them to do. That is why Jesus asked Peter, James, and John this question as recorded in Matthew 26:40: "So, couldn't you stay awake with me one hour?" (CSB).

Think about this for a minute. In the middle of the most difficult night of Jesus' life, the disciples lacked the personal discipline to stay with Jesus in prayer.

Peter, James, and John did not fulfill Jesus' desire for them. They overestimated their ability in these difficult moments to deny themselves what they naturally wanted to do—sleep. Then within hours, Peter denied Jesus three times. Three times of neglected prayer led to three denials of Jesus. *No prayer, no power. No prayer, no courage. No prayer, no victory.*

Would you take an inventory of your life right now? Pride is the self-life. Pride always leads you to point fingers at others. Pride never takes the blame for anything. Pride leads you to think more of yourself than you do of God. Do you have any pride?

God's Word gives us numerous cautions concerning the sin of pride. The writer of Proverbs declared, "A man's pride will bring him low, but a humble spirit will obtain honor" (29:23). And again, he said, "When pride comes, then comes dishonor, but with the humble is wisdom" (11:2).

The caution lights are going off right now, aren't they? God is warning you that pride will always bring you down. The result will be the dishonoring of yourself and the dishonoring of God. None of us would ever do this intentionally, but pride is deceitful. Remember, pride blinds you. Pride deceives you. Be very careful. Pride can sneak into your heart. Before you know it, you will be down and dishonored.

Pride keeps you from praying because it overestimates the power of self. You cannot make it on your own. Your enemy, Satan, wants you to believe you can. But the result will be prayerlessness followed by spiritual defeat.

Force yourself to pray. Make yourself go down on your knees. Do whatever it takes to get before God daily. Walk and pray. Sit and pray.

Do whatever you need to get into a mode of prayer. You will never be stronger and your enemy will never be weaker than when you pray.

Reason #2 Christians Do Not Pray: Unbelief

When Jesus walked on this earth, He did many mighty and supernatural works. It was in His nature to move beyond the natural. Everyone who demonstrated one small degree of faith experienced the power of God. The New Testament is filled with eyewitness accounts of the mighty acts of Jesus Christ.

However, when Jesus went to His hometown of Nazareth, these miracles were limited. When I go to the city of Nazareth, I am reminded of this very story.

The people were amazed at His teaching in the synagogue and asked, "Where did this man get this wisdom and these miraculous powers?" (Matthew 13:54). But in verse 58, Matthew makes an interesting observation about this occasion: "He did not do many miracles there because of their unbelief."

Jesus impressed the people in Nazareth with His teachings. The only problem was they chose not to believe in Him or His teachings. *As a result of their unbelief, Jesus chose not to do many mighty acts among them.* Everywhere He went, the miracles were plentiful—except for places where a lack of faith was prominent, such as Nazareth.

There is an element of Nazareth that each of us faces in prayer. There are moments when we just cannot believe. Even though we know about Jesus' ability, we are not certain that He is willing to intervene in our situation. Rather than choosing to pray, we choose to trust in ourselves. *Our unbelief keeps us from praying.*

Unbelief is another major reason we do not pray. Why does our unbelief keep us from praying? Never forget this: ***unbelief underestimates the power of God.***

Wake up, my friend, and hear these words that God wants each of us to hear. Are you listening? Are you ready to be challenged? *Whereas pride overestimates the power of self, unbelief underestimates the power of God.* The result of each of these sins is prayerlessness.

I have had the opportunity to travel across America to speak to various churches, denominational meetings, and conventions. Many times I have felt that God wanted to do something mighty in our midst. Yet, like the synagogue in Nazareth, there was a bondage of unbelief among the people. They simply could not do what the Spirit was asking them to do because of their unbelief. Instead of believing in the power of God, they made excuses as to why God cannot do the mighty work.

The eleventh chapter of the book of Hebrews comprises the Great Hall of Faith, featuring men and women who exercised big faith. Even though many of their circumstances seemed hopeless, they pursued God through prayer. This chapter makes an insightful statement about prayer and its connection with faith: "Without faith it is impossible to please Him, for he who comes to God must believe that He is and that He is a rewarder of those who seek Him" (v. 6).

According to this scripture, when we pray we must first believe that God is. What does it mean to believe that God is? It means to believe that God is who He says He is and that He can do whatever He says He can do.

When you do not believe that God is who He says He is and that God can do whatever He says He can do, then you do not have faith in God. Without faith, prayer will not occur. Remember: *unbelief underestimates the power of God. Unbelief is a major obstacle to prayer.*

Satan wants you to think God is too busy to listen to your prayers. Your enemy places into your imagination the false idea that God is limited in His power. I trust you know better: *God is who He says He is and He can do whatever He wants to do. He is God!*

What are you facing right now in your life that is bigger than you? What is your biggest problem? Does it have to do with business, family, finances, or friendships? God is bigger than your problem.

God is bigger than your greatest crisis. God is bigger than cancer. God is bigger than your greatest critic. God is bigger than anything you face in your life today.

Therefore, talk to Him about your life. Talk to Him about your problem. There is nothing that God cannot do. When you exhibit even the smallest degree of faith, God will step into your life and care for you through your circumstances. Just as Jesus moved in the lives of those who had faith in Him while He was on this earth, He will move in your life when you exercise faith in Him.

> *Whereas pride overestimates the power of self, unbelief underestimates the power of God. The result of each of these sins is prayerlessness.*

Unbelief moves you away from God and prayer. Faith moves you toward God and prayer.

Any reluctance that you have toward prayer is a sign that you are struggling with unbelief. Identify this unbelief for what it is. Refuse to yield to its magnetic hold on your life. God is who He says He is. God can do whatever He says He can do. Therefore, whatever you are facing—big or small—pray! Trust God. He is able!

Reason #3 Christians Do Not Pray: Ignorance

Over thirty years ago I was called to serve as the senior pastor of the First Baptist Church in Springdale, Arkansas; today it is called Cross Church, a large multi-campus church with multiple ministries.

Early on in my ministry here, when I was just a boy preacher, God began to open up opportunities to meet some influential people. I met well-known politicians such as former Arkansas congressman John Paul Hammerschmidt, who has now passed away. I also met early on our former governor and now two-term president of the United States, Bill Clinton. And I met national and international religious leaders in my younger years such as Billy Graham, Jerry Falwell, Tim LaHaye, James Dobson, W. A. Criswell, and Adrian Rogers.

I will never forget how I felt prior to meeting these people. I would rehearse in my mind what I would say to them. My stomach would churn with stress. I felt I was out of my league even to carry on a conversation with any of them. I am confident each of them noticed it. I am certain that some of the things that I said were inappropriate.

My mistake was that I overestimated the difficulty of talking with these influential people. I did not know they were just like me. I was not aware of their desire and interest in others. You see, I made a terrible mistake. I did not know I could talk to these influential people like I talked to common people. I did not have to impress anyone. My problem was that I was ignorant—I simply did not know any better.

Ignorance is one of the major reasons we do not pray. How does ignorance keep us from prayer? *Ignorance overestimates the difficulty of talking to God.*

God is not difficult to talk to in prayer. Just as I once overestimated the difficulty of talking to influential people, I used to overestimate the difficulty of talking to God. What I know now is that God is easier to talk to than any person on this earth. God wants you to talk to Him. He wants you to come to Him anytime, anywhere, about anything. He wants to fellowship with you.

Forget trying to impress God with your language. *He is not interested in your words. He is interested in your heart.* Share your heart with God. Real prayer occurs when you share your heart with God. Ignorance can no longer be a reason why you do not pray.

Ignorance is when you do not know any better. Stupidity is when you know better but choose not to do it.

Now that you know God is easy to talk to—share your heart with Him. Let Him hear your deepest concerns, regardless of your ability (or lack of ability) to articulate them to Him. Be honest with Him. Let Him hear from you today.

It is not difficult to talk to God. Just talk to Him. Respect Him for who He is, but talk to Him like you talk to other people. Prayer is a conversation with God.

Pride keeps you from praying because it overestimates the power of self. Forsake your pride and talk to God.

Unbelief keeps you from praying because it underestimates the power of God. Rebuke unbelief and believe that God can do anything in your life. God can do anything, anytime, with anyone, including you!

Ignorance keeps you from praying because it overestimates the difficulty of talking to God. Ignorance is no longer an excuse—just share your heart with God.

Reason #4 Christians Do Not Pray: Time

Time is one of the most precious commodities you have in life. In the business world, time is money. Each person in this world has 168 hours a week and 24 hours a day. Time places everyone on equal ground.

If you were to ask one hundred people why they do not pray, the subject of time would likely be mentioned. The typical excuse, "I am too busy," is given by most people who want to avoid something that they do not deem as important.

One of the major reasons people do not pray is time. How does time keep you from talking with God? *Time underestimates the value of being with God.*

Remember, each person has the same amount of time. Time only becomes the problem when you underestimate the value of being with God.

When I first met Jeana, I was attracted to her immediately. I wanted to spend each waking hour with her. She was very important to me. I had plenty of other things to do; however, I valued spending time with Jeana. Therefore, I always had time for her.

Time with God is essential for life. Whenever you do not take the time to pray, you have a problem with your values. You simply do not deem God as important and worthy of your time.

Make time to talk to God. Time with God is critical to a successful Christian life. Quite honestly, you cannot walk with God effectively if you do not take the time to spend a few moments with God daily.

I start every day in my life having a time with God. Even when my schedule is bulging with many demands, I always make sure that the first thing I do every day is spend time with God. This is a non-negotiable for me.

However, there have been a few times in the past when my schedule has seemed to force me to cut short my time with God. This has never been beneficial to my day. *Rushing my time with God is never advantageous to my spiritual health.*

When you take time for God, He will meet with you. Invest your time wisely with God, and He will make your effort worthwhile. Remember what Hebrews 11:6 says: "He is a rewarder of those who seek Him."

Take time for God today. Do not put Him off. He is the King of kings and Lord of lords. He is more prominent than any person you will ever meet in life. No one is like Him.

What if you were informed that you could spend time with the wealthiest person in the world who is also a major business leader and influencer? What if you were told that you could spend some time with Michael Jordan the basketball star, or Bill Gates the billionaire computer guru, or national championship football coach Nick Saban, or even the president of the United States or one of the former living presidents of our great nation? Would you rearrange your schedule to spend some time with these people?

I guarantee you would do whatever it took to spend time with one of these people or someone else whom you deemed important. And I imagine you wouldn't just spend a few short minutes with these people; you would want to sit down and talk to them for as long as they gave you time.

What is my point? *The point is that you will spend time with whomever you value in your life.* How much do you value God? How much do you honor Him? Do you honor Him with your time? Do you spend time with Him every now and then, or do you value Him enough to spend time with Him every day? Do you take the time to linger with God, or do you give Him merely a token couple of minutes as you fly out the door to go to work or school?

Prayer is your means of spending time with God. It is the way that you express yourself to Him. *Never underestimate the value of spending time with God.* All God needs with you is a moment. In that moment, He can transform you. He can fill you with hope. Never forget these words: *God can do more in a moment than you can do in a lifetime.*

Take time for God today. Do not put Him off. He is the King of kings and Lord of lords. He is more prominent than any person you will ever meet in life. No one is like Him.

What is keeping you from praying? Pride? Unbelief? Ignorance? Time? Now is the time to identify what is standing in the way of becoming a person committed to prayer. Will it take a crisis to make you want to pray? I hope not.

None of these obstacles are too big to be conquered. Just as David brought down Goliath in the name of the Lord, you can bring down these giants of prayerlessness in the name of the Lord. One by one, take authority over them in Jesus' name and with the power of the Holy Scriptures undergirding you!

God wants to be with you. Do you want to be with God? I believe you do, or else you would not be reading this book. Therefore, I want to lead you in how to experience a meaningful time with God each day. It is possible. You can do it! Do not stop reading now! Read on!

CHAPTER 3

HOW TO HAVE A MEANINGFUL TIME WITH GOD

If you could do anything in your life, what would it be? If your time and resources were unlimited, what would you do? I am not talking about something noble or spiritual but something fun. If my time and resources were unlimited, let me tell you what I would do.

Each Friday afternoon during football season, I would board a private jet and fly to watch the high school football game my son is coaching in Alabama. If one of the grandsons was playing on Thursday night, I would fly in just in time to see his game, stay over for Friday night's game, and then on Saturday morning, I would board that private jet and fly to the college football game of the week that I wanted to see.

I would wear the colors of the team I was supporting that day. I would have a great time, sitting in the private box I had rented, accompanied by several friends or family members who had traveled with me.

You see, I love the game of football, especially college football. I like the atmosphere. The excitement. The enthusiasm. The glamour. The drama. I like it from the beginning of the warm-ups to the very end when the last player walks off the field. I love the thrill of victory and dread the agony of defeat.

Football is a special sport because of the many things it can teach its players about life: The value of teamwork. The value of personal performance. The value of having a great work ethic. The value of winning. The value of rebounding from defeat.

One of the constant challenges of a football coach is to keep the team focused on the importance of the fundamentals of blocking correctly, tackling effectively, and running tirelessly. If the offense is pass-oriented, they must allot time each day to throwing and catching the ball. Timing is critical, and the only way to develop this timing is to practice the fundamentals of throwing and catching the football daily.

One of the things that makes college football so great is that, on any given Saturday, the "Davids" of the game can defeat the "Goliaths." No one likes to be on the losing end of any major upset, from the high school level to the collegiate level to the pros! These periodic upsets remind all of us that on any given day, anyone can lose.

When the defeated team's football coach has to face the press in his postgame press conference, he looks as if he has lost his best friend. His team's loss surprises even him. After reviewing the game film, the next day he stands before the alumni and fans in his next press conference and says something like the following: "Yesterday, we were very disappointed in our team's performance. After reviewing the film, it is obvious that we have got to do a better job of blocking, tackling, running the football, as well as passing and catching it. I have to do a much better job of coaching and preparing our team to play. This week our staff will focus on going back to the fundamentals of the game. We will be more than ready to play next week."

I have heard that speech several times from several of the game's greatest coaches. The "back to the basics" speech is always the key to a dominant team remaining dominant and not losing to the so-called lesser teams on their schedule. One of the key ways to avoid defeat in the game of football is always to do the basics of the game better than your opposition. If you do, victory is likely. If you fail in the fundamentals, defeat is inevitable.

We Are Making It Too Hard

I am convinced that we are making the Christian life a lot harder than God ever intended for it to be. Our enemy, Satan, has confused our intention, our direction, and our goal. We know that we ought to be winning in the Christian life, yet we are losing much of the time because we are making it too hard.

I believe that the most important action you can take in the Christian life is to have a meaningful time with God daily. This action must be the heart of all that we do. It is the most basic of the basics. It is the one key fundamental that even the greatest Christian had better not fumble, or else defeat is inevitable.

Our enemy's strategy is deliberate and deceiving. Satan wants to destroy us. He wants to get us out of God's game plan. He wants us to think that living the Christian life is virtually impossible. He has gotten us involved in knowing more about Christianity instead of doing what we know. He has the church of Jesus Christ in disarray over pointless issues and many times in the weeds so much that no positive outcome for the advancement of God's kingdom throughout the world occurs.

It is time to stop dumbing down to the devil's level by saying that the Christian life is too hard. This wise and crafty schemer's strategy is extremely focused. He wants to get followers of Christ involved in so many things that they will not make the time to have a meaningful time with God daily. Some of these things might even be good, but they are not essential.

The issue is *not* that the Christian life is too hard. The issue is that *we* are making it too hard. We have to understand that the only way to experience spiritual power, direction, and purpose is to have a meaningful time with God daily. The only way we are going to defeat the schemes of Satan is to have a meaningful time with God daily. The only way our families and our churches will function properly is for us to have a meaningful time with God daily.

As Christians, we ought to be winning in life. Our enemy has already been defeated through the death and resurrection of Jesus Christ. We already have the victory. We are to be even greater than a dominant football team over its inferior opposition. Like a dominant football team that makes itself vulnerable to defeat by not performing the basics of the game well, we ensure our defeat by neglecting the most fundamental of all fundamentals: *having a meaningful time with God daily.*

> *We have to understand that the only way to experience spiritual power, direction, and purpose is to have a meaningful time with God daily.*

I don't have all the answers, and I can learn from each of you. But with great conviction, I am not going to assume anything. I am not going to assume that you know how to have a meaningful time with God daily. I am not going to assume that you are a strong, praying Christian who has a strategic plan of prayer for your life.

It is obvious by the wreckage of broken lives, broken families, and powerless churches that many Christians are not spending daily time with God. Therefore, I want to share some guidelines for you to consider implementing in your life today to help you have a meaningful time with God daily.

Six Special Guidelines for a Meaningful Time with God

The number one priority in the life of a true disciple should be having a meaningful time with God daily. If nothing else gets done in your day, this must get done. Do not ever underestimate the value of meeting with God daily.

Since a meaningful time with God every day is essential for spiritual victory, we need to learn from every great Christian we know about how to do this. When you meet Christians whom you greatly respect, ask them, "What has helped you have a meaningful time with God daily?"

I do not consider myself a great Christian at all. In fact, I am always curious to see how other Christians, especially Christian leaders, spend their personal time with God daily. I am a learner and I am always in need of learning more.

But I am aware that God has taught me a few things about walking with Him daily. Therefore, I want to share with you six special guidelines I have followed that have assisted me in having a meaningful time with God each day.

1. A Special Time

As I mentioned in the introduction, God taught me the importance of having a time with Him years ago. Even before that defining moment, I was passionate about how to have a meaningful time with God daily. Quite honestly, I do not even remember the last day of my life when I did not begin my day by spending time with God.

All the times we have with God may not be as meaningful as we would like them to be. Each time my wife and I spend time together is not always as meaningful as we would like it to be. Yet this does not negate our need as a couple to be together, and it does not negate your need to spend time with God. Sometimes I feel as if many Christians decide not to spend time with God because, for various reasons, the time has not been as meaningful as expected.

The first guideline to having a meaningful time with God daily is to designate a special time that you meet with Him. It is your *most* important appointment, and you need to make and keep it daily.

Ask yourself right now, "What time am I going to meet with God every single day for the rest of my life?" Since this is the number one priority in the life of a true disciple, I believe that your appointment with God should take place before anything else in your life.

Your time with God should take place before you go online, check your phone or email, turn on the television, check social media, or read the newspaper each day. Since a meaningful time with God is imperative for you to have a vital relationship with God, then the priorities of your day should reflect this truth. The moment you wander around the house or leave for work or school in the morning without having a meaningful time with God, you make yourself vulnerable to attacks from your greatest enemy.

You have to determine to make your time with God a special time. My time with God happens within moments after I throw water on my face to prepare myself physically for this spiritual activity. It does not matter if it is a routine day for me, a travel or vacation day; God is going to get the prime time of my day. The thing I have learned to do first each day is to spend meaningful time with God.

In the routine days of life, which normally happen for me on Sunday through Thursday, I have a time set aside for God. I meet God for private devotion at 3:00 a.m. There may be a slight rescheduling of this time periodically due to travel schedules or crossing time zones, but I always meet with God the first thing every day.

I begin each day with God. Whether the day is considered a workday like Sunday through Thursday, time off like a Friday, or during a vacation time, I begin my day with God. For example, while my own Fridays and Saturdays are different unique days, I usually wait until 6:00 a.m. to have my special time with God.

Some of you may protest greatly, declaring, "I am not a morning person!" It may surprise you, but neither am I. Even if you are not a morning person by nature, it is still important for you to make your time with God the first thing every day. When you meet with God, it shows you depend upon Him. When you do not, it shows you depend upon yourself. If you are going to be involved in effective praying—talking to God and listening to what He is saying—then you must set aside a time for this to happen, or else it probably will not happen.

While a few of you may spend the major time you have with God later in the day or even into the evening, I would encourage you strongly, still begin your day with God. At least talk to Him briefly, but much more importantly, let Him talk to you through reading the Scriptures daily.

One of the ways you can make your time with God a special time is for you to work on it being special daily. Begin each day with God.

2. A Special Place

You may not remember the day or the hour that Christ came into your life, but you will remember the place that you surrendered your life to Jesus Christ to be your Lord and Savior. I remember the exact place where I repented of my sins and placed all of my faith in Jesus Christ and Him alone for my salvation.

Places are important to God. All through Scripture, we read various accounts of God's activity, and often the place of the activity receives special attention.

If you are going to have a meaningful time with God every day, then set aside a special place to meet with Him. This special place needs to be somewhere you enjoy. It needs to be somewhere private. The fewer interruptions you have, the easier it is for you to have a meaningful time with God.

I meet with God every day in my study at home. This is my special and private place to be with Him. He has been so real to me in this place. You see, in this special place, He has spoken to me through His Word. He has built me back up when I have been discouraged. He has put me back together when I am broken. Yes, it is a special place. God meeting with me there makes it special. It is not special because of the chair I sit in, the color of the walls, or even the beautiful windows I often gaze through as I think, meditate, and pray. The thing that makes this place really special is that it is where God and I hang out together.

Where is your special place that you meet with God daily? It does not have to be in a private study. It can be on a worn-out lounge chair that sits beside a dim light. It can be at the kitchen table. It may be in your bedroom. For some, it could be on the outside porch.

Wherever you meet God is a special place. Meeting Him daily at the same place will make that place very special over the course of time. Let this place be your hiding place, a private place you meet with God daily.

3. A Special Plan

If you do not have a plan to meet with God and pray, then you probably will not do either one. If you are going to have a meaningful time with God daily, you need to develop a game plan.

Every day is game day for the Christian. There are no off-days or off-seasons. In order to be ready for your game day every day, you need a plan to follow and then to follow that plan to meet with God daily.

When I was a new believer, I came across a prayer notebook that helped me through those young years in the Lord. Later on, I began to use the Lord's Prayer as my personal plan for prayer. Over the years, I have followed many plans, and today I have a plan that works for me.

Just remember this: *if you do not plan to pray, you will not pray.* In order to have an effective prayer life, you need to plan to meet with God daily.

I am a deep believer in meeting with Jesus at a special time daily. I think it is also important to meet with Jesus in your special place. I also know that when you arrive there, you better have a special plan to follow.

4. A Special Book

The special Book that you need to read is a compilation of sixty-six smaller books. This Book contains literally thousands of promises made to you from God Himself. This Book is so powerful that people have died for its message. It is not a Book written by man but a Book that is written by God. It was breathed into existence by a personal and perfect God. Therefore, it is a perfect Book.

This Book is called the Bible. The Bible is essential for your life. It needs to be read daily. It needs to be studied continually. It needs to be memorized periodically.

Please understand clearly: The Bible is God's Holy Word. It is the infallible Word of God. It is God's Truth without any mixture of error. When God's Word speaks, God speaks. What God says, He means.

Just remember this: if you do not plan to pray, you will not pray. In order to have an effective prayer life, you need to plan to meet with God daily.

There is no way that you can have a meaningful time with God without reading the Bible daily. The Bible is the main way God speaks to you. The Bible is His love letter to you. God's Word is intended to be a lamp for our feet and a light for our path. This kind of guidance is possible when you read it and study it during a daily time with Him.

Consider developing a plan for reading through God's Word daily and even annually. For my first many years of reading through the Bible, I used *The One Year Bible.* It is fantastic! *The One Year Bible* will have a specific reading of God's Word every day, rather than flipping aimlessly through the Bible, hoping something may come alive to you. Since you are interested in having a meaningful time with God every day, strongly consider reading through God's Word on an annual basis.

I have now read through the Bible no fewer than twenty-eight times. In 1990, I began reading through the Bible annually. While I do not use *The One Year Bible* plan any longer, I have developed my own plan of reading through Scripture. Usually sometime in September or October, I have finished reading through the entire Bible. Then, I often read through the entire New Testament again or read through additional books of Scripture I believe God is leading me to read.

Get involved in reading this special Book daily. Read it slowly. Your goal should not be to hurry through a chapter or a reading assignment. Your goal should be to hear God speak to you through the words of the Bible, because when the Bible speaks, God speaks! I promise you that God's words in His Book have the power to change your life. Let this special Book called the Bible become the special Book that you read daily as a part of your time with God.

5. A Special Letter

On January 1, 1990, I began a spiritual discipline that has really impacted my personal walk with Christ. I have not missed one day in doing this spiritual practice. It has blessed me and touched my life in a powerful way. It helps document my walk with Christ daily.

At the conclusion of my time with God each day, the final thing I do is write a one-page letter to God. I begin the letter the same way every day by writing the words, "Dear God . . .". In this letter I try to do two things. First, I write down anything that I sense God has specifically spoken to me about through His Word. Second, I write down the main things on my heart that I have prayed about during this time with God. Journaling is powerful because of the release that comes when you write down some of your greatest burdens and know you have given them to God.

This special letter that you write to God becomes the documentation of your spiritual life. If you take the time to read through these letters, you will discover God's activity that has been taking place in your life. It also reminds you of some special moments when you handed over some burdens to God.

Therefore, my walk with Christ has been documented daily since 1990. This means that I can go back and look at how God saw me through the challenges of Jeana's cancer, the challenges my children were facing, the challenges I was facing in my church, or the challenges I was facing as president of the Southern Baptist Convention, or challenges later serving as the president of the National Day of Prayer, or simply the challenges of living life for God daily.

Do you realize what this does? *It increases your faith!* Since you know God has seen you through before, you know that He will see you through again.

Consider developing the practice of writing a daily letter to God. You can use something as simple as a notebook or as sophisticated as a leather-bound journal. You can even do this online. While I write continually using my laptop or iPad or phone, I still write this one-page letter by hand in a simple notebook. I find it so releasing and freeing to write it by hand and then close the notebook. To me it signals, "I have given it to God."

Regardless of how you do it, begin to write God a letter every day. In time, I believe you will regard it as being one of the most dynamic things you have ever done in your spiritual growth plan.

6. A Special Goal

I have often heard that in order for something to become a habit in your life you have to do it for at least twenty-one days in a row. This is true whether the habit is a new diet, a new exercise plan, or a new spiritual discipline.

You should desire for your daily time with God to become a habit in your life. You do not want to live the rest of your Christian life with the inconsistencies of the past. *The greatest habit you could ever establish in your life is to have a meaningful time with God daily.*

Do you believe God is able to help you have a meaningful time with Him daily? Set a goal of meeting with God consistently for at least twenty-one days in a row. Mark your calendar. Do not let anything come before this in your life. God wants you to do it. He will empower you to keep your commitment. Begin it now, even while you are learning how to pray more effectively through this book.

Remember, the number one priority in the life of a true disciple of Jesus Christ should be to have a meaningful time with God daily. Jesus is waiting to meet with you daily. Do it.

Set a goal of meeting with God for a specific amount of time every day. Always have a goal in mind. For example, as you begin this journey, how long would it take if you read one chapter in God's Word, spent time in personal prayer through your plan to pray, and then wrote a letter to God? You are not on someone else's level right now—you are on your own level. Start there and grow! Just begin!

Let Me Introduce You to Gene Layman

One of the finest laypersons I have ever met is a man named Gene Layman. Gene was a private businessman who still to this day has an insatiable passion for God. Even in his eighties, Gene rises early to meet with God daily.

It is like clockwork to him. He prepares himself for the day, grabs his books, and heads out to a local restaurant to meet with God. You might think that a restaurant is not a very private place, but it is when you are there by 4:00 a.m. Gene goes to his special corner, where he pursues his relationship with the living God.

Many mornings in my early days at Cross Church, Gene would call me to tell me what God had said to him that morning. Sometimes he wanted to share a special word for me from his time with God. This word was never a harsh word of rebuke but a word of edification for me. His words were always meant to build me up, and believe me, they have.

Gene Layman models these six guidelines that I have given to you in this chapter. If you could spend time with him, in a few short moments you would learn of his depth in his walk with Christ. Still to this day, so many young men are inspired by Gene's walk with Christ.

For years and years, he has practiced what I have written about in this chapter. I guarantee that he would tell you today the same words I have already stated: *the number one priority of a true disciple of Jesus is to have a meaningful time with God daily.*

What a Meaningful Time with God Will Do for You

When you pursue your relationship with God by having a meaningful time with Him daily, you will begin to discover some great things this does for you personally. I hesitate taking this approach because I detest the consumer mentality that is infiltrating our lives personally and the church collectively. At the same time, I know that having a meaningful time with God daily will do some things for you that I definitely want you to know because of the potential impact it will have on your life. I am convinced that a meaningful time with God daily will result in you experiencing a new level of . . .

Spiritual Power

You cannot make it spiritually without a meaningful time with God daily. The fight through life is too ferocious, and you are too fragile. Your goal should not be simply to survive in this world, but to experience genuine spiritual victory over this world. Is this really possible? Yes!

When you have a meaningful time with God daily, you will begin to experience a new dimension of spiritual power. God will use that time to fill you with His Spirit and His power. He will use this time to take back the control of your life from you. Why settle for what you can do when you can experience what God can do? His power flowing through your life gives you spiritual power for daily living.

A meaningful time with God daily will not just result in a greater spiritual power in your life, but it will also give you a clearer . . .

Spiritual Direction

Everyone needs a clearer direction for his or her life. In fact, have you ever wondered what God wants to do in your life? I am sure you have. You see, one of the greatest benefits of having a meaningful time with God daily is the sensitivity God places into your life that leads you to follow His guidance. This time with Him daily becomes your spiritual GPS!

> *Why settle for what you can do when you can experience what God can do? His power flowing through your life gives you spiritual power for daily living.*

God does not will that you just wander around without His clear direction. Like any Father, He wants to make His will clear to His children. You are God's child! He *will* make His will and His way clear to you when you are having a meaningful time with God daily.

Furthermore, you will also discover that God will begin to build within you His . . .

Spiritual Purpose

Few things are more important than having purpose for your life. A lack of purpose has driven many people to hospitals and some to their graves. God wants to give His followers purpose.

When you have a meaningful time with God every day, you will begin to experience purpose for your life. You will discover that God wants to use you wherever you are in life. He wants to use you to make a difference with your life. He wants you to join Him in His purpose of seeing a spiritually lost world come into a dynamic personal relationship with Him.

His heart will become your heart. His purpose will become your purpose. When you have a meaningful time with God daily, He will give you true spiritual purpose for your life.

If you want to know more about what it means to live purposefully, take a look at my recent book *Living Fit*. I dedicated the first chapter to teaching what it means to live purposefully. I think that chapter alone can change your life and build within you a confident expectation that God has a powerful, exciting plan for your life.

But always understand, my friend, it all begins with having a meaningful time with God daily. When this begins to happen in your life, God will give you a new dimension of spiritual power, a clearer spiritual direction for your life today, and a spiritual purpose that will make every day of your life much more meaningful.

Back to the Basics

God's game plan for your life is discovered through having a meaningful time with Him daily. God is pursuing you. He wants a relationship with you. God wants to fellowship with you. When you draw near to God, He will draw near to you.

Experiencing a meaningful time with God is the most basic of the basics of living the Christian life. Just as football teams cannot win games while neglecting the basics of the game, Christians cannot experience God's work in their lives while neglecting the basic of having a meaningful time with God daily. It is the most fundamental part of the Christian life.

Is it not amazing how Satan, our greatest enemy, does all he can to keep us from meeting with God daily? Even Satan knows where the spiritual power is discovered in the Christian life.

If you genuinely desire to walk with God and to develop a more effective prayer life, then follow the six guidelines in this chapter about how to have a meaningful time with God daily.

The time is short. It is past time for Jesus' disciples to get back to the basics. *There are no shortcuts to spiritual victory.* Stay with the fundamentals. When you do, the benefits will be innumerable and the blessings will be bountiful.

PART 2

KEYS TO A POWERFUL PRAYER LIFE

CHAPTER 4

HOW TO PRAY ACCORDING TO GOD'S WILL

Years ago, our Cross Church Springdale campus constructed an office facility that is still to this day a special workplace for our staff team that serves this campus. When my office was being built, the designers asked what I wanted in my office. I requested only that the space allotted to me for ministering to people would remind me of God's purpose for my life and ministry. This was accomplished by printing the Great Commission of our Lord Jesus Christ on the walls of my office and placing a large picture of the world behind my desk.

My office may be uniquely decorated, but in reality it is like any other pastor's office. It contains incredible memories. It also contains important information. Much of this information is confidential—no one needs to see it or know it other than me.

Although everyone is welcome to visit while I am in my office, the key is not given out to anyone who wants one. In fact, few persons have direct access to this office. Not any key will get you into my office; only the key uniquely designed for my office will give you access into this place.

Just like the key that opens the door into my office, prayer is the key that unlocks the door into God's throne room. Would you like to have a key that unlocks the treasure chest of heaven? A key that would unleash the power of God in your life and future? This treasure chest contains the powerful blessings God has created for you and wants to distribute to you. God's throne room is the place where you talk to God. It is the place where you offer your prayers to God and He answers them. Prayer is the key that unlocks the door to this treasure chest of heaven, God's throne room.

In this special place, through your prayers, you get hold of God. In this special place, through your prayers, God gets hold of you. As a believer in Jesus Christ, you have the awesome privilege of experiencing the presence of God in this special place because the key of prayer gives you access to God.

Imagine this because it is so: *You can go to God anywhere at any time about anything!* You have direct access into God's throne room, the place where you talk to God.

In this place, you pray. In this place, you offer praise. In this place, you worship. In this place, God changes you. Leaving this place, you are never the same.

I want the treasure chest of God made available to me. However, let me be honest with you about something. I do not seek the treasure chest of God; I seek God Himself. When I seek God first, I receive all that He wants me to have from His treasure chest. I receive the peace of His presence and the confidence of knowing that He is working in my life. In this secret place, God answers my prayers.

Prayer is a secret adventure. I like to refer to the experience of abiding in His presence through prayer as the secret place. One reason prayer seems difficult at times is because we have the challenge of bowing in humility before the Lord in prayer in secret. No person may see us. Yet God sees us. And when we determine to pray, regardless of our physical posture, it is bowing the heart in humility before

God that becomes the deliberate decision to depend upon the Lord rather than ourselves.

May I inform you of something that you may not know or may have forgotten? This treasure chest of God contains all the answers to your needs. In other words, even before you ask or know you have a need, your wonderful God has the supply. He has the answers to all of your prayers. Prayer is the key that unlocks the door to God's throne room.

In this section I am going to share with you three keys to a powerful prayer life. If Jesus Christ is your Lord and Savior, you have all three of these keys. The result is that you can have a powerful prayer life.

I have never met a Christian who does not want to have a powerful prayer life. I have heard hundreds of Christians say they wished they could pray like this person or that person. The good news is that you do not have to go to a prayer conference to receive these keys. You already have each of these keys if you are a genuine follower of Jesus Christ.

God's throne room is the place where you talk to God. It is the place where you offer your prayers to God and He answers them.

A key to a personal office or a key into your home gives you direct access. You are afforded this access not because of simply having a key, but because you have the authority to experience this immediate access. Through having a personal relationship with Jesus Christ, you are given the keys to access God's throne room.

Would you etch the next statement deep into your memory? *Prayer leads you to the power of God.* Jesus verified this when He said, "For Yours is the kingdom and the power and the glory forever. Amen" (Matthew 6:13).

Prayer is your immediate entrance into the power of God. God is power. Prayer is the means by which you communicate to God and He communicates to you.

Are you ready to enter into this treasure chest of God? Are you ready to enter into God's throne room? Are you ready to experience His power like never before? Are you ready to experience the confidence of God in your life by knowing He will answer your prayer? If you are ready to take your prayer life to a new level, let me inform you that the first key to entering God's throne room of prayer is for you to . . .

Pray According to God's Will

I am the father of two sons. These two young men are still the joy of my life. When they were teenagers, Josh and Nick would earnestly seek to know my will by asking, "Dad, what do you think?" They still ask this question today, just not as often. This question demonstrated when they were teenagers, and even today, a teachable spirit. Even now, if a situation they are facing has major significance in their lives, they will make sure that they know my desire about that situation. Just as with many of us, when the stakes are so much higher, we want to do all we can to make sure our decisions are right.

Children get frustrated when they cannot discern what their parents really want them to do. Many times, parents are very poor at relating their desires to their children because the parents really do not know their desires. Or they may be somewhat afraid of their children's response to these desires.

As a child of God, you should have a teachable spirit. You should desire to know the will of your Father in heaven—not simply in moments of crisis but at all times in all things. There are moments as a child of God that you may act like a teenager who is afraid to know your Father's will because you know He will not agree with your will. Can you relate to this?

One of the great comforts you can have as a child of God is that your Father in heaven does not operate with the same margin of error as human parents; in fact, He operates at a zero margin of error. He has a perfect plan for your life. He wants to share this plan with you daily and even momentarily. He never keeps His will from you because He is afraid of your reaction or rejection of it. He reveals it to you in His perfect timing. Count on this in relation to God's time-table: He is never too early or too late, but He is always on time. He knows what is best for you even when you do not know what is best for you. He is ready to share with you what His will is for your life.

Prayer is the vehicle of communication by which you can understand God's will for your life more clearly. The challenge is that you have to learn to pray according to His will. First John 5:14–15 states, "This is the confidence which we have before Him, that, if we ask anything according to His will, He hears us. And if we know that He hears us in whatever we ask, we know that we have the requests which we have asked from Him." There is no need to come into prayer with a tentative nature. It is clear from these verses that you can enter God's throne room with confidence.

Confidence in prayer means that you can have freedom of speech in prayer. You can say anything to God you want to say. Confidence in prayer also means that you come to God and tell Him your needs. In other words, you can go to God anytime, anywhere, and about anything. Knowing this should give you great confidence in prayer. This is why having confidence when you pray results in praying with great expectation. You know God is hearing you and He will reveal to you His will for your life and future.

As you are praying, you are to pray about what *God* wants, not what *you* want. In fact, I am not sure God will give you an answer concerning some of your prayers until your will is totally surrendered to Him. The attitude that you should have is, "Lord, I am willing to receive Your will. If You want me to do it, I am ready. If You do not, then that is fine." At this point of self-denial, God brings into reality the heart of Jesus' prayer, "Not My will, but Yours be done" (Luke 22:42).

Therefore, your ultimate goal in prayer should be to pray according to what God says in His Word, the Bible. Remember, when the Bible speaks, God speaks. Knowing what God says in His Word should move you to following what God says in His Word—not simply relating to a personal decision or issue, but about everything.

God hears your prayers when you ask for the things that are in line with His Word, which always reveals His will, His intention, and His desire. In fact, our prayers should reflect what God says in His Word.

Do you want God to hear your prayers? Do you ever wonder if He hears your prayers? Do you want God to answer your prayers? I believe the secret to God hearing your prayers is for you to ask for the things that are in line with His Word, which reveals His will.

Humble and passionate prayer conforms your will to the will of God as revealed through the Word of God, the Bible. You can have the confidence that God hears you when you pray about the things that are in line with His Word, which again, reveals His will. Furthermore, when God's timing is right in your life and your requests are aligned with God's Word, then God may choose to grant your requests.

Let me pull up a chair beside you as you read this. While all the above can be true, I also take great comfort in knowing that for whatever reason there may have been in God's sovereign will and knowledge, God has not always answered my prayers, even when they were aligned with His Word and prayed with the purest of motives. Why? I will tell you why: God knows what is best for me even when I do not know what is best for me.

God is a great and perfect Father. He is a good, good Father! He wants to show you His will. He wants to meet all of your needs. Just as an obedient and teachable son will earnestly seek the will of his earthly father, as an obedient and teachable child of God you need to seek the will of your Father in heaven.

But just as your father on this earth may have chosen to not grant your will at certain times because he may have known things that you did not know at the time, your God and Father in heaven always does this even better than any earthly dad could ever do.

In relation to the truths discovered in 1 John 5:14–15, what is God saying to you? You can go to God anywhere, anytime, and about anything. When you go to God in prayer, you can freely express your heart with the words that He gives to you in prayer. There is no special formula to use in prayer, but the key is for you to pray about His desire for your life. When you go to God, talk to Him about His desire for your life, His desire for your family, His desire for your job, His desire for your church, and His desire for your country. Use caution about always exploding with your intentions, or else you may forfeit God's activity in your life.

The result of this kind of praying is that you will receive the confidence that you should have in prayer as you pray about what God wants in all situations rather than what you might want. This kind of praying also results in your prayers being answered. Have you prayed according to God's will for your life? Have you prayed about God's will for your family? Have you prayed about God's will for your church? Have you prayed about God's will for your job? Have you prayed about God's will for your country? Since it is important to pray about God's will in these areas and others, there are three important questions I want to address in the remaining pages of this chapter.

> *There is no special formula to use in prayer, but the key is for you to pray about His desire for your life.*

Question #1: How Do You Know God's Will?

This is a critical question. If God has promised that He will answer when you pray according to His will, then you should ask, "How do I know God's will?"

In the Bible, God reveals to you His will about all matters. When the Bible speaks, God speaks to you. If you are going to know God's will, then you are going to have to know the Scriptures. Learn to pray according to the Scriptures. Learn to search the Scriptures about the burden on your heart. See what God says about this burden, and then pray about your burden by using God's activity in the Scriptures.

God has a unique way of speaking to you about the matters of life when you are reading through the Scriptures in a systematic manner. The breadth of life is covered in the breadth of the entire counsel of God. This is why it is important to read the entire Bible.

There are times when a major need comes into a person's life. For example, suppose you are a single adult in a dating relationship with someone, and things are getting rather interesting. You think about this person most of the time. When you are around this person, your heart flutters. The stars of love are in your eyes. If you have not gone to God yet about this relationship, then approach the Word of God and discover what God says about dating and marriage. Through your investigation of this subject in the Word, you are opening yourself up for God to speak to you.

Through His Word, He will speak to you about this person. Pray about this person from God's point of view. Release the relationship in its entirety to God. Ask God for His will to take place, and in His time, He will either penetrate your heart with His peace or saturate it with restlessness. Pray about what He wants you to do about that relationship. When you are willing to go forward and also willing to walk away, it is then God may reveal His ultimate intention for this relationship.

When I pray, I often say to God, *Now, Lord, I have laid out several needs to You today. As I read Your Word now, if You so choose, speak to me about some of these needs.* When I sense God is speaking to me through the Scriptures about one of these needs, I write the verse down beside the need and pray over it for a while. In His timing, God will confirm to me His will. The observation I have made through the years is that as

I pray according to the Scriptures concerning this need, God conforms my will to His concrete direction concerning the need.

Sometimes I feel the bondage of sin taking hold of my life. Whenever I feel this pressure from the enemy or sense my own lack of repentance over this sin, I open my Bible to Psalm 51, where David confessed his sins before God. I read this psalm back to God, personalizing it for me and my sin. If you want to know the will of God, learn to personalize the Scriptures and pray them to God in relation to your need.

Sometimes Christians have a poor view of God. They seem to think that God plays hide-and-seek with them concerning His will. God is a loving Father who wants you to know His will. He reveals His will in the Bible. I want to encourage you to follow this practice: do not begin to pray seriously without the Bible in your hand.

Prayer and the Bible are like two wings on an airplane—you will not reach your destination without both of them. Your destination is discerning the will of God about all matters of life. The way you do this is through prayer and through the Bible.

By the way, the Father loves to hear His Word. Remind Him of what He said in it. Read it to Him. He loves to hear it! How do I know this? As a father of two sons and now the "poppy" of seven grandchildren, I love to hear my boys or my grandchildren say, "You know, Dad," or "You know, Poppy, you said . . .". A loving father or grandfather will not back away from his word to his children, and God, who has zero margin of error, never backs away from His Word to His children. The Bible is the most relevant book in the world today. God honors all of His words in this Book for all ages and peoples.

Are you praying according to God's will? I can tell you how you will answer this question by asking another question: *Are you praying according to the Scriptures?* When you are praying according to the Scriptures, you are praying according to God's will. When this occurs, it is like praying with power from on High!

Spend time in the Word of God. Read through the Bible. It will change your prayer life. It will change your thought life. It will change your life.

Question #2: Do You Always Know God's Will?

There are times when you may not know God's will about a certain situation. This should not cause you to have a spiritual wreck. It should cause you to move with caution about the matter on your heart. The apostle Paul experienced this. He told the church in Rome that he was "always in my prayers making request, if perhaps now at last by the will of God I may succeed in coming to you" (Romans 1:10). Paul wanted to go to Rome. Several times he requested from the Father that he be permitted to go to Rome.

Notice the conditions Paul placed on his prayer. Let me paraphrase for you what I believe Paul was praying: *Lord, I have come to You several times about going to Rome. I really want to go, Lord. If You would grant me this request, I would sure appreciate it. Yet, I only want to go if You want me to go.* Let me take it another step for you. He was saying to the Lord: *Lord, I do not want to go to Rome unless You really want me to go. I just pray You will let me go.*

Be honest, do you ever pray like this? I do not believe there is anything wrong with praying like this because the emphasis is still on God's will, not your own, even though you may have a personal desire about the situation. Perhaps you are unsure about a job that you would like to have. Maybe you are interested in a promotion. Seek God's will about these matters. If He does not speak to you through His Word, then come to Him and pray, *Lord, I would really like to take this new job* or *God, I would really like to take this new promotion.*

I do not think it is good to trust in yourself in regards to prayer. Place all of your trust in God. So add these words to your prayer: *Lord, if it is not Your will for me to have this new job or this new promotion, take the desire away from me. If it is not Your will, keep the decision away from me.*

If you truly want to seek God and His will, He will be faithful to make His will known to you. Through this process of seeking God's will, you learn the walk of faith.

In times when you do not clearly understand God's will from His Word about a particular need or situation, do not hesitate to pray as Paul did. Just pray, *Lord, if You want me to . . . I will* or *Lord, I would like to do this, but I only want to if You want me to do it.* God will always honor a person who seeks Him with his or her whole heart.

Question #3: Why Do You Need to Pray If God's Will Is Going to Be Done Anyway?

God is sovereign, which means He is able to accomplish anything He chooses to accomplish. At the same time, you have a free will that may not always be in conformity to God's will. Yet, God is able to engineer the circumstances in life to bring your will into conformity with His will. Knowing all of this, you might ask, "Why should I pray if God's will is going to be done anyway?"

There are two reasons why you should pray. First, you should pray because God commanded you to pray about all things. He wants you to spend time with Him talking to Him about your life. Remember, God wants to have fellowship with you. Through reading the Bible and praying to God, you experience His fellowship.

Another reason you should pray is that God has chosen prayer as the means to meet your needs. *Dependence upon God builds faith.* When you see God respond to your requests, your trust in God is enlarged.

Prayer does not move God as much as it moves you toward God. Prayer changes you. It conforms your will to His will. It places you in a posture to receive what God has for your life.

When you pray, God is more likely to meet your needs. His will

> *Through prayer, God establishes a trust relationship with you and me. Our faith is enlarged when God's activity becomes evident in our lives. Therefore, prayer is an act of obeying God.*

is for you to talk to Him, abide in Him, and know that without Him you are nothing. This spiritual posture moves you into expecting God to do something in your life. Through prayer, God establishes a trust relationship with you and me. Our faith is enlarged when God's activity becomes evident in our lives. Therefore, prayer is an act of obeying God. It is always God's will to obey His Word and to talk to Him through the means of prayer.

A Spiritual Insight

God's Word clearly states that God wants you to pray. You pray for the purpose of communing with God, not for the purpose of getting something you want or think you need in your life. I want to share a spiritual insight with you that will bring this subject to an appropriate conclusion: *you are to pray, and God will determine when and how those prayers are answered.*

This may cause some problems from your perspective. You may struggle with the issue of when God answers your prayers. He never seems to move as quickly as you might desire. Remember: *God alone is in charge of the timing of His answer to your prayers.* Rest assured that God always answers your prayers. At times, He says yes. At other times, He says no. There are other times when His answer is, *Wait.* God is in charge of the "when" of life, not you.

Furthermore, God is also in charge of when He says yes, when He says no, and even when He says, *Wait.* God always knows what is best for you even when you do not know what is best for yourself.

Another struggle you may face in prayer is how God may answer your prayer. It is impossible to see all God sees. There were times in your life when you really wanted God to answer your prayer in a certain way, but He did not do it. At that time, you were somewhat despondent about it. Yet when you look back at it now, you see that He was protecting you. He was caring for you when you did not know how to care for yourself.

A Personal Story

When I was about to graduate from seminary with my master of divinity degree and was waiting for entry into the doctoral level of study, I preached at a church that wanted to call me as their pastor. It was a new church, located in the suburbs of a major metropolitan city in Texas. I dreamed of giving my entire life to that church.

When I preached in view of a call, everything went great. On the way back to the airport, the chairman of the pastoral search committee informed me that I needed to receive at least 95 percent of the vote for the church to call me as their pastor. I was concerned, because even Jesus Christ would do well to get that kind of vote in any church I have ever been in.

Plus, the church waited to vote the Sunday following my time of preaching. That week seemed so long as we waited with great enthusiasm to hear from the chairman the following Sunday. As soon as I completed preaching at the church I was serving, Jeana and I walked into the parsonage, which was next door to the church.

Early on that Sunday afternoon, I received the call from the chairman of the committee. He informed me that as well as things had gone the Sunday before, when the church voted, I received less than the required 95 percent vote. The chairman was devasted. I was devastated. Jeana was devastated.

My ministry life was turned upside down. I became downcast about being rejected by this church and for a while had difficulty staying focused on the church I was serving at the time. But, as stated earlier, God knows what is best for us even when we do not know what is best for ourselves.

In the course of time God put me back together, healed my heart, and lifted up my spirit. Then while working on my doctorate degree, God called me to the First Baptist Church in Palacios, Texas, one of my favorite church experiences of all time. The power of God fell on that place, and in three years the church tripled in attendance. God used that ministry to define me and prepare me for the future. It still impacts me to this day.

Listen carefully and focus on these words: God protected me from what I had previously prayed for, initially thinking it was God's will for my life and ministry. But then, in His timing, He provided a wonderful church that was truly in His will for my life—a church that shaped not just my life but my ministry even to this day. As a result, I experienced the blessings of God that can only come when you trust and live in the providence of God.

It would be great to have 20/20 spiritual vision on the front side of certain situations, but that would take away the faith and the joy of the journey in prayer. No matter what your current situation may be, you can trust that God's will is always the best answer for your life, even if it's not the answer you expect at the time.

God wants you to pray. He will determine when and how your prayers are answered. The joy of the Lord is yours when you realize the reality of His protection in your life. *He knows what is best for you, even when you do not know what is best for yourself.*

Begin today to practice praying according to God's Word, always seeking God's will. This key, given to you by the Master Himself, will open up the treasure chest of God to you as you abide in this secret place, God's throne room. Enter into this special place by praying according to God's will.

CHAPTER 5

HOW TO PRAY IN
JESUS' NAME

I am grateful for the many doors of ministry God has opened up for me around the country and even the world. It is always a joy to go to another setting and relate God's truth with people. Even though I enjoy the privilege of ministry around the country, I do not enjoy the challenges of travel. The challenges of airlines and hotels seem to keep things interesting while I travel.

Security has, understandably so, become a big issue for the airline and hotel industry. Several years ago I arrived at a hotel and needed to check into my room before a meeting downstairs. I was already late due to my flight being delayed. I checked into the hotel, hurried to prepare for my meeting, and walked out of my room to attend the meeting in the hotel's conference room.

After a long meeting that went until late that night, I got on the elevator and went to the floor to go to my room for the evening. As I stepped out of the elevator, I reached into my pocket to get the entry card to my room. I had been successful in bringing the entry card, but in my hurried state I had failed to bring the brochure that had my room number on it. Therefore, the guessing game began.

I was really tired, and I did not want to go all the way downstairs again. So I tried to remember my room number. I thought I had done so; however, when I placed the entry card into the door of the room that I supposed was mine, the code on the card did not activate the lock. I determined that I probably had the wrong room number. So I attempted to open another door. Again, the code did not activate the lock. At this point, frustration after a long day was setting in, so I hurried downstairs to the front desk. The clerk was busy checking in several people as well as answering the phone.

As I waited, my frustration increased. Finally, the clerk got to me. I told him my story, and then I had to be checked out, for security reasons, to make certain I was telling the truth. Approximately forty-five minutes after my initial attempt to get into my room, I received the correct room number. Not only did I not have the correct number to my room, but I was not even on the right floor when I tried to enter the two rooms!

When I finally got into my room that evening, I was relieved that my clothing was there. At last, I was home for the evening. There is nothing like the joy of travel.

Do you ever wonder if the Lord has a sense of humor? One week after this experience, my wife and I went to spend the weekend in New York City. I was scheduled to preach for Jim Cymbala, pastor of the Brooklyn Tabernacle church in Brooklyn, New York. When we arrived at the hotel and received the information about our room, I was determined not to forget my room number again. The Lord helped me to not forget it: I was assigned room 666. Jeana and I laughed and proceeded to our room with the blessed assurance we would not forget our room number in that hotel.

One of the pivotal things I learned from my hotel experience is that the entry card, when coded correctly, will give you entry into your room. If the card has been coded incorrectly, the lock will not allow entry into the room. Even if the card is coded correctly, it is necessary to use it on the right door in order for successful entry to occur.

When you go to the Father in prayer, there is a code you can use that will give you immediate access into God's presence. This code is never in error, and it will open all that God has for you when you enter into God's throne room. This code is the name of Jesus. When you use the name of Jesus in your prayer, you have access to all God has for you.

Pray in Jesus' Name

Those of us who have grown up in church life have had the privilege of experiencing some wonderful blessings of God. I have been very active in church my entire life. As a result, I have been mentored in prayer through the years by observing others' prayers in worship services and prayer meetings.

I remember in a distinct way how people would pray in the church I attended most of my life. One of the normal prayers at my church sounded something like the following:

Dear Father, we are grateful for this day. We thank You for the blessings of our life. We thank You for the blessing of our family. Now, Lord, be with our pastor today as he preaches. In Jesus' name, amen.

This generalized praying probably did not grab the horns of the altar, but there is something that I will never forget about all the prayers in that small church. Every person I ever heard pray in that church would conclude their prayer by saying, "In Jesus' name, amen." At this point in my life I do wonder how many people who used that phrase really understood what it meant or if they used it simply out of habit.

What does it mean to pray in Jesus' name? Just before Jesus went to the cross to die for your sins, He had an important conversation with His closest followers. In the sixteenth chapter of the gospel of John, Jesus spoke about the relationship the Holy Spirit would have with His disciples. Jesus instructed His disciples about the role of the Holy Spirit in prayer. In verses 23 and 24, Jesus said, "Truly, truly, I say to you, if you ask the Father for anything in My name, He will give it to you. Until now you have asked for nothing in My name; ask and you will receive, so that your joy may be made full."

When you go to the Father in prayer, there is a code you can use that will give you immediate access into God's presence. . . . This code is the name of Jesus.

Jesus gave His disciples a key to a powerful prayer life. That key is to make all requests known to the Father in Jesus' name.

Jesus encouraged you to ask the Father for anything. When you go to the Father in prayer, you are not going to your buddy. You are not going to the man upstairs. You are going to the King of kings and the Lord of lords. Jesus has given you the privilege to go to His Father and ask Him for anything. The word *ask* depicts the image of requesting something from someone who is your superior. The Father is your superior. You cannot simply yank His chain and "name it and claim it." You need to understand who God is, live under His authority, and receive His will for your life as you make your requests known to Him in Jesus' name. When you ask the Father for something in Jesus' name, you need to understand that this phrase is neither a magical formula that attempts to bargain with God nor a vain repetition.

In this section of the book, I am giving you three keys to a powerful prayer life. In the previous chapter, you read about the first key: *praying according to God's will*. In this chapter, you are reading about the second key: *praying in Jesus' name*. Since praying in Jesus' name is the code for us to enter God's throne room, I want to address the question . . .

Why Should You Pray in Jesus' Name?

There are many reasons why you should pray in Jesus' name. I want to highlight three of these reasons.

1. Jesus' Name Is the Gateway to God

In the city of St. Louis, Missouri, a large white arch called the Gateway Arch stands in the heart of downtown. This arch symbolizes that the city of St. Louis is the gateway to the West—the city where you enter the western part of the United States.

A gateway is an entry point. Jesus' name is the entry point into the presence of God. It is the code of entry into God's throne room. Coming to the Father in Jesus' name gives you the assurance of being able to approach God.

You cannot approach God in your own name. You cannot approach God in your own ability. *You can approach God only in the name of Jesus Christ. He is the gateway, the entry point, into the presence of God.* This initial entry point takes place at your salvation experience. In John 14:6, Jesus said, "I am the way, and the truth, and the life; no one comes to the Father but through Me."

The Bible teaches that Jesus is the only way to have a personal relationship with God. Jesus regarded Himself as the only way to God. He said He is the only truth. There is no truth apart from Him. He also understood that He is the only One who can grant spiritual life. Jesus is the only gateway to God!

If you are going to do serious business with God, then you must pray in the name above all names—the name of Jesus. An example of this would be:

Father, I do not come to You today in my own name or my own ability. I do not even have a right to talk to You except by and through the person of Jesus Christ. I approach You, but not in my own name or my own ability. Father, I approach You in the strong and powerful name of Jesus Christ, amen.

When you pray in Jesus' name as illustrated for you here, you have punched the code. You have used the key that will get you into God's presence.

The first reason you should pray in Jesus' name is because His name is the entry point, the gateway to God. Jesus' name alone gives you access into the presence of God, where you can do some serious communication with God.

2. It Reminds the Father of Jesus

I tend to live a hurried life. The schedule I keep is very busy, but if you want to stop me for a moment, all you have to do is talk to me about my sons, Josh and Nick. I will immediately stop and talk about either one of my boys. The mere mention of either of their names brings everything else to a halt for a few moments, and you will have my immediate attention. If you have a few good things to say about them, I can add to those with a whole lot of other good things. As a father, I love to be reminded of my two sons.

When you go to the Father in prayer, mention the name of His Son, Jesus. He loves Jesus' name. He is reminded of His Son and all He has done every time you mention Jesus by name. Whenever God hears Jesus' name, He is reminded of being one with Him. He is reminded of the preexistence of His Son. He is reminded of how Jesus substituted Himself to die for your sins. He is reminded of how Jesus died in your place. He is reminded of how Jesus is at His right hand right now and lives to make intercession for you. Therefore, anytime I pray in Jesus' name, I am reminding the Father of all these things and more about His Son, Jesus Christ.

Let me give you an example of this truth about reminding the Father of His Son, Jesus Christ, in prayer:

Father, thank You for letting me come to You and talk to You today. Thank You for the privilege of letting my requests be made known to You in Jesus' name. I lay my life and these requests before You in the name of Your wonderful and beloved Son, Jesus Christ, amen.

When the Father hears you pray something like these words, He says, *Yes! My Son is wonderful and He is My beloved!* By using the name of Jesus Christ in prayer, you are reminding the Father of His Son and all His Son has done. At the mere mention of Jesus' name, you get the immediate attention of the Father.

3. Jesus' Name Is Your Authority to Tie Your Request to the Father's Will

The name of Jesus is the most powerful name in heaven and on earth. Any time you take a request to God the Father in Jesus' name, you are tying it to the most authoritative name that has ever been given anywhere in the world. *This means that you are taking your requests to God with authority.*

Much of the time, prayer is uncertain ground for many believers. By observing the tentative nature of many Christians, you might think the ground is filled with more land mines than blessings. This is not the kind of praying I am writing about here. You should not feel as if you are walking on eggshells with God. You should sense you are walking with the authority of His Son, Jesus.

By offering your request to the Father in Jesus' name, you are tying your request to great authority. The Father loves Jesus' name. Offering your requests in Jesus' name gains the Father's attention. By tying your requests to Jesus' name, you are submitting to the will of God about each request. Remember, it is not "My kingdom come and my will be done"; it is "Your kingdom come" and "Your will be done, on earth as it is in heaven" (Matthew 6:10).

For example, let's imagine for a moment that you have a child who has drifted away from God. This child's departure from God's life has worn you down. How should you pray about this?

Lord, my heart is broken over my child. He is away from You and the way he has been raised in his life. I come to You today in the strong name of Jesus, asking for Your authority to take place in this situation. Bring him back to You. In Jesus' name, reign in this situation, amen.

When you pray in this way, you are submitting your will to God's will about this situation. You are tying your request in an authoritative manner to the Lord Jesus Christ. You are asking God to do a miracle in your child's life.

Can God do a miracle? Absolutely! God can always do a miracle!

When you tie your requests to the name of Jesus Christ, you offer them to God with authority. At this point, God becomes personally involved in the situation.

Pray Specifically, Not Generally

I want to encourage you to get out of the generalities of prayer. Stop praying in a general way. Stop offering general requests before God. Generalities are portrayed in prayer with statements like, *Thank You for all things* or *Bless me with everything*. Get away from this kind of praying. This will not lead to a powerful prayer life.

When I was in college, a professor told my preaching class that he did not appreciate "GWOT" sermons. He defined "GWOT" sermons as sermons that were about "God, the World, and Other Things." He was gently rebuking our class for preaching in generalities. The end result of that kind of preaching is that no one will understand what the preacher is trying to say.

Much prayer that is done today is "GWOT" praying. Our praying is so general at times, it is as though we are praying for God, the World, and Other Things. Do not pray like this. Get away from the generalities.

When you begin to pray about specific requests and tie them one by one to the authoritative name of Jesus Christ, God is drawn to you quickly. He wants to know your heart. His specific interest in you and His interest in your specific prayer requests prove that God wants a personal relationship with you. This relationship is developed through practicing effective prayer principles. God will answer specific prayers that are directed to Him and linked with the authoritative name of Jesus.

> *Any time you take a request to God the Father in Jesus' name, you are tying it to the most authoritative name that has ever been given anywhere in the world.*

A Closing Word

I cannot write a chapter about the importance of praying in Jesus' name without sharing a climactic passage with you from God's Word. Since praying in Jesus' name is a key to a powerful prayer life, His name must be very powerful. Philippians 2:9–11 proclaims,

> For this reason also, God highly exalted [Jesus], and bestowed on Him the name which is above every name, so that at the name of Jesus EVERY KNEE WILL BOW, of those who are in heaven and on earth and under the earth, and that every tongue will confess that Jesus Christ is Lord, to the glory of God the Father.

This passage is such a dynamic word about the name of Jesus Christ. The name of Jesus is the name above every name. His name is better than any other name. His name stands for Savior. His name stands for purity, righteousness, and holiness. There is no blemish at all in the name of Jesus. His name is perfect. His name is powerful!

One day each knee on this earth will bow out of honor and respect for your Savior, Jesus Christ. It may not be cool in today's church to be on your face before God; however, one day you will be on your face before God every time the name of Jesus is mentioned. Even the demons in hell will bow at the mention of the name of Jesus. Why? Because they know that Jesus is Lord.

You cannot get to God on your own merit. You cannot pray to God in your own name. You cannot bribe God to answer your requests. It is impossible!

There is no need for any of these things because God has given you the key to a powerful prayer life.

This key to a powerful prayer life is praying in Jesus' name. By praying in Jesus' name, you enter into the very presence of God. By praying in Jesus' name, you remind the Father of all that Jesus has done. By praying in Jesus' name, you link your requests to the Father for His will to take place and His authority to occur in every situation.

You will never go wrong when you link your prayer requests to the most powerful name under all of heaven, the name of Jesus. There really is something about that name!

HOW TO PRAY IN THE SPIRIT

I magine for a moment that you are alone in a quiet and beautiful place. While sitting at a table, you look out the window at the beautiful mountain range that surrounds you. As you look down on the table, you see a blank piece of paper and a writing pen. Your assignment is to write on that blank sheet of paper all that you know about the subject of praying in the Spirit. What would you write? Would you even know enough to fill the blank sheet?

I have often wondered what the results would be if I led a congregation in this exercise on a Sunday morning. Perhaps many people would turn in a blank sheet of paper. Beyond that, I am confident that a variety of answers would be erroneous. Few answers would be on target about this subject.

I am disturbed how a biblical truth like praying in the Spirit is treated by some Christians. Many Christians never even discuss this subject; they just ignore it. Others look at it as a fanatical teaching that is practiced only by those who are too emotional about their faith. Since they equate praying in the Spirit with extremism, they do not want to have anything to do with it. Others abuse the phrase "praying in the Spirit" by saying it is something that it is really not. The result of this mistreatment is that ignorance and confusion abound on an essential teaching of the Christian life.

A Man Named Jude

Jude was the half brother of Jesus Christ. Even though he could have boasted about his relationship to Jesus, Jude instead referred to himself as a "servant of Jesus Christ" (Jude 1:1 csb). Jude was a man for his times. He was concerned about his culture and burdened that the godless culture in which he was living was invading the church.

Jude intended to write a letter to Christians that instructed them on the basics of salvation and the Christian life. However, Jude received word that false teachers were invading the church with counterfeit teachings. These false teachers were twisting the truth of the grace of God and making it appear as a license to sin. Jude was startled that this false teaching was rampant and yet no one was addressing it. He knew that someone needed to stand against these false teachers and their wrong teachings so the church of Jesus Christ would not tolerate their poor doctrine.

This courageous leader named Jude stood for Christ. He contended for the faith just like an athlete agonizes to cross the finish line, stretching every nerve and muscle to that mark of completion. Jude's defense of the faith was an experience of agony that demonstrates to everyone that defending the faith may be costly.

The faith that Jude defended was the faith that kept him. He knew God would protect him and guard him as he did what was right. Jude had this kind of courage because of his commitment to biblical truth and to prayer. In the twentieth verse of his letter to these Christians, Jude wrote, "But you, beloved, [are] building yourselves up on your most holy faith, praying in the Holy Spirit." What does this scripture mean?

The "most holy faith" mentioned in this verse refers to the doctrines and the teachings of God's Word. Faith cannot be holy without the Word of God. Faith does not even exist without the Word of God. Remember that Jude was calling for Christians to contend for the faith. In this verse he was saying that believers are built up on the concrete truth of God's Word.

If Jude lived in our culture today, he would be a very unusual Christian. The reason for this is because he had . . .

A Most Holy Balance

Jude was not a wild-eyed religious radical but a man of God who was theologically balanced. He was a man who not only understood the importance of truth and faith but also understood the power of prayer. In fact, he understood prayer in a unique way: he understood how prayer relates to the Holy Spirit. This is why he instructed Christians to pray "in the Holy Spirit." Praying in the Spirit is one of the keys to a powerful prayer life.

This courageous leader named Jude stood for Christ. He contended for the faith just like an athlete agonizes to cross the finish line, stretching every nerve and muscle to that mark of completion.

Notice the balance in verse 20. As a Christian, you are to be built up in the most holy faith, and at the same time, you are to pray in the Spirit. When you pursue the Word of God, you pursue a relationship with the Holy Spirit. When you pursue a relationship with the Holy Spirit, you will pursue the Word of God. The Holy Spirit will always point you to Jesus Christ and lead you to the Word of God. When you know the Word of God, you are equipped to pray in the Spirit.

Effective prayer cannot be accomplished without knowing, believing, and practicing God's Word. It is more important for you to know what God says to you than for you simply to say things to God. What you say to God in prayer will be determined by what God says to you in His Word.

If you will implement the truths of the twentieth verse in Jude's book, you will achieve this most holy balance. You will join the Word of God with your relationship to the Holy Spirit. How balanced are you at these two truths in your life? Do you lean toward one of them and ignore the other? If you lean to God's Word without a personal relationship with the Holy Spirit in prayer, you will have knowledge with no life. If you lean to a personal relationship with the Holy Spirit without an understanding of God's Word, you will have an appearance of life with no spiritual depth.

In order to have this most holy balance, consider these two observations.

1. When You Have the Word and Little Prayer, You Have Some Spiritual Light but Limited Spiritual Power

Most Christians who take the time to read books like this one have some commitment to the Word of God. Usually, their commitment is much stronger to the Word of God than to a relationship with the Holy Spirit of God. You may understand what the Bible is saying, but if the Holy Spirit is not moving mightily in your life, you will have little spiritual power. If the Holy Spirit is not empowering you daily, you cannot teach, preach, witness, or communicate God's Word in a way that will capture the attention of this generation.

Your challenge is to grow in your knowledge of the Word of God and in your relationship with the Holy Spirit. Maybe you can teach good lessons from God's Word. Perhaps you can even preach good sermons from God's Word. Yet, when you allow the Holy Spirit to accompany you as you communicate God's truth, you will capture the attention of your generation.

Your goal should not be just to have spiritual light but to have spiritual light accompanied with great spiritual power. Only a balance of the Word of God and the ministry of prayer will bring about this holy balance that is a powerful combination.

2. When You Have Prayer and Not Much of the Word, You Have Spiritual Zeal but Limited Knowledge

This imbalance is so dangerous. People who live in this spiritual imbalance think they have spiritual life, but in reality they only have simple enthusiasm. Spiritual zeal is meaningless if it is not built up by the Word of God.

The way this dangerous extremism occurs is that some people do not balance reading the Word and praying in the Spirit. If all you have is spiritual zeal, without having a commitment to being built up by God's Word daily, then you have dangerous extremism. Spirit-led prayer must be blended with biblical knowledge in order for you to have spiritual power rather than meaningless zeal.

Your goal in your spiritual life should not be merely acquiring information or achieving a powerful experience. Your goal in your spiritual life should be spiritual transformation. This takes a personal relationship with the Holy Spirit combined with a growing understanding of God's Word. Accomplishing this most holy balance will cause you to grow in your Christian life.

As a Christian, you have the privilege of entering God's throne room, where you can receive numerous blessings from God's treasure chest. One key that will get you into this special place of prayer is praying according to God's will. The second key that will open this special place for you is praying in Jesus' name. The third key is praying in the Holy Spirit. Each of these keys will give you a powerful prayer life.

Let's go deeper now about what it means to pray in the Holy Spirit. Let's begin here.

What It Does Not Mean to Pray in the Spirit

I want to make sure that you interpret what it means to pray in the Holy Spirit in the context of what Jude wrote in his letter to Christians. I want to challenge you not to interpret this through your personal experience or through your religious tradition. These are not your authorities for what you believe or practice—*the Bible alone is your authority.* Looking again at this letter from Jude, let's interpret what Jude is *not* saying about praying in the Holy Spirit.

Since this powerful reference is in Jude's book, we must understand there is no indication that praying in the Holy Spirit refers to praying in other tongues. In fact, Jude doesn't even mention the gift of tongues in his letter.

The gift of tongues (or languages) is a spiritual gift that was demonstrated on the day of pentecost. As people gathered in Jerusalem from all over the world for the Feast of Pentecost, God sent His Spirit upon the Christians in Jerusalem. They began to speak in languages and dialects they did not know but that others knew. They spoke in these languages and dialects for the sole purpose of sharing the gospel of Jesus Christ in a way the people could understand it. The result was that at least three thousand people came to Christ. The emphasis was not the phenomenon of the gifts of tongues; the miracle was that God provided a way for all people gathered for the Feast of Pentecost to be able to hear the gospel of Jesus Christ in their own languages and dialects. I believe it is important that there is no reference to praying in the Spirit in Acts 2, where this experience is recorded.

In 1 Corinthians 12 and 14, the apostle Paul's references to the gift of tongues do not refer to praying in the Holy Spirit. In fact, the tongues mentioned in 1 Corinthians were causing problems in public worship. The Corinthians were rebuked for attempting to duplicate the tongues of Acts 2 by the works of the flesh and given specific guidelines on how they were to worship.

I mention these passages because it is important that persons do not put their theology together like a jigsaw puzzle. When you piece together a puzzle, you will attempt a great deal of trial and error. But God doesn't work like that. He spoke His truth about praying in the Holy Spirit in the same verse that He spoke of being built up by the Word of God. God knows the need for balance. He knows the tendency of believers to run after an emotional experience without having the foundation of God's Word. He also knows the tendency of believers to run after more intellectual knowledge without having spiritual life.

Praying in the Holy Spirit is a biblical truth. We cannot let the extremism of some, the misinterpretation of others, or the deadness of a few people negate the truth of praying in the Holy Spirit. We cannot let others and their preferences rob us of one of God's wonderful truths. Let's permit this truth to stand on its own as mentioned by Jude. Let the Word of God be the Word of God. Let the truth of praying in the Spirit stand on its own.

What It Means to Pray in the Spirit

Since truth is built on God's Word and not upon our own personal experience, we need to continue our search for truth that is found only in the Word of God, the Bible. What does the Bible mean when it says to pray in the Spirit? I believe it means the following three things.

1. Praying in the Spirit Means to Pray According to the Leadership of the Spirit

When you pray, are you praying under the leadership of the Holy Spirit? Do you run through a prayer agenda without considering the Spirit's guidance in your time of prayer? When you pray under the Spirit's leadership, you cannot be in a hurry.

How can you begin to pray according to the leadership of the Holy

Spirit? One way you can begin is with moments of saying nothing at all. Be quiet before God. Meditate on the Word of God and the work of God.

I would encourage you to begin by praying something like, *Lord, I come to You in the name of Jesus today. Please show me what to pray for right now.* It is important to have a plan to pray, but that plan is simply a guide, not a rule book. You always want to pray under the leadership of the Holy Spirit. Be flexible and learn to let the Holy Spirit lead you in your prayer time. A prayer gives you a general direction; it should never place you into personal bondage.

When you pray under the leadership of the Holy Spirit, He will lead you to pray by the Word of God. At times, I have had some people say to me, "Pastor, I am praying about getting a divorce, and I really sense the Holy Spirit is leading me to do so." Yet, when I quiz the person, there is an admission that there are no biblical grounds for divorce. It is just the person's personal preference at this time in life.

The Holy Spirit will always lead you to fulfill the Word of God. Therefore, the Spirit will not lead you to be divorced if there are no grounds for it to occur biblically. *You cannot let the phrase "the Spirit is leading me" become a means to justify an action that is contrary to God's Word.*

Praying under the leadership of the Holy Spirit means that you will pray by and with the Word of God. When you pray under the leadership of the Holy Spirit, you will let God show you what you need to pray for and about in your time of prayer. God will show you what to pray for. Read His Word. Listen to His Spirit. Let His Spirit talk to your spirit. At times, just be quiet. Be silent. Then let God lead you as you pray.

2. Praying in the Spirit Means to Pray with Assistance from the Holy Spirit

Decades ago, I followed the green and gold of Baylor University football. While pastoring in my home state of Texas, I traveled with a family in my church to several Baylor Bear football games. I will never forget going to Texas A&M University's Kyle Field to watch the Bears play the Texas Aggies. It was a memorable experience. At that time, I had only seen Texas Aggie football on national television. I assure you, there is nothing like being at a game in their home stadium. The crowd at Aggieland is known as the 12th Man. Fans stand the entire ball game, symbolizing their strong support of their team, and they are always ready to suit up for the game if they are needed. They hunch over and yell for their team at the top of their lungs. They sway from right to left to the music of the dynamic Aggie band. What a great tradition!

The eleven Texas Aggies on the field are not by themselves. They are supported and assisted by thousands and thousands of Texas Aggie fans. Whoever goes onto Kyle Field to play the Aggies goes onto this field with a great disadvantage. The zeal, passion, and commitment of the fans of the Texas Aggies assist the players as they play the game of football.

As great as this is, in a much greater way, the Holy Spirit assists you when you pray. As the fans of Texas A&M football push their team to victory, the Holy Spirit pulls you toward God and to experience your spiritual victory. Romans 8:26 says, "In the same way the Spirit also helps our weakness; for we do not know how to pray as we should, but the Spirit Himself intercedes for us with groanings too deep for words."

There are times in the Christian life when you do not know how to pray. This passage is speaking of how the Holy Spirit comes to assist you in prayer when you do not know what to pray. The Holy Spirit is praying for you to have victory. He is praying for you to fulfill God's will in your life. He is praying for you and pulling for you in every way.

When you pray with assistance from the Holy Spirit, your prayer will be something like this: *Lord, I do not know how to pray about this matter. I must have Your help. I must have Your assistance. As You lead me to pray about this, may Your Spirit utter to the Father what the depths of my heart feel about this matter. Assist me, Holy Spirit, right now as I pray.*

Praying in the Holy Spirit is letting the Spirit assist you in your time of prayer. Oftentimes, when I do not know what to pray or how to pray about what is on my heart, I pause and just sit before the Lord. I listen. I read Scripture. I listen to what the Holy Spirit is saying to me.

Then I respond by praying what is in my heart at that moment. Through giving God time to prepare me, He leads me to pray more effectively and specifically. Yes, the Holy Spirit does assist us at all times when we pray.

3. Praying in the Spirit Means to Pray with Power from the Spirit

In October 1997, more than one million men filled the Washington, DC, National Mall to beseech God to send revival to America. This event, called Stand in the Gap, was a great moment in the history of American Christianity. In fact, it could have been the largest gathering of Christians in the history of the world at that time.

I was asked to speak on the program on this historic and significant day. On the evening prior to this event, the speakers and participants gathered together in a prayer meeting. The power of God came upon the meeting as we prayed for one another. As we laid hands on various people, the power of God was ushered into that place. We prayed with true spiritual power.

One of the reasons Stand in the Gap was so powerful in the lives of many Christians was that the power of God first fell upon the leadership. *The power of God in prayer usually precedes the power of God demonstrated in a public meeting.*

Prayer leads you to the power of God, both in personal times of prayer and in public meetings of believers. God is attracted to men and women who admit their weakness and know they need the Spirit to help them when they pray. God will bless those who will pray in the Spirit with power.

Prayerlessness means you are depending on yourself. Prayer in the Spirit means that you are depending on God. When you depend on God, you will receive His power when you pray.

When His power comes upon you, mighty things begin to happen—He fills you with Himself, He leads you, and He empowers you to live and to pray more effectively. The more surrendered we live to God, the more we will place ourselves in a position to pray with power from on High.

This takes prayer to a different level in your life. You begin to pray for things you did not have a burden to pray for before this time. You are energized, filled, and empowered by His Spirit. You are granted the authority of Jesus Christ. You will experience boldness, courage, and faith like never before. It is a faith-building moment. A powerful moment. A true God moment! When you are praying in the Spirit, experiencing His power, you become God's tool. At times, you are simply a vessel in the hand of God as you represent His people and their needs before God. Yes, prayer leads you to the power of God.

One of the reasons Stand in the Gap was so powerful in the lives of many Christians was that the power of God first fell upon the leadership.

The Southern Baptist Convention gathers annually to discuss programs, policies, and budgets that affect the local church. When I was president during two back-to-back years of leadership, the first convention in Columbus, Ohio, and the second in St. Louis, Missouri, the entire Tuesday evening session was given to leading thousands of Southern Baptists in the Word, worship, and mostly, prayer. Prayer moments were set up through brief episodes of someone sharing the Word of God that was applicable to the moment.

God moved powerfully. It was one of the great highlights for these gatherings with thousands of people attending on each of these evenings, and was life-changing for many spiritual leaders.

Why? Even though we had a direction, we let the Holy Spirit lead us in how to pray in the moments we were experiencing together. There was always order spiritually, as all was built upon Scripture, but the Holy Spirit moved powerfully.

We experienced moments of great energy and power! Faith was enlarged! Worship was powerful! God was in the room and everyone knew He was orchestrating all of us in these grand and spiritual moments. The two hours we were together were not about a man or a group of men or women; they were about Jesus. He was the focus. The Word was our foundation. The Spirit was our life!

The Chalk Talk

As a football player, it was always a great experience to be in a locker room just before kickoff and hear the final talk given by the coach. This used to be called the coach's final "chalk talk."

In this setting, the coach goes over the final details. You faintly hear the bands playing and the fans yelling. You are trying to focus on the final details the coach is giving you. His final words to you are words of motivation.

Moments before Jesus ascended into heaven to be with the Father, He gathered His disciples for His final chalk talk. He gathered them together in Jerusalem and shared with them that the Holy Spirit would soon come upon them. He stated that they would be endowed with God's power from on high.

His disciples did not respond with, "We do not want that" or "Oh, that sounds charismatic." Oh no! They were in tune with what Jesus was saying. He told the disciples that the power they would receive would be their power to let everyone in the world know that He died for their sins and rose from the dead.

In this Spirit talk, Jesus was preparing His disciples to pray in the Holy Spirit. He was preparing them to enter into real God power in their lives. This is why Paul wrote in Ephesians 6:18: "With all prayer and petition pray at all times in the Spirit."

The apostle Paul knew that the wardrobe of the believer had to be empowered by praying in the Spirit. *Real warriors are prayer warriors!* Prayer warriors are people who know the importance of praying in the Spirit at all times—praying under His leadership, praying with His assistance, and praying in His power. This is what it truly means to pray in the Spirit.

These Three Keys

In this section, I have given you the three keys to a powerful prayer life. It is my desire that you feel you are more equipped to pray more effectively. A person who wants to pray effectively must use the three keys I discussed in this section.

Remember, God's throne room is that special place where you experience the presence of God and all God has for you. The three keys for you to access God's throne room are:

- Pray According to God's Will
- Pray in Jesus' Name
- Pray in the Spirit

These three keys will lead you into greatness with God. They will unlock the chest that contains the fullness of God's blessings.

As you practice praying in the Holy Spirit, pray according to the leadership of the Holy Spirit in your life. Practice praying with the

Holy Spirit's assistance in your life. Practice praying with power from the Holy Spirit. When you begin to pray like this, you will pray with power like never before. You will begin to pray like it really matters.

Now that you understand these things, you are prepared to go to a new level in your prayer life. Continue to join me now in the following pages, as we enter this powerful journey of navigating together and moving to a new level in prayer.

PART 3

MOVING TO A NEW LEVEL IN PRAYER

CHAPTER 7

HOW TO CALL
UPON THE LORD

It was a defining spiritual day in our lives. On a hot summer Sunday morning, Jeana and I departed from our hotel and traveled into the city of Brooklyn, New York. Our tour guides were a humble and modest couple who had been believers in Jesus Christ for only a few short years. Their excitement and servant hearts captivated our attention as we chatted on the drive.

Coming into Brooklyn, we saw numerous buildings. Finally, we slowed down, and I noticed a great number of people walking away from one particular building. Lined up beside the same building that hundreds of people were exiting was a crowd of people wanting to go into the building. No, they were not standing in line to attend a Broadway show. The people were leaving and preparing to enter one of America's great and unique churches, the Brooklyn Tabernacle.

The church has now relocated from the building in which I preached that summer Sunday years ago. The Brooklyn Tabernacle church continues to be a miracle story of Jesus Christ. Years ago, this church could barely operate, but then the wind of God's Spirit began to blow. Now the church stands as one of the greatest testimonies to Jesus Christ in all of the world.

The summer I was asked to preach there, the invitation was extended by the senior pastor, Jim Cymbala. He asked me to spend a Sunday ministering to his people. At the time I was there, they had four services taking place each Sunday. Each service lasted at least two hours. Pastor Cymbala had asked me to preach two of the services: at noon and 7:30 p.m. We left the hotel at 10:30 a.m. and returned just before midnight.

What a church this was! What an experience this was to minister to this unique, Spirit-empowered church of Jesus Christ. There was no time limit. There was no celebrity pastor or singer. The day was about Jesus. This church is about Jesus. This church is a true Jesus church.

When the Brooklyn Tabernacle church gathers for worship, congregates are there to meet God in His timing, regardless of how long it takes. They are an example of Christian unity, as people of various colors and ethnicities come together to compose this unique church in metropolitan New York City.

Convenience is not even an issue because most come to the church not by car but by subway. Pastor Jim Cymbala is a real servant. He walks slowly among the people, praying and touching people with his genuine Christian life. He is a real example of a true man of God.

This church truly knows how to worship God. Its pastor leads worshipers to meet God weekly. Pastor Jim spends the entire day expending himself for the sake of the gospel. In the one service I attended but did not preach, Pastor Cymbala expounded the Word like a true shepherd. It was not a simple sermonette but a strong biblical message that was true to the text in every way.

When the Brooklyn Tabernacle church gathers for worship, congregates are there to meet God in His timing, regardless of how long it takes.

Then when the pastor prayed, it was not in some flowery manner. He led the people to pour out their hearts toward God and call out to the Lord in prayer. No one said, "Hush, hush, do not disturb anyone else." It was a loud and noisy moment that was signified by genuine brokenness and prayer.

Yes, the people of this church called out to the Lord to meet them on that day. I have to admit that I was a little taken back by it, not because it bothered me but because I was surprised that a growing church like this had such openness in worship and prayer. The Lord was blessing this church then and still is today in an incredible manner.

In his best-selling book *Fresh Wind, Fresh Fire*, Jim Cymbala recounted the story of how God turned this church upside down. He is careful not to attribute this turning to a church growth method but to the Lord alone, who gave the church fresh spiritual wind and real spiritual fire.

The key of the Brooklyn Tabernacle church is its ministry of prayer. Each week, the worship center overflows with people who come to call out to God in prayer. In each worship service, deep, genuine prayer occurs.

In *Fresh Wind, Fresh Fire*, Pastor Cymbala wrote:

The Bible [says], "My house will be called a house of prayer for all nations." Preaching, music, the reading of the Word—these things are fine; I believe in and practice all of them. But they must never override prayer as the defining mark of God's dwelling. The honest truth is that I have seen God do more in people's lives during ten minutes of real prayer than in ten of my sermons. . . . Have you ever noticed that Jesus launched the Christian church, not while someone was preaching, but while people were praying? . . . Am I the only one who gets embarrassed when religious leaders in America talk about having prayer in public schools? We don't have even that much prayer in many churches![1]

Prayer is not confined to special services at the Brooklyn Tabernacle. As I stated already, each worship service is filled with deep, abiding, serious prayer that exudes what the Scriptures tell us about calling upon the Lord in prayer.

When I think back on that special day in our lives when I preached at the Brooklyn Tabernacle, I will never forget what I witnessed personally. I witnessed that Sunday a church that operates on a different spiritual level from most churches I have ever attended or pastored. The works of the flesh were not manifested, only the works of the Spirit of God. It was truly refreshing!

This work of the Spirit has taken this church to a new spiritual level because of its emphasis on prayer. This church really knows how to pray. It knows what it means biblically and practically to call upon the Lord. If you are a skeptic or a cynic, I would remind you of one thing: This church has not been raised up on the side of an interstate on one hundred acres of land, or in a region overflowing with an exciting population explosion where everything is new. This church stands as a testimony in Brooklyn, New York, as a spiritual tower of God's power! And I believe this amazing growth is all because of the grace of God upon His people and the prayers of the people of God.

Are you ready to go to a new level in your prayer life? Are you ready to leave normal church and begin to experience biblical Spirit-empowered church? Are you aware of what you need to know to go to a new level in your prayer life?

In this section, I will share with you some things you need to know about moving to this new level. If you want to go further with God than you have ever been, then read and implement the truths discovered in these chapters. They have taken me to new heights in my prayer life, and I know they will do the same for you.

What Does It Mean to Call Upon the Lord?

Prayer shows that you are depending upon God. Prayerlessness demonstrates that you depend upon yourself. Are you a praying Christian or a prayerless Christian? Are you depending upon yourself, or are you depending upon the Lord? Calling upon the Lord in prayer indicates that you are a praying Christian who depends upon the Lord.

Too many evangelical Christians would view this concept of calling upon the Lord as a foreign practice. What does it mean to call upon the Lord? The word *call* in the Old Testament means "to summon His aid." When you call upon the Lord, you are summoning, or inviting, God's aid to come into your life. This word *call* also means "to cry out loudly" in order to get someone's attention. This indicates that God wants you to call out loudly to Him like you really need His help. Pride will not permit you to call upon the Lord, but humility opens the door for you to move to a new level in your prayer life. When you call upon the Lord, you are inviting His activity into your life.

The word *call* also means "to shout." This principle calls for us to shout to God in prayer. You may view shouting as a disruptive and irreverent practice, but remember, I am talking about shouting to God in prayer. You shout at a pep rally. You shout at a ball game. The Bible teaches that one day God is going to call us home to heaven "with a shout" (1 Thessalonians 4:16). Please understand what I am sharing with you here. I am sharing what the Bible says when it uses the word *call*.

There is another word in the Old Testament Hebrew language for *call* that refers to calling upon the Lord in a public worship setting on the Sabbath Day. I interpret this to mean that the day of worship that we celebrate should be a day when we call upon the Lord by summoning His aid into our lives. In the church that you attend weekly, how many minutes in the service are allotted for Christians to call upon the Lord?

This is one of the great things I learned from the ministers of the Brooklyn Tabernacle church. They give opportunities for their people to come before the Lord—summoning Him, inviting Him to be involved in their lives. *This practice may be unique to us, but it is not foreign to the Word of God.*

I believe that one of the sad commentaries on Christians today is that many only desire "neck-up" religion. They want their intellect increased and disregard emotion as needless. Your goal should be balance in regard to intellect and the heart. Refrain from labeling fellow believers who may be out of balance one way or another. They are not the issue. God's Word calls upon each Christian to call upon the Lord.

I want you to notice how the word *call* is used in several scriptural passages. Jeremiah 29:11–13 says, "'For I know the plans that I have for you,' declares the LORD, 'plans for welfare and not for calamity to give you a future and a hope. Then you will call upon Me and come and pray to Me, and I will listen to you. You will seek Me and find Me when you search for Me with all your heart.'"

God's Word affirms that He has a future and a hope for everyone who calls upon Him. Our goal should not be to seek this future or this hope but to seek God in prayer by summoning His aid into our lives with all of our hearts.

The word *call* is used again in Jeremiah 33:3, which says, "Call to Me and I will answer you, and I will tell you great and mighty things, which you do not know." When you are willing to call out loudly to the Lord, summoning His aid into your life, God will do great and mighty things.

Psalm 145:18 says, "The LORD is near to all who call upon Him, to all who call upon Him in truth." God does not play games. He wants His people to summon His assistance with truthfulness. In prayer, let God see your heart and hear your heart as you invite Him into your life for assistance.

The practice of calling upon the Lord began in Genesis 4:25–26: "Adam had relations with his wife again; and she gave birth to a son, and named him Seth, for, she said, 'God has appointed me another offspring in place of Abel, for Cain killed him.' To Seth, to him also a son was born; and he called his name Enosh. Then men began to call upon the name of the LORD." The Bible is very clear that the origin of calling upon the Lord in prayer began in Genesis. Under the leadership of Enosh, people began to summon God and invite Him into their lives.

Another passage that I believe you need to consider today is Psalm 80:18, which says, "We shall not turn back from You; revive us, and we will call upon Your name." In this verse, God's people declared that they were not going to turn back from God anymore. They cried out to God to give them new life so that they would call upon Him again in prayer. What Christianity needs today is revival in calling upon the name of the Lord. Perhaps pride and timidity are not the reasons Christians fail to call upon the Lord. The real reason is that they need spiritual revival.

> *When you are willing to call out loudly to the Lord, summoning His aid into your life, God will do great and mighty things.*

Remember, prayer is work. The hardest thing you will ever do in your life is call upon the Lord in prayer. Satan's strategy is to get you involved in anything that will keep you from praying. Satan will make you sleepy, make your mind wander, make you find reasons you cannot pray, and make things come your way that will keep you from praying.

Determine today to begin to summon God's assistance into your life daily. Commit to being a genuine prayer warrior who will call upon the Lord in prayer. If you will follow this practice daily, you will move to another level in your prayer life.

When Should You Call Upon the Lord?

Scripture is clear that each Christian should practice calling upon the Lord in prayer, individually and corporately. When should believers call upon the Lord? I want to highlight five situations in which Christians should call upon the Lord.

Call Upon the Lord All the Time

Do you call upon the Lord all the time or only when you need something? Do you call upon the Lord out of conviction or out of crisis? Your spiritual life should not have to be in an intensive care unit for you to call upon the Lord. You should call upon the Lord all the time.

Prayer should be your first choice, not your last choice! Again, prayer is not inaction; it is your greatest action.

Are you spending time calling upon the Lord daily? Do you have a prayer plan that allows time for you to call upon the Lord in prayer? If you don't already have such a plan, the last chapter of this book will help you design a plan for prayer in which you can call upon the Lord each day.

In our church, we have begun to dedicate certain services solely to prayer. We have dedicated an entire Sunday morning service and services on all campuses solely to the ministry of prayer. In fact, we have done so for the past few years. These prayer services have been filled with God's power. My prayer of preparation is always, "Lord, give me the spirit and burden for prayer." In these times, our church calls out to the Lord in prayer. As Christians, we need to be willing to speak out to the Lord in prayer in a public setting, to call upon the Lord earnestly and deeply.

Without any question, each Christian and each church should call upon the Lord all the time. *Calling upon the Lord continually demonstrates that we are depending upon the Lord rather than ourselves.*

Call Upon the Lord in a Time of Need

Just as parents love for their children to call upon them in a time of need, God loves for His children to call upon Him likewise. Calling upon the Lord in a time of need does not indicate a lack of faith but an understanding that God is the ultimate object of our faith. God can do anything, anywhere, and at any time. He can provide for your need.

What kind of need do you have today? I do not believe God categorizes our needs as big or small. At times, we may be tempted to handle the small things and let God handle just the big things. It is as if we are saying, "God, we know You are really so busy that we will bother You with just the things that we know we cannot handle by ourselves." This attitude is wrong. God wants us to come to Him at all times to pray about all of our needs. As I have heard Pastor Cymbala say, "The Lord is attracted to our weakness."

What is your need today? Do you need healing? All healing takes place because of God. Do you need money? Honor Him with what you have, and He will provide for your need. Do you have a relationship that is strained? Only God can bring two hostile or opposing persons together. The cross shattered all walls between people. Do you have a material need? Call upon the Lord! He is able to meet even your material needs. Bear your heart to Him in prayer by summoning His aid into your life. Remember, God can make a way when there seems to be no way.

I believe God creates needs in your life for the purpose of causing you to depend upon Him. He wants you to rely upon Him. He wants to do the impossible. He loves to show others that with Him all things are possible. *Even before your need exists, God already has the supply.* Call upon the Lord in a time of need.

Call Upon the Lord in a Time of Pursuing the Future

Some of the most important decisions you will make in your life have to do with planning your future. If you are still young, in the future you will have to make decisions pertaining to college, career, marriage, and children. If you are middle-aged, you will have to make decisions pertaining to the care of your parents and your children, job opportunities or career moves, and even retirement. If you are in the senior years of your life, you may have to make decisions regarding where you live, what kind of care you want, how long you want to continue to work full-time, and how close you want to be geographically to family members. Regardless of your age, the future demands that you make decisions.

Each of my sons has worked through challenging decisions relating to his future. For Josh, after winning four state championships as a head football coach here in Arkansas, the Lord opened up a powerful opportunity in the largest public school division in the state of Alabama. God has blessed his work there and has verified again and again his calling to this school in the greater Birmingham region.

Bear your heart to Him in prayer by summoning His aid into your life. Remember, God can make a way when there seems to be no way.

My preaching son, Nick, has the favor of the Lord upon his life in ministry. He leads our entire staff of Cross Church and also is our lead teaching pastor. God has so favored his leadership at our Fayetteville campus, even opening up opportunities over these past few years to serve as chaplain to the Arkansas Razorbacks football coaching staff and team. God is creating a major legacy through this young, gifted leader and preacher of the gospel.

There is no telling what God will do with both of my sons. How blessed they are, and God is seeing them through to the future He has for each of them. They are praying it through, and as their parents, we are crying out daily to God for each of them in regard to their futures.

When pursuing your future, call upon the Lord. He is able to give you guidance and wisdom in regard to your future. The Bible promises you a great life, wonderful welfare, and God's peace as you call upon the Lord in prayer. As Jeremiah 29:11 states, "For I know the plans I have for you . . . to give you a future and a hope."

One of the pivotal questions each person must ask pertaining to his or her future is, "God, what do You want me to do?" My life is not my own; I belong to God. I am not owned by any man or any system. I am not the property of this world. I am God's property. Since He owns the title to my life, I must take directions pertaining to my future from Him.

I still talk daily to God about my future. I will do whatever the Lord wants me to do in my life. I have one shot to live, and I want to position myself to take my best shot to be all God wants me to be. Whatever it takes to make the biggest impact for the gospel is what I am committed to doing until my dying breath.

The only way that your future is secure is when you call upon the Lord. He will come when you invite Him to be part of your life. He will help you walk through all of the transitions of your life. He will provide you peace when you feel there is no way that peace can exist. He will be there for you in your future when no one else will. Therefore, trust Him. Rely upon Him. Call unto Him. Summon Him. Invite Him to make your future and all of its decisions clear to you.

Call Upon the Lord in a Time of Worship

In moments of public worship, are you calling upon the Lord? Is your day for worship set aside for the purpose of calling upon the Lord? When you go to worship at your church, call upon the Lord. Summon Him to meet with you and the entire body of Christ that is sharing this experience with you. The day of worship should be set aside as a day in your life that you call upon the Lord in prayer.

Much of the worship in church life today is stale and powerless. As a result, lives are left unchanged. Could this be happening because we do not spend time calling upon the Lord in worship?

Much of worship today centers on personalities and performance, songs and sounds, rather than the Lord, His Word, and His work in the lives of people. Prayerlessness indicates dependence upon ourselves. Worship should never be about ourselves. Worship should exalt the Lord Jesus and be focused on calling upon Him in prayer. Call upon the Lord in a time of worship.

Call Upon the Lord in a Designated Prayer Time

Do you have a designated time of prayer in your life? As I mentioned previously, make a date with God daily. Find a plan to follow, such as the one outlined in the last chapter of this book, that will instruct you on how to pray.

> *First things first! Get alone with God at the first of the day. Use this time to call upon the Lord in prayer. Let it be the time every day when you share your heart with God about your life and your greatest needs in life.*

First things first! Get alone with God at the first of the day. Use this time to call upon the Lord in prayer. Let it be the time every day when you share your heart with God about your life and your greatest needs in life. Take the time to listen to what He says to you as you do this.

Appeal to the pastors and leaders in your church to set aside services that are dedicated solely to prayer. God can do more in a moment of prayer than in all the programs one church could do in a lifetime. Determine to make your church a praying church. Decide today how you can walk alongside your pastor, helping him create a fellowship of believers who practice calling upon the Lord in prayer. I can assure you that his office is not being flooded with calls by people who want to help him make the church a praying church. Stand up and be different. Be a Christian who calls upon the Lord in prayer.

Prevailing Prince of Prayer

During my visit to the Brooklyn Tabernacle church, Jim Cymbala mentored me in prayer. I watched him with his people. I watched him in worship. We talked a lot about prayer. I learned a great deal from him about prayer.

In between one of the services, Pastor Cymbala handed me a booklet entitled *Daniel Nash: Prevailing Prince of Prayer*. This booklet, written by J. Paul Reno, would be very worthy of your time to read. It will stir your heart to pray and to change.

Who is Daniel Nash? Perhaps you will be able to answer this question more accurately: Have you ever heard of the historic evangelist by the name of Charles Finney? If not, let me tell you briefly about both of these men.

Charles Finney was a converted lawyer. Finney's life was so changed by the power of Christ that he never counted on anything other than prayer to win lost souls to Christ. According to this booklet, 80 percent of Finney's converts stood the test of time and were committed to Jesus Christ all the way to the end.

In later years, Dwight L. Moody was converted to Christianity. He was a shoe salesman who became a great evangelist and pastor. Fifty percent of Moody's converts stood the test of time.

Evangelist Billy Graham once stated that if 20 percent of his converts stood the test of time in their commitment to Jesus Christ, he would be pleased because of the spiritual depravity of our culture.

When I read this information, I immediately asked myself one question: "Why did 80 percent of all of Finney's converts stay committed to Jesus Christ?" I discovered the answer. Charles Finney had a prayer warrior who traveled with him everywhere he went. Many times, this prayer warrior would go into the city or region two to three weeks ahead of the evangelistic emphasis that Finney would lead. He would rent a room and gather two or three saints of God from that city to prostrate themselves before God in prayer for their city or region. They would call upon the Lord in prayer, agreeing for God to do a mighty work of revival and evangelism in their midst. The power of God was evident before Charles Finney ever came to town.

Daniel Nash was this prayer warrior. You do not read about him in history like you read about Charles Finney, Dwight L. Moody, or Billy Graham. In fact, you may never read about Daniel Nash at all. Let's get it straight: although the percentage of Finney's converts is a subject of debate, no one disputes that Daniel Nash was the key to Charles Finney's evangelistic accomplishments. He became known to some as Father Nash. Others referred to him as "The Prevailing Prince of Prayer."

Daniel Nash expended his life calling upon the Lord in prayer. History records that many times people would hear him as far as three-quarters of a mile away calling unto the Lord in prayer for the souls of many people in that city to come to Jesus Christ. Inscribed on Daniel Nash's tombstone are the following words: *Laborer with Finney. Mighty in Prayer.*

What an awesome statement to have written about your life! Daniel Nash was a man of prayer who understood the value of calling unto the Lord.[2]

Are you ready to move to another level in your prayer life? I certainly hope so. The key to moving to this next level is learning to call upon the Lord in prayer! It is time for all of us to learn the value of calling upon the Lord.

Who is going to be the Daniel Nash of our generation? How many people of this present generation will take on the burden and ministry of Daniel Nash? Most people expend their lives on things that really do not matter at all. Will you give your life, your all, to being a Christian who has a passion to call upon the Lord in prayer? Now is the time to call upon the Lord in prayer!

CHAPTER 8

HOW TO PRAY IT
THROUGH

I n my collegiate years, God began to deeply impress upon me a greater conviction and passion to pray. My world of friends expanded greatly and I began to listen to men of God preach on the subject of prayer in ways I had never heard before.

I was raised in a small Texas church with thirty to forty people during weekly worship services, though at times we might even climb to fifty people. Every pastor I had growing up was a bi-vocational pastor. Growing up in this kind of church may have limited me in many ways, but if it did, I did not know it then and do not know it today. It was God's plan for me.

My parents raised me with a tremendous love for the church and for the role of the pastor. We were in church every time the doors were open, and if something was happening, we were there. Church was first and most important in our family. When Wednesday evenings came, we were there in prayer meeting. Yes, every Wednesday night, no compromise, we were present. All ages, except the youngest of preschoolers, were in those gatherings for prayer.

While the phrase "praying it through" was first heard in some of these Wednesday night prayer meetings, it was when I began to hear other preachers and pastors say it in my collegiate years and seminary years that it popularized the phrase in my mind. Praying it through means being persistent in praying for something until the breakthrough comes and the prayer is answered. The answer may be yes or no or to wait; but we keep praying until we know what the answer is.

When I fast-forward my life and experiences a few decades to today, I understand this phrase more than ever before. Pastoring a church, raising a family, leading in all kinds of settings, serving my Southern Baptist Convention family as president and now serving as the president of the National Day of Prayer, I can assure you there have been many times when I was involved in just trusting God and praying all kinds of matters through.

In fact, when I get real about this entire journey of my life and leadership, it has been this principle that my small church initially taught me, deepened through my collegiate years, that has carried me through much of my life. Where would I be today if I had not learned the power of what it means to pray it through?

What does it mean to pray it through? I hope by the end of this chapter you will understand what this phrase means more than ever before. It is important we all go to school again on this because we cannot walk with God as powerfully and effectively as we need to if we do not learn what it means to pray it through.

How Long Should You Pray for Something?

I have often been asked, "Pastor Ronnie, how long should I pray for something?" I do not believe there is a Christian anywhere in the world today who has not asked at one time or another, "How long should I pray for something?" Years ago, some began to teach that if you really had enough faith, you would only have to ask God once for something. In fact, it went beyond that. If you did ask more than once, you were doubting God and not having the kind of faith God wanted to see.

I did not believe that principle then and I certainly do not believe it now. I believe this teaching is in total contradiction to the teaching of Jesus Christ.

Why do Christians struggle with the question of how long we should pray for something in life? I believe there are three reasons.

1. The Issue of Faith

Every growing Christian wants to live by faith. However, when a prayer request has been continually presented to God with no outward response from God, a tension occurs within us. This tension has to do with the subject of faith. *How long is too long to pray about something? Does my need to keep praying indicate a lack of faith? Where does faith fit into what I am presenting to the Lord in prayer?*

2. The Issue of Guilt

If you are committed to prayer in your life, you know that you will continually battle with Satan. In fact, you will endure some of the toughest battles with him while you pray. Many times he will come to you while you are praying and attempt to discourage you. He will tell you, *If you had any faith, you would not keep on asking God about that.* Or Satan may whisper in your ear, *Your heart is filled with doubt, so God is not going to answer your prayer.*

All of a sudden you begin to wonder, *How long should I pray for this?* Guilt begins to flood your soul because you are asking God about it so much of the time when you talk to Him. Satan has been the author of creating doubt in your heart about whether or not you are doing the right thing by praying to God.

> *If you are committed to prayer in your life, you know that you will continually battle with Satan. In fact, you will endure some of the toughest battles with him while you pray.*

3. The Issue of Uncertainty

When you do not know how long you are to pray for something, you experience an element of uncertainty. When you operate in the lane of uncertainty, your faith seems to come to a standstill. Uncertainty breeds doubt in your life.

You see, what you may struggle with at times are the same things each of us struggles with. The issues of faith, guilt, and uncertainty do not need to invade any of our hearts.

So how long should we pray for something in life? Let me answer this for you: I believe you need to pray it through until the breakthrough comes and the answer becomes clear.

What Jesus Taught about Praying It Through

Jesus was the Master Teacher of prayer. Your prayers and your prayer life should be a mirror of His prayers and His prayer life.

In the Scriptures, Jesus taught us the following truth about prayer:

> He said to them, "Suppose one of you has a friend, and goes to him at midnight and says to him, 'Friend, lend me three loaves; for a friend of mine has come to me from a journey, and I have nothing to set before him'; and from inside he answers and says, 'Do not bother me; the door has already been shut and my children and I are in bed; I cannot get up and give you anything.' I tell you, even though he will not get up and give him anything because he is his friend, yet because of his persistence he will get up and give him as much as he needs. So I say to you, ask, and it will be given to you; seek, and you will find; knock, and it will be opened to you. For everyone who asks, receives; and he who seeks, finds; and to him who knocks, it will be opened. Now suppose one of you fathers is asked by his son for a fish; he will not give

him a snake instead of a fish, will he? Or if he is asked for an egg, he will not give him a scorpion, will he? If you then, being evil, know how to give good gifts to your children, how much more will your heavenly Father give the Holy Spirit to those who ask Him?" (Luke 11:5–13)

When you understand this parable, you will know what it means to pray it through. Let me place this passage in context for you.

One of Jesus' disciples admired His prayer life so much that he asked Him, "Lord, teach us to pray" (v. 1). Jesus immediately responded by teaching the disciples what is called the Lord's Prayer. After He presented this model prayer, Jesus used a masterful illustration.

Suppose you had a friend who came to your home unexpectedly at midnight. This friend did not have anything to eat the entire day. Since you had not been expecting his visit, you were not prepared to give him anything to eat. Desperate to find some food to offer him, you crossed the street to a neighbor's house and began to knock on your neighbor's door. You yelled, "I need three loaves of bread." Your neighbor was sleeping when you awakened him, and he yelled back at you, "Leave me alone! My family and I are trying to sleep, and I am not going to get up and give you anything." You were tempted to walk away from the house, but you decided not to do so. Instead, you knocked on the door again and repeated your request. Because of your persistence, your neighbor eventually got out of bed and gave you whatever you needed.[1]

After giving this illustration, the Master Teacher, Jesus Christ, made the following declaration: "So I say to you, ask, and it will be given to you; seek, and you will find; knock, and it will be opened to you" (v. 9).

The literal translation of this in the original language of the New Testament reads something like the following: "Ask and keep on asking, and it shall be given to you. Seek and keep on seeking, and you will find. Knock and keep on knocking, and the door will be opened to you."

I want you to pay close attention to what Jesus was saying to us about prayer. He wants us to be persistent in our prayers—to keep on asking, to keep on seeking, and to keep on knocking until God answers our request.

Asking is a very important element in prayer. When you ask God for something in prayer, you are recognizing His authority over you and submitting your request to Him in faith that He will answer.

Seeking is another important element in prayer. Jesus taught you not only to ask Him for things in prayer but to seek after God in prayer. If you need a job, it's not good enough to pray, *Lord, I need a job. Give me a job. You know my phone number, so have them call me or text me.* This is a low view of God, because He wants you not only to seek Him in prayer about the job but to pursue that job at the same time.

> *He wants us to be persistent in our prayers—to keep on asking, to keep on seeking, and to keep on knocking until God answers our request.*

Knocking is another important element in prayer. Knocking indicates that you go beyond asking and seeking in going after what you need. It is being *persistent* with your request. It is taking the request to a new and different level.

Jesus taught you to ask and keep on asking. He taught you to seek and keep on seeking. He taught you to knock and keep on knocking. Jesus was teaching the importance of not giving up in prayer. Jesus was teaching the importance of praying something through.

Think back to Jesus' masterful parable of persistence. When you ask someone for bread, you are submitting to his or her authority to give you the bread. When you are seeking, you are traveling to the neighbor's house for the purpose of having your need for bread met. When you are knocking persistently at your neighbor's door, the neighbor will meet your need.[2]

As the Lord Jesus instructed His disciples in prayer, He began to ask them some questions. He asked, "How many of you as fathers would give your son a snake if he asks you for a fish?" (v. 11). My children know I am no snake handler, so they would definitely not receive a snake. Then Jesus asked, "If your children ask you for an egg, how many of you would give them a scorpion?" (v. 12). I do not handle scorpions either, especially after I was once bitten by a brown recluse spider.

As a father, I do not know another father who would give these kinds of gifts to his children. But then Jesus turned the discussion into another question in relationship to the heavenly Father: "If you, since you are evil, know how to give good gifts to your children, how much more shall I as your heavenly Father know how to give good gifts to you?" (v. 13).

Jesus assured us that the heavenly Father will be a better father to us than any earthly father could ever be to his children. God always knows what is best for you. Just as you would only give to your children what they need, your Father in heaven will only give you what you need. God is the perfect Father.

What does all of this teach you about prayer?

Identify the Principle

How long should you pray for something? In his excellent book entitled *When God Doesn't Answer*, Woodrow Kroll goes to the heart of the matter: "If persistence was the key to the unwilling heart [of a neighbor], how much more effective will persistence be to the willing heart of God?"[3]

Do you remember when the man first asked his neighbor about the bread, and his neighbor responded, "Get out of here, it is midnight!" yet the man pursued his need being met? It seemed as if the neighbor almost got up but chose not to do so. But the man just knocked and kept on knocking on the door. Was the neighbor's heart willing to assist him? It appeared not! However, the man kept asking.

Jesus taught that if the key to the unwilling heart of your neighbor is persistence, *how much more effective will persistence be to the willing heart of your heavenly Father?* Wow! This is so powerful! If the unwilling neighbor is finally going to give you what you need due to your persistence, then *how much more would your Father meet your needs when you pursue Him persistently?*

What does it mean to pray it through? How long should you pray for something? The answer is in this principle.

The Principle of Persistence in Prayer

The entire passage of Luke 11:5–13 has one basic teaching: if you ask and keep on asking, seek and keep on seeking, and knock and keep on knocking, God is going to hear your prayer and meet your need. God will honor your persistence in prayer as He comes alongside you to help you be successful in your life.

In this passage, *persistence means to be steadfast, to continue, to persevere, to endure, or to be tenacious in prayer.* Jesus was saying to His disciples and to us, "Do not give up in prayer." Pray it through! Jesus wants you to persevere in prayer. Even when you do not want to go on, just go on praying. Even when you want to give up praying, keep on praying. Jesus wants you to endure in prayer. When you want to quit, just keep on praying. Jesus wants you to be tenacious in your prayer life. Hold on to the promise in the Bible and do not let go until God absolutely closes the door and tells you emphatically, *No!*

> *Jesus was saying to His disciples and to us, "Do not give up in prayer." Pray it through!*

How do you pray something through? You pray with great persistence. Just like I told you in the opening paragraphs of this chapter, praying it through is what has carried me all these years in my life and in my leadership. You see, I believe God is attracted to a believer who never gives up in prayer.

In the remaining paragraphs of this chapter, I want to attempt to answer the all-important question I mentioned earlier.

How Long Should You Pray It Through?

This is the major question that I want to answer for you. I want to suggest to you that you pray something through until one of the following three things occurs. Pray it through . . .

Until You Know It Is Not God's Will

Since God speaks to you mainly through His Word and at times through your circumstances, you should pray it through until God affirms to you that it is *not* His will for your life. If the Word is not for it, do not bother to even pray about it. *You must remember: God's Spirit will never lead you opposite of God's Word.*

Some years ago, I was asked to consider taking a position away from the pastorate in the evangelical world. This position was one of great influence and vision. As soon as I was approached about this position, I felt God wanted me to draw aside in fasting and prayer in order to pray it through. The position was highly visible, so I did not want even to be considered if I knew God did not want me to do it. I prayed it through until I knew for certain that it was not God's will for my life at that time. I called the person who wanted me to talk with this search committee and with confidence informed him that I really sensed it was not God's will for my life at that time, so I would not let my name be considered for the position.

For those seven days, I was persistent before God in prayer with fasting. By praying it through, God affirmed me as a pastor and confirmed that the position was not His will for me at that time in my life. I was committed to go on with God in prayer until I prayed it through. God does not always answer that quickly, but I am thankful He did.

When I reflected upon this even more recently, I was reminded this decision was not an evil-versus-good choice for me. Both choices were wonderful. But at that specific time, it was about timing, not the position itself. I could have done the job with great vision and passion. But again at that specific time in my life, family, and church, it was just not God's timing. Thank God I knew the principle of praying it through!

I want to encourage you to pray your burden through until you know it is not God's will for your life. Pursue your dream. Activate your passion. Get before God and stay there until you know it is not right in the eyes of God. If it is God's will, you will soon know. If you do not know, do not do it. *When in doubt, don't!* This is an important rule to follow in your life. Pray it through until you know it is not God's will.

You should also pray it through . . .

Until God Answers Your Prayers

Pray it through until you know the doors are shut tightly. Pray it through until you know it is just not right. Pray it through until God says no or until God says yes. Sometimes it is difficult to let it go when you know God says no. Yet when He says no, walk away. The worst place you can be spiritually is somewhere God does not want you to be in your life.

Pray it through until God says yes. Thank God for the times in life when your persistence in prayer resulted in God saying yes. What an encouragement! What faith is created through God saying yes to our persistent praying.

If you are praying for someone who does not know Christ, then claim God's expressed desire in 2 Peter 3:9: "The Lord . . . is patient toward you, not wishing for any to perish but for all to come to repentance."

God is willing for all persons to repent of their sin and be saved. He does not want anyone to perish. Therefore, upon the authority of God's Word, you know it is God's will for this lost person to be saved. So pray it through! Claim this verse before God. Hang on to it! Remind God of what He said. Pray with confidence, believing that God will save this person.

For example, Elaine had prayed for Jim to come to Jesus Christ for more than forty years. She prayed with great passion and persistence for her lover and husband. Through the years she was tempted to get discouraged, but she clung to the promise of 2 Peter 3:9. Finally, in a unique way, God prepared Jim's heart. In God's way and in His timing, God prepared him to be saved. Jim came to Jesus Christ after forty years of his wife's persistent prayers for him. Elaine prayed it through until God answered her prayer about Jim. She practiced the principle of persistence in prayer. This is just what Jesus taught her in Luke 11.

Whatever you are facing today, pray it through until God gives you the answer. Do not stop! Hang in there and pray. Pray with persistence. Pray with faith! You may be praying for your house to sell, but it has not sold. Keep praying until God gives you the answer. You may be praying for a new job. Keep praying until God gives you the answer. You may be praying for a financial breakthrough. Keep praying until God gives you the answer. You may be praying for someone's salvation. Keep praying until God comes through. Yes, pray it through! Pray with persistency.

How long should you pray something through? Pray it through . . .

Until God Releases You

Many times what you pray about is a burden to you. I believe a burden is something that you go to bed with, wake up with, and live with all through the day. I am talking about something that is very heavy on your heart. I have learned that you should pray that burden through until God releases you. If He does not release you from that burden, then keep on praying persistently about it.

When Nehemiah learned of the condition of Jerusalem, he was burdened for his homeland's main city. This was truly a burden as he entered days of fasting and prayer. He continued with that burden until God released him. God did not release him until he completed the task of rebuilding the wall around Jerusalem. This all occurred because he prayed it through. He kept on praying about it until God released him.

The burden that God gives you is a wake-up call. If God gives you the burden, it signifies He is active in the situation. Therefore, you keep praying it through until He releases you. How do you know when He releases you? He releases you when the situation is answered just the way you have prayed for it. He releases you when the situation is just not right. He releases you when He removes your burden and replaces it with His peace. You will know when He releases you. Until then, pray persistently!

Do not give up in prayer. Keep on praying until God releases you. Sometimes that burden may last one year, ten days, or even forty years. Yet pray until God releases you. Persistent prayer is effective prayer.

Persistency in your prayer life demonstrates that you have great faith in God. It does not indicate a lack of faith. Persistency in prayer develops your character. It does not show you are inferior or prone to worry. Persistency in prayer guarantees God's activity—not in the sense that He will answer it the way you want it answered or even that He will answer it at all—but by indicating that God is active in the situation as long as He wants you to pray it through. Stay involved in prayer until God speaks to you in the situation.

> *Do not give up in prayer. Keep on praying until God releases you. . . . Persistent prayer is effective prayer.*

Do you want to move to a new level in your prayer life? I hope so. One of the great ways that you can move to a new level is to learn to pray things through. Remember, you have a perfect Father in heaven who is willing to meet your needs. So pray them through! Give God the opportunity to receive the glory when you can announce to others that He answered your prayer as you prayed it through. I promise you, this will help you take a quantum leap in your prayer life.

CHAPTER 9

HOW TO PRAY FOR
ONE ANOTHER

From the moment I first met Helen Graham, I knew she was a very special woman. Godliness was her apparel. Her gray hair was truly her crown of glory. Everyone who knew Helen loved and respected her.

Helen Graham was a special person for many reasons. When I followed God's call to serve this church in Arkansas, she was a member. She loved young people, so that is where she spent her time on Sunday mornings during the Bible study hour. She loved worship, so the choir was her place in the Sunday worship services. If Helen was healthy, she was present and praying.

I was only thirty years of age when I accepted God's call to this rather large congregation. I followed a godly and gifted leader who had invested sixteen years of his life in leading this church into spiritual greatness. Remarkably, while there were moments when the transition was challenging as any would be, to God's glory alone, the church made the transition in a wonderful way because of people like Helen Graham.

Helen Graham loved the pastor of her church, regardless of who the pastor was. She had a respect for the office of the pastor like few people do today. The reason for this was that she was a great woman of prayer.

Every time I saw Helen, she encouraged me and assured me of her prayers for me. She devoted the senior years of her life not to criticism but to intercessory prayer. Helen always wanted to know how she could pray for me. Intercessory prayer was not a put-on for her; it was the passion of her life. Because of Helen's faithfulness, the glory of God was all over her life.

In 1996, I addressed the Southern Baptist Convention in the New Orleans Superdome. I was assigned the pivotal message, the convention sermon. At that time in our denomination, thousands upon thousands came to our annual convention meetings. I took this assignment very seriously. I did not want simply to prepare an impressive sermon that my peers would applaud, but I wanted to have a true word from God that would shake the convention.

I really sensed that God wanted me to fast and pray for forty days so that I would be prepared to receive His message for this convention. In this fast, I truly sensed that I was standing in the gap between God and the largest evangelical denomination in the world. The burden was great upon me to relay His message to this denomination, which at the time consisted of more than forty thousand churches composed of more than sixteen million members. This convention, which is attended mainly by pastors, staff members, and lay leaders, was an outstanding opportunity for any preacher.

God really impacted my life through my forty-day fast. I sensed His message for these convention messengers. As I preached the convention sermon on that Wednesday morning, God fell upon the Superdome with His favor. I can honestly tell you it had nothing to do with me but everything to do with our sovereign God, who was attentive to the prayers of His people. I sensed God's leadership to offer an altar call at the conclusion of my sermon, which was a call to action for Christians and churches to get serious about meeting God through prayer and fasting for the purpose of spiritual renewal for our churches and our nation.

The response was God-sized! Lives were impacted. Some churches were truly changed, as evidenced by the testimonies that have been shared with me even after all these years. God did more than I ever asked Him to do. It was truly a "God moment."

Why did this happen? Prior to that event, several members of my church committed to fast and pray for that specific moment. While I was in New Orleans, our worship center became a mighty place of prayer for the time of the convention sermon. Many of our laypeople gathered to agree in prayer and to intercede for me and the preaching moment before the Southern Baptist Convention. I thank God for the people who dedicated that day to the ministry of intercessory prayer.

On that strategic morning, Helen Graham committed to be part of this time of intercession. Toward the end of the prayer meeting, Helen prayed. When she returned to her place in the worship center, she had a stroke, and God soon called her home.

This is truly an amazing story. Helen Graham gave the senior years of her life to intercession. In fact, she spent one of the last moments of her life praying for God to fall upon the convention in New Orleans. She expended her life for the cause of Christ and for intercession for God's people.

Helen Graham knew how to pray for others. She knew how to pray for me. She knew how to pray me through. She was not content merely to pray for herself; she wanted to move to the high level of praying for others. If you want to move to another level in your prayer life, then you must learn how to pray for one another.

What Is Intercessory Prayer?

The term *intercessory prayer* may not mean a great deal to you, but it is vital to your Christian life. I believe one of the highest callings in the

Christian life is the call to intercession—to pray for others. This call comes to every Christian who is growing in his or her faith.

When you intercede for others, you plead or offer petition on behalf of another person who is in trouble or in difficulty. You get before God in a very serious mode of prayer. When you are before God in this manner, you are praying for others who may really need your prayers.

Therefore, intercession is when you offer a prayer on behalf of another person or a group of persons. An intercessory prayer asks God to meet with those people and to provide for their needs. Intercessory prayer is not focused on yourself but on others. It is a call from God to stand in the gap between a holy God and a person in need. Intercessory prayer is one of the highest callings in the Christian life.

If you want to move to another level in your prayer life, then you must learn how to pray for one another.

Due to the me-driven cultural Christianity that is rampant in churches in the world today, Christians do not hear a great deal about intercessory prayer. In fact, in most churches the term and the practice have been placed on the shelf. What we want is to have others pray for us, meet our needs, teach us, help us, fill us, and have God touch us. The focus is always on ourselves and our interests. This self-centered Christianity is a far cry from what God teaches in His Word.

What Is an Intercessor?

An intercessor is a Christian who prays for another person. When the Holy Spirit places a person upon your heart to pray for and you are obedient to pray for that person, you become an intercessor. *When you pray for your church, you become an intercessor.* Every growing Christian will perform the ministry of intercessory prayer. As you grow in your faith, the Holy Spirit will place certain people upon your heart so that you will pray for them.

Are you an intercessor? Do you let the Holy Spirit place persons upon your heart so that you can pray for them? If you are a parent, you should intercede for your children. If you are a grandparent, you should intercede for your children and grandchildren. If you are married, you should intercede for your spouse. As a Christian, you should intercede for your local church and for the work of Christ around the world. You should also intercede for your country.

Improper conduct by a friend, family member, church leader, church body, leader in our nation, or our nation itself does not eliminate or disqualify the dire need for us to become intercessors. Undoubtedly, each growing Christian will become an intercessor by faithfully praying for others.

Two Insights

When you pray for others, you move into a high moment in the Christian life. Each Christian who intercedes in prayer does so in many ways. I believe that two insights must be understood by anyone who wants to be an effective intercessor. The first insight is that an intercessor must . . .

Pray Specifically

Are you a parent? If so, have any of your children ever come up to you and asked, "Mom and Dad, will you just meet my needs today?" Probably not, because then you would have had to spend time trying to guess what they wanted you to do. Children usually articulate specific needs to their parents. There is no need for a guessing game. They are requesting you to meet a specific need.

When you pray for others, you need to pray for their needs specifically. This means that you need to know these needs in order to pray specifically. Effective intercessory prayer articulates specific needs of others. You are not to pray, *Lord, help this person. Bless him.* This kind of generalized praying is neither productive nor effective.

Our church's intercessory prayer ministry has changed throughout the years. Today, we currently have over three thousand people each week who have committed to pray weekly for thirty minutes specifically for their church. Our Cross Church Circle, which is what this intercessory prayer ministry is called, agrees in prayer over five to six specific needs through a monthly prayer guide that I personally write each month.

Even though our church is a multi-campus church and we have thousands of people who attend one of at least ten worship services we offer each weekend, I do not delegate this intercessory prayer ministry. A praying church will only occur if a praying pastor is leading the church.

When you pray for others, you need to pray for their needs specifically. … Effective intercessory prayer articulates specific needs of others.

In fact, going back to the early 1990s, we had an intercessory ministry called Warriors on the Wall. It was a different day, before modern-day technology that we each enjoy.

In the days of our Warriors on the Wall ministry, we did a handoff hour by hour, creating accountability for each of us by calling the person who was to be next on the wall of prayer. For many years, I have called the same man in our church each Sunday morning at 6:00 a.m.

As I commend him to pray for our church, he always asks me, "How can I pray for you specifically this week?" Billy Ussery understands this insight of praying specifically. He wants to pray specifically for my needs when he intercedes for me through our Cross Church Circle, but also as he prays for me throughout the week.

Praying specifically is really important when you intercede for others in prayer.

The second important insight about intercessory prayer is to . . .

Pray Biblically

One of the most effective ways to pray for others is to pray specific biblical passages for people. Pray according to God's will for their lives. You can know God's will in prayer by studying the Scriptures. Pray biblically for others by praying according to God's revealed will in the Scriptures.

Pray the Word of God into the lives of other people. Ask God to give you a verse that He may want you to pray for them. You can always ask the person you are praying for to give you a Bible verse to pray into his or her life.

Pray for people straight from the Word of God. Pray the Bible into the lives of other people.

In our Cross Church Circle intercessory prayer ministry guide that I create each month, I always place a scripture for us to stand upon in agreement and ask people to pray through this need in specific ways. Additionally, as president of the National Day of Prayer, I release three prayer priorities to pray for our nation each month. In this intercessory prayer guide for America, I do the same thing. I always place a Scripture to stand upon as we intercede in prayer together for our nation. Therefore, we always pray biblically.

How can you pray the Word of God into the lives of others? Let me show you how this can be accomplished.

How to Pray for One Another

You can learn a great deal about prayer by evaluating the prayers of other people. When the apostle Paul described his prayers for the church in Colossae, he gave us an example of how to intercede for others. Colossians 1:9–12 records Paul's prayer:

> For this reason also, since the day we heard of it, we have not ceased to pray for you and to ask that you may be filled with the knowledge of His will in all spiritual wisdom and understanding, so that you will walk in a manner worthy of the Lord, to please Him in all respects, bearing fruit in every good work and increasing in the knowledge of God; strengthened with all power, according to His glorious might, for the attaining of all steadfastness and patience; joyously giving thanks to the Father, who has qualified us to share in the inheritance of the saints in Light.

This prayer illustrates three specific and biblical ways that you can pray for others.

1. Be Filled with God's Will

Paul prayed that these Christians would be "filled with the knowledge of [God's] will" (v. 9). Why was this so important?

There was a detrimental philosophy in Paul's day known as gnosticism. This anti-Christ philosophy taught that man could attain a higher knowledge of God and that salvation came by this special knowledge. Paul's prayer for this specific people was not to have superior knowledge, but for them to have "God knowledge," a full knowledge that is discovered in the will of God.

The problem at Colossae was similar to the problem in many modern churches in America. At times, spirituality in the American church is equated with some kind of superior knowledge about the Bible. This is why arrogance exists and the pride of knowledge is celebrated. Yet, knowledge in and of itself is not the source of spiritual power and understanding. This is why it is important to pray that others are filled with God knowledge, the knowledge of His will.

The Holy Spirit imparts the wisdom of God. Paul prayed for these Christians to be filled with the knowledge of God's will "in all spiritual wisdom and understanding" (v. 9). Spiritual wisdom is applying God's knowledge to life's situations and seeing life from God's perspective. Spiritual wisdom is dependent upon the knowledge of God's will. For spiritual wisdom to be realized in your life, you must know what God says in His Word and how His truth applies to situations in your life.

Spiritual wisdom should be accompanied by understanding. To have spiritual wisdom with understanding is to use this information to make wise decisions in your life. Good decisions are made from God knowledge, not human knowledge alone. This is why quick decisions can be detrimental to your life.

Take the time to discover the facts and information about what is going on. Know what God says about it in His Word because it will always lead you to His will. Do not seek to have mere human knowledge but God knowledge. Pursue the will of God and His wisdom in your life.

Spiritual wisdom is applying God's knowledge to life's situations and seeing life from God's perspective.

When you have the privilege to intercede for other people, pray for them to be filled with the knowledge of God's will. Pray for them to have God knowledge. Pray for them to discover God's will in His Word. Pray for them to see life the way God sees it. Pray for them to have spiritual wisdom and understanding. Pray for them to be able to gather the needed information for their situation and then proceed to discover the will of God.

Whether you are praying for your spouse, your children, your friends, your church, your pastor, or your country, it is fitting to pray that these people are filled with God's will.

2. Walk in God's Ways

As you pray for others, pray for them to walk in God's ways. The way a person walks is the way he or she witnesses. If people do not walk in the right manner, they cannot witness through their lives or their words with integrity. In his prayer for these fellow believers, Paul prayed for them to walk in a certain way. How should you pray for people to walk in God's ways?

Worthily

Paul prayed that the Colossians would "walk in a manner worthy of the Lord" (v. 10). The only way to walk worthily in the Lord is to walk in the ways of the gospel message with the goal of pleasing the Lord. Our intercessory prayers should not be, *Lord, help this person to do what they want to do* or *Lord, help this person to be satisfied in life.* These prayers do not honor God. The intercessory prayer that should be prayed is, *Lord, help this person to walk in a manner worthy of You and to please You in all respects.*

Your goal is not to be the public-relations person for another person, organization, or your church. Your goal should be to please the Lord in all things and to live a life worthy of Him. Your goal is to please God, not men.

As you pray for others, pray for them to walk in God's ways in a worthy manner. Pray for them to represent the gospel in every way in their lives. Pray for them to please the Lord at all times. Another way you can pray for them to walk in God's ways is for them to walk . . .

Fruitfully

Paul prayed that the believers in Colossae would be "bearing fruit in every good work" (v. 10). For you to bear fruit means that you will bear fruit of the seed. The seed is the Word of God, which was placed in you at salvation. This seed is also the person of the Holy Spirit, who is the down payment given to you at salvation and guarantees your future inheritance.

You are to bear fruit of this seed of salvation by living a holy life. You are to bear fruit of the seed by reproducing the life of Christ in you into the lives of others. You are to bear fruit by winning others to faith in Jesus Christ. God does not want you just to be faithful; He wants you to be fruitful. *A faithful Christian is a fruitful Christian.*

When you pray for others to walk in God's ways, ask God to help them walk in a fruitful way.

In Maturity

Paul prayed that the Colossians would be "increasing in the knowledge of God" (v. 10). The only way you can get to know God is to increase in your understanding of God, revealed in His Word. Through the practice of prayer—talking to God and listening to what He says to you—you can get to know God more intimately. This is the process of maturing in the Lord.

Are you maturing in the Lord? Are you further along with God than you were one month ago? A year ago? Real knowledge is not knowing more facts about God. Real knowledge is God knowledge. It is demonstrating in your own life what God says in His Word.

When you pray for other people to walk in God's ways, pray for them to walk in a mature manner. Pray for them to walk in such a way that they will practice the Word of God and be ever-increasing in the faith.

Bert Miller served beside me on our staff team for several years, and then upon his retirement he began to serve on our church's board of directors. Bert is a former businessman who in his latter years of life chose to serve the Lord's church in a full-time manner. God used Bert on our staff team in a great way. Beyond just building up our team through his servant heart, he was used to oversee the building of many of our buildings, including our entire project at our Pinnacle Hills campus.

Bert and his wife, Wanda, have prayed so much for me through the years. I love them dearly and they have been in our lives for over thirty years. If I used Bert as an illustration of how I could pray Colossians 1:9–11 into his life, it could go something like this:

> Lord, I thank You and bless You for Bert. I pray for him to be strengthened today and filled with Your will in his life. I pray that he would be committed to hear what You say to him, not just what man says. I pray that his greatest passion will be to learn about You by being nurtured in You. May You continue to draw Bert to Your Word so that when he makes decisions for his life, for his family, and for our church he will be filled with the knowledge of Your will. I pray that he will be able to take Your Word and apply it to his life. God, fill Bert with Your will. May his wife, Wanda, see a man who walks in Your ways. May the members of his family see a man who walks in Your ways. I pray for him to walk worthily, fruitfully, and in maturity. Help him to desire to learn Your knowledge through Your power. In the name of Your Son, Jesus Christ, I place these requests before You for my friend Bert, amen.

As you intercede for others in this manner, you will rejoice as you see God mature this person and progress him in his faith. This is the power and result of intercessory prayer. The Lord instructs you to pray that others would be filled with God's will, walk in God's ways, and . . .

3. Be Strengthened with God's Power

Paul prayed that the believers in Colossae would be "strengthened with all power, according to His glorious might" (v. 11). When you pray for others, pray for them to be strengthened with God's power. Pray for them to experience the power of God in their lives. As you pray for others in this way, you are praying for them to be strengthened in God's power so they can be . . .

Steadfast

Paul prayed that the Colossians would attain "steadfastness" (v. 11). When you pray for others to be steadfast, you are praying for them to be faithful. This means that God will endow them with His power to bear up under affliction. Whatever they are going through in life, God will give them the power necessary to see them through. God wanted them to be strengthened with His power so they would be steadfast and also so they could be . . .

Patient

In addition to steadfastness, Paul prayed that the Colossians would attain "patience" (v. 11). Patience can only take place in a person's life when he or she is being strengthened with God's power. When the person you are praying for is suffering or facing an injustice in his or her life, this person needs to be able to put off his or her fury. This is what it means to be patient. It means to be able to put off your fury through the challenges of life. When you are praying for a person to be patient, you are praying for that person to be nonretaliatory, regardless of what others do to him or her.

Pray for others to be patient. This kind of patience cannot exist without the power of God. God's power is the only way that one can become patient. God has instructed you to pray for others to be strengthened with God's power so they can be steadfast, patient, and . . .

Thankful

Paul prayed that these Christians would be "joyously giving thanks to the Father" (vv. 11–12). God's power enables you to be thankful in life. As a Christian, thanksgiving should flood your heart because Christ's sacrifice on the cross has qualified you to live forever with God.

One of the missing ingredients in this present generation is

When you pray for others, pray for them to be strengthened with God's power. Pray for them to experience the power of God in their lives.

thankfulness. The entitlement mind-set plagues our churches, our families, and our nation. When people think they are entitled to certain things, they will not be thankful. God's power gets Christians beyond this deceit and trains them to be thankful.

When you have the privilege of interceding for others, pray for them to be strengthened with God's power so that they will be steadfast, patient, and thankful.

Earlier in this chapter I talked about my good friends Bert and Wanda Miller. Just over two years ago, Bert and Wanda lost their son in a tragic accident. Craig was not only their son but a husband and a father of three children. He was a dear friend of mine and a great minister of the gospel with a massive heart to reach the world for Christ.

Can I illustrate how I can continue to pray this passage for Bert and Wanda? It would go something like this:

Lord, help my friends Bert and Wanda to continue to live their lives before the world in a way that demonstrates You are strong. May they know You are not attracted to strength but to weakness. You are with them! Lord, their loss of Craig is beyond my imagination, but help them, Lord, to bear up under this affliction. Strengthen Bert and Wanda with Your power. Grant them faithfulness and patience. Help them to be patient with all going on in their lives and to continue to permeate the character of Christ. Remind them periodically of how each was once a sinner but now each of them is a saint of God. Fill my friends Bert and Wanda with an overflowing attitude of gratitude, always thanking You for all You have done for them. In Jesus' name, amen.

When you pray for others, pray for them specifically and biblically. Pray for them to be filled with God's will, to walk in God's ways, and to be strengthened with God's power.

Will you be open to God's Spirit calling to you to pray for other people? Will you hear Him speak to you about the importance of praying for others? Will you let Him speak to you about whom He wants you to pray for in your life? Will you learn to pray for others specifically and biblically?

Take up the call to be an intercessor. There is not a higher moment of prayer than when God leads you to pray for others.

Who Will Step Up?

I began this chapter talking about a dear woman of God and prayer intercessor named Helen Graham who so often prayed for me. I have often wondered about who is praying for me now like Helen Graham prayed for me so many years ago. In God's sovereign way and by His will, I know there are others who took on her mantle for intercession, and some have prayed me through and interceded for me for years. I am grateful for each one of them. May their tribe increase. I need prayer desperately. Our church needs it also.

Who will step up now? Will you step up for your friends, for your pastor, for your church, for your family, and for your nation and intercede in prayer? Will you step up and stand in the gap for other people?

Will you be the one? God told Ezekiel, as recorded in the twenty-second chapter of his book, that He searched all over the land for one man to stand in the gap for His people, but He could not find one who was willing to do so. I hope

Take up the call to be an intercessor. There is not a higher moment of prayer than when God leads you to pray for others.

this tragic indictment cannot be said about you or me in respect to our families, our friends, our churches, and our country.

We need to be praying Christians. We need to be Christians who pray for others—the kind of Christians who experience the high calling of intercessory prayer.

Take up the call to be an intercessor. There is not a higher moment of prayer than when God leads you to pray for others.

Praying for others will move you to a new level in your prayer life!

HOW TO DO WARFARE PRAYING

When I was a young preacher, I had several opportunities to preach the Word of God in my region. People were so gracious to put up with me. I believe my enthusiasm is what drew them to ask me to preach because my content was probably rather questionable. All I knew to do at that time was to do what I had seen done and what I had heard thus far in my life.

One of the opportunities that came my way was to preach at a vibrant African-American church that was hosting an area-wide youth rally. I had never attended this church, so I was in for a real treat. The singing was rather lengthy, and I was the last of several preachers. When my time came, I preached all I knew to preach. The more they praised the Lord, the longer I preached. It seemed like I preached and preached and preached some more. As long as they appeared to enjoy it, I just kept on preaching.

An older preacher preceded my time to preach. He was preaching on Satan that night and made a statement I have never forgotten. He said, "If you are not having a head-on collision with the devil every day of your life, that probably means you are going in his same direction."

What a word! I have never forgotten what that man said. I do not remember his name or even the name of the church, but I have never forgotten that statement. This statement is really true about the Christian life. If you are not having a head-on collision with the devil every day of your life, then you are probably going in his same direction.

Satan is our enemy, and he is very strong. He comes against us in so many ways. If you are not colliding with him regularly, then you had better check out where you are spiritually. The last place you want to be going is in his same direction.

The Principle of Spiritual Conflict

Most Christians assume that all conflict is bad. Yet, this is just not so. I have been a Christian for many years and have learned so much in this journey. One of the things I have learned that I believe will help you understand spiritual conflict in a greater way is this: **the closer you get to God, the more spiritual attacks you will face in your life.**

This principle may seem strange to you, but it is reality! I thought for years that my problems would be solved if I would just pray more and be with God more in my life. I thought that conflict was bad and only happened when something was not right in my life. In fact, I faced a lot of guilt when conflict did occur.

I saw this principle lived out in my early years of serving as a pastor. I was consumed with enthusiasm to reach the community with Christ. I guess my enthusiasm was somewhat contagious because usually the vast majority of the church wanted to assist in the task of taking the gospel to the community. I would lead the church to pray and lead the church to witness. Both of those spiritual disciplines were very important. I thought everyone would agree.

Little did I know, not every person in the church wanted to share the gospel with the community. Not every person in the church wanted to get before God in serious prayer to pray for the lost of the community. I do not know if my seminary classes did not teach me that not everyone would want to evangelize and pray, but if they did, I was asleep or not listening. Quite honestly, I was absolutely surprised that not everyone was fired up to make a difference for Jesus.

This led to spiritual conflict. Years ago, I equated this conflict with certain people, due to my own immaturity, but now I know better. This conflict came from Satan, the devil, our enemy. I did not understand as a young pastor what the problem was, so I would try to convince everyone in the church to come along with us. I would use all kinds of persuasive techniques in the pulpit, most of them even spiritual, but the conflict still occurred every time we tried to do something for God.

I kept wondering, *Why is this conflict occurring? Why don't these people want to embrace Jesus' mission for His church?* Then I began to learn the principle of spiritual conflict. I began to understand that the closer I got to Jesus, the more spiritual attacks I would face in my life.

I began to understand this principle of spiritual conflict as it related to the church. The closer the church got to the Lord by doing His will, the more spiritual attacks the church would face. It was serious business to take the gospel to the lost and attempt to win them to faith in Christ. I finally realized that Satan was not just going to hand people over to the Lord without a fight. When I began to understand this principle of spiritual conflict, I began to be freed from the guilt I had experienced. I also began to gauge the success of our ministry not so much by our numbers but by the level of disarray that Satan attempted to cause within the church.

The closer you get to God, the more spiritual attacks you will face in your life.

I am firmly convinced that any time we get serious about prayer and walking intimately with God, there will be spiritual conflict. Through national leadership opportunites that have come my way, I have had to learn this the hard way. Any time I take on prayer or the Great Commission, conflicts occur.

In this chapter, I will be covering exciting ground. Yet I need to remind you that the ground is sprinkled with land mines. However, you can make it through if you will just pray as you read this chapter and be ready for the impending attacks of the evil one.

This chapter is for Christians who really want to move on with God. It is for Christians who want to do some serious praying to God. It is for Christians who want to move to a new level of spiritual growth in their prayer lives. Get ready! I am praying that God will teach you in this chapter how to do warfare praying. Before you read on, pause for a moment and pray a prayer to God something like this:

Dear Lord, I want to learn how to do warfare praying. I want to learn how my praying can penetrate the territory of Satan. As I read the remaining pages of this chapter, cover me with the blood of Jesus Christ. Let nothing happen to distract me from completing this chapter and implementing its content. I surrender these moments to You. You are Lord. Yes, You are greater than our enemy, Satan. In Jesus' name, teach me how to do warfare praying, amen.

I have prayed a similar prayer in writing this chapter, so I really encourage you to pray a similar prayer in reading it. This chapter is written to lead you into the journey of learning about and doing warfare praying.

Warfare Praying Consists of Praying against Satan

One of the most familiar passages of Scripture concerning spiritual warfare is Ephesians 6. This chapter describes what is known as the spiritual armor of the believer. The verses that precede the description of the believer's spiritual armor are especially insightful:

Finally, be strong in the Lord and in the strength of His might. Put on the full armor of God, so that you will be able to stand firm against the schemes of the devil. For our struggle is not against flesh and blood, but against the rulers, against the powers, against the world forces of this darkness, against the spiritual forces of wickedness in the heavenly places. (vv. 10–12)

Since the Word of God serves as our authoritative source for faith and practice, let's investigate what the Bible says about praying against the power of Satan.

One thing you need to understand is how limited you are in relationship to Satan's power. He is much stronger than you and can overcome you. You are inadequate in and of yourself to overcome his power. He will defeat you if you attempt to engage him in your own power.

This is why Ephesians 6 calls for you to be strong in the Lord and in the strength of His might. This means that you are to have God's power in your life as you pray against Satan. You are to operate at a high spiritual level by being empowered by the Holy Spirit rather than by yourself. If you are in Christ, your authority is great. *You have the name of Jesus as your banner, the blood of Jesus as your covering, and the Word of God as your sword.* You are prepared to pray against Satan when you are being controlled by the Spirit.

When you lose the battle against Satan in your life, it is because you are operating in your own strength. Defeat comes as a result of your choice to handle your own affairs rather than to let God handle them for you. Even though defeat may come periodically in your battles against Satan, it is always God's intention to grant you victory through His power flowing through your life.

This chapter is for Christians who really want to move on with God. . . . It is for Christians who want to move to a new level of spiritual growth in their prayer lives. Get ready!

One of the alarming things happening in the church is that believers are asleep and rather lethargic about being in a war with Satan. Status quo and defeat are accepted as the norm in the Christian life rather than being seen as abnormal. If your spirit is down and your heart is experiencing some despair, understand that you are in a war! Satan is out to destroy your life. You are not to wave the white flag in surrender to him, but you are to stand firm against his schemes (1 Peter 5:8–9). The Bible says, "Be sober-minded, be alert. Your adversary the devil is prowling around like a roaring lion, looking for anyone he can devour" (1 Peter 5:8 CSB).

Each one of his schemes has the ultimate goal to bring you down in your life. As you are in a spiritual war, stand your ground against Satan. Do not surrender anything. In fact, be aggressive enough to take back what you may have already surrendered to him.

Satan is real. He is cunning and sly. He is the angel of light. He will not walk down the aisle of your church and say, "Look at me everyone—I am the devil." You often cannot recognize him because he is the greatest con artist ever to have existed. Remember, he exists to bring you down.

More can be understood about your enemy when you understand what his name means. The name *devil* means "accuser and slanderer." Satan does all he can to malign you, your name, and, most of all, the name of Christ and His church. He is the one who comes and whispers in your ears thoughts like, *You can't win. You can't do it. You can't live the Christian life.* He wants to make you question all you are doing in your life, especially those things that are right. He will bring people into your life who will operate his scheme, which is to bring you down in some way. These people may say or write things about you that are not true at all.

The people who come against you in this manner are deceived. They are tools in the hands of the devil and do not know it. These people can even have good intentions. They may even be people who are close to you—people you love. For example, it could be your father, who always has a way of putting you down. It could be your mother, who never encourages you and constantly tells you how you should have done things another way. It could be your children, who are struggling with authority and periodically have their tongues ablaze with accusations about what a poor parent you are. It could be your boss, who has the gift of criticism and exercises it with you daily. Their goal seems to be to choke life out of you with their hateful words rather than put life into you through encouraging words.

This is why it is so important that you are careful with your words. When you are accusing someone of something, be careful. Remember, Satan is an accuser. If you choose to slander someone's character, be careful to remember that Satan is a slanderer. Do not participate in maligning someone else. Satan is Mr. Maligner.

This is why the Bible instructs you to remember that your enemy is not flesh and blood, but Satan. "Flesh and blood" is a reference to people (Ephesians 6:12). This may be difficult to grasp, but you never fight against people, only against Satan. If you can prick the finger of someone and it bleeds, this person is not your enemy. Your enemy is Satan.

This struggle that you will face with Satan calls you into hand-to-hand combat against him. This combat will not take place on earth but in the heavenly places, where you pray against the spiritual forces of darkness and wickedness. In a spiritual sense, you have been raised up to live in the heavenly places. It is here, in the heavenlies, that you do this warfare praying.

One of the best ways to prepare for combat is to know everything you can know about your enemy. You need to study your enemy thoroughly, along with his tactics and strategies. You can never assume you know these things. If you do, your defeat is inevitable.

What You Need to Know about Your Enemy

There are four critical facts about Satan that you need to know.

Fact #1: You Are in a Spiritual War with Satan

Let me reaffirm to you that you are not in a war with people. Stop seeing people as the source of your problems and conflicts. You are in a spiritual war with Satan. If you don't wake up and go into combat, you will be continually defeated.

Fact #2: Satan Is Your Only Enemy

You need to understand that Satan is your only enemy. It is critical that you stop viewing persons, institutions, systems, and circumstances as your enemies. Yes, Satan can operate through each one of these, but the essence of your problem lies with the spiritual force of darkness, Satan himself. I like to say it this way and I also pray it this way: *Lord, help me to keep perspective—Satan is my enemy, not people, situations, or circumstances.* Put on your spiritual glasses and begin to see what God sees. Satan is your only enemy.

Fact #3: Satan Wants to Destroy You, Your Family, Your Church, and the Work of Jesus Christ across the World

Satan is never interested in building you up. He does not desire for you to experience victory or success. He wants to destroy every person in this world so they will experience an eternity of destruction with him in hell.

He wants to destroy your marriage. Your spouse is not where the combat really is; your war is against Satan. Satan is ending as many marriages as he can. Satan will do anything to take out the man of God called your pastor. He hates men of God. He hates women of God. He hates church planters. He hates missionaries.

Satan wants to destroy the church. This is why so many churches are in never-ending battles over insignificant things. The church is supposed to be a unified body of Christ, but this is rarely the case due to the level of division going on in the body of Christ.

Satan wants to do anything he can to put a stop to the work of Jesus Christ around the world. He does not want the good news told, so he will get the church involved in many good things in order to keep them away from the main thing of taking the gospel to the world.

Yes, Satan is out to destroy all he can. You are his target! If you are questioning whether this is reality, you are right in the middle of his deceitful plan. Satan has deceived you, and you have bought his lies. Remember this about Satan: he always plays for keeps. His wins are not just short-term wins. Many times his wins are eternal.

> *Satan wants to do anything he can to put a stop to the work of Jesus Christ around the world.... Yes, Satan is out to destroy all he can. You are his target!*

Fact #4: Even Though Satan Is Alive and Well Today, His Doom Is Certain

Satan is tearing up and wrecking lives all across the world today. It is obvious how destructive he is when you witness the dysfunctional relationships in every segment of society. Our enemy is wreaking havoc upon our culture. We read daily about the torment and adversity that he is bringing into the lives of people. He appears to have the upper hand in the lives of people everywhere. Yes, Satan is alive and well.

However, Satan's doom is certain! One day, the evil one will be thrown into hell once and for all. *When Satan points you to your past, which may be filled with defeat and despair, you should point him to his future, which will be finalized with guaranteed defeat.* As a believer in Jesus Christ, you will win in eternity and Satan will lose.

This is why your praying must become warfare praying. Periodically, you need to pray something like the following:

*Lord, I stand against the power of Satan in my life today. I
declare him powerless over me because I am a child of the King.
I am born again by Your Spirit. I am forgiven because I am
covered with Jesus' blood. First John 4:4 says, "Greater is He who
is in you than he who is in the world." So therefore, Satan, I
stand against you in Jesus' name. You have no authority over me,
my family, or my church. You are a defeated foe. You have no
authority in my life. In Jesus' name, I stand my ground, amen.*

This warfare praying calls upon God for strength. It reminds
Satan that you are not his prey because of what Jesus has done for
you and in you. This kind of praying equips you to not give up any
ground at all to Satan in your life. This kind of praying will lead you
to experience true spiritual victory.

As you practice warfare praying, it is important to be covered
daily with the armor of God. As I mentioned in chapter 1, one of
the spiritual practices I follow daily is to place God's armor upon the
members of my family. As the spiritual leader of the home, I have the
responsibility to put the armor of God upon my family. This now
includes my grandchildren.

How do I do this? I pray in the following manner:

*Dear God, in Jesus' name, please place upon me, Jeana, Josh,
Kate, Peyton, Parker, Jack, Nick, Meredith, Reese, Beckham,
Norah, and Maya the armor of God. On our heads, put on
the helmet of salvation. On our breasts, the breastplate of
righteousness. On our waists, the belts of truth. On our feet, the
preparation of the gospel of peace, putting in our right hands
the sword of the Spirit, which is the Word of God, and in our
left hands, the shield of faith that extinguishes the flaming
arrows of the evil one, and finally, Lord, praying at all times
in the Spirit with every prayer and request persevering and*

*interceding for one another and for all the saints of God. So
Father, from the top of our heads to the bottom of our feet,
cover us with Your armor in the name of Jesus, amen!*

This kind of praying brings rest upon your heart, knowing that you have placed the members of your family under the armor of God. They are now truly dressed for spiritual success. They are ready to face the day, and even Satan. The armor is now on, and they can stand firm against their enemy.

Warfare praying consists of praying against Satan. But there is more to warfare praying.

Warfare Praying Consists of Praying against Strongholds

What is a spiritual stronghold? A stronghold is an area of your life that you have given over to Satan. Would you take a moment to read that definition again? A stronghold could be a habit, a bad thought, or even a vain imagination in which you followed your own selfish desires and fulfilled the lusts of your flesh. These expressions are against the will of Christ and are expressions of disobedience to God's Word.

When you give in to the desires of your flesh, you usually think that it is no big deal. However, the moment you give in to your flesh, Satan gains some ground in your life. Eventually, this area of your life can imprison you. The results can be spiritually devastating to you.

This is why you deal with the same sins over and over again in your life. You confess them to God repeatedly, yet you have no victory. This creates a defeatist attitude spiritually where you eventually accept mediocrity in your faith. Satan convinces you that this is "just you" and that you cannot ever overcome these sins because they are just a part of your human nature. What has occurred is that Satan has built up a fortress in your life. Every time you disobey God in this area, Satan gains a little more ground in your life. This is a stronghold!

Would you imagine with me for a moment one of the speakers connected to your home entertainment system? When you look at the speaker, all you see is a case covered with some kind of cloth or external covering. All you know is that sound comes out of that speaker when it is activated. This speaker has the power to penetrate your home with sound. If you were to remove the cloth or external covering, you would be able to see the speaker. Otherwise, all you see is the cloth or external covering.

A stronghold could be a habit, a bad thought, or even a vain imagination in which you followed your own selfish desires and fulfilled the lusts of your flesh.

This is exactly what a stronghold is like. The real issue is the difference between what God sees and what you see. For example, you see the cloth or external covering over the speaker. Only when this is removed do you see the speaker itself. With or without the cloth or external covering, the function of the speaker is the same. This is the same way it is with a stronghold. A stronghold is the difference between what God sees and what you see.

For example, what you see is worry about your job or finances. What God sees is the stronghold of worry. What you see is fear of the future. What God sees is a stronghold of fear. What you see is someone you do not like because of something he or she may have done to you. What God sees is a stronghold of unforgiveness. What you see is the lure of seeing any form or level of nudity on a video, a magazine, or the web. What God sees is the stronghold of pornography.

When the Lord opens your spiritual eyes to see what He sees and removes the cloth or external covering, you will begin to recognize that many of these sins are major strongholds in your life. At some point in time you handed over a specific area of your life to sin, and then

Satan gained ground in your life. From God's perspective, you will see a stronghold in which Satan's wicked power resides in your life. Yes, he can influence your mind, your will, and your emotions.

The Bible is very clear about spiritual strongholds. Second Corinthians 10:3–5 describes this struggle: "For though we walk in the flesh, we do not war according to the flesh, for the weapons of our warfare are not of the flesh, but divinely powerful for the destruction of fortresses. We are destroying speculations and every lofty thing raised up against the knowledge of God, and we are taking every thought captive to the obedience of Christ." What does this passage mean in relationship to spiritual strongholds?

Would you take a moment and touch your arm with one of your hands? Would you touch one of your legs with your hands? This is your flesh. The Bible says in these verses that you cannot war against the spiritual strongholds in a physical way. If you try to fight the devil with your own might, you will lose. We are simply not powerful enough on our own to overcome the power of Satan.

God has given you some weapons to use in this spiritual war. In a few moments, you will read about some of these spiritual weapons God has given to you. The problem is that when the world takes up fleshly weapons against you or your flesh, you are tempted to retaliate immediately with your flesh. Your weapons of warfare are divinely powered. Your flesh is not empowered like this. The Bible says that your spiritual weapons are so powerful they can destroy spiritual fortresses or strongholds. This means that you can regain the ground you gave up by your sinful choices by using your God-empowered spiritual weapons to destroy strongholds.

The Bible says that these spiritual weapons can even destroy various speculations or imaginations that we have in life. An example of one of these vain imaginations would be when you think, *I wonder what they think of me?* In time, you begin to imagine things that may not even be true. Before you know it, a devastating paranoia begins to take place in several areas of your life. How many times have you imagined something to be a lot worse than it really turned out to be? You may justify this kind of thinking by saying, "Well, I am just playing it safe. I wanted to prepare myself for the worst possible scenario." The problem with speculations or vain imaginations is that you are not able to enjoy the present life because you are too busy worrying about what might happen in your future.

The Bible goes on to say that all disobedience will be punished. When you get to heaven, your obedience to God will be ultimately complete and your disobedience will be ultimately punished. The secret to overcoming a spiritual stronghold in your life is to take captive every thought you have and place each of them under the lordship of Jesus Christ.

> *The secret to overcoming a spiritual stronghold in your life is to take captive every thought you have and place each of them under the lordship of Jesus Christ.*

Yes, the Scriptures verify that God has given you some weapons to carry on this spiritual battle. Remember, it is not a fleshly battle, so you cannot fight it with the flesh. It is a spiritual battle that must be fought with spiritual weapons. As you pray against Satan and spiritual strongholds, you will be successful only when you use spiritual weapons.

The Weapons of Your Warfare

What are the weapons of your warfare? I want to mention five weapons that God wants you to use in your daily spiritual battles.

1. The Name of Jesus Christ

The name of Jesus is the most powerful name under heaven. You are to stand firm against Satan in the name of Jesus Christ. You are to destroy spiritual strongholds in the name of Jesus Christ. At the name of Jesus, Satan will flee and spiritual strongholds will be obliterated, regardless of their apparent strength. Activate the power of God by using the weapon of the name of Jesus.

2. The Blood of Jesus Christ

When Jesus died on the cross, His blood became the atonement for your sin; in other words, His blood covered over your sins. His blood was so powerful that His unblemished sacrifice became the provision for the forgiveness of your sins.

If you want to make Satan angry, just sing about the blood of Jesus Christ. Remind Satan that you are covered by Jesus' blood and that you stand in His grace alone. The blood of Jesus is a spiritual weapon that can destroy any stronghold because all of your sins were paid in full on the cross.

3. The Word of God

The Word of God is the only offensive weapon in the armor of God described in Ephesians 6. It is also the most powerful weapon because the battle comes down to God's Word versus Satan's word. God's Word is always more powerful than Satan's word. This is why it is imperative that you read the Word, hear the Word, grow in the Word, study the Word, and memorize the Word.

Any time Satan comes against you with false accusations, speak the Word of God and he will flee from you. The Word of God is the Truth. Satan is a liar, and he hates the Truth. The Word of God is a powerful weapon in your spiritual artillery.

4. The Word of Your Testimony

Satan hates to hear your testimony of how Jesus Christ changed your life. This is why you are sometimes hesitant to witness. Satan has convinced you that you cannot do it or that your testimony is ineffective. Satan does not want to hear you recite what Jesus did for you on the cross. He does not want to hear about how Jesus died in your place for your sins. He realizes that the moment you share your experience of the life-changing power of Jesus Christ, people will want what you have. Then they will embrace the cross, and Satan will have lost another soul to God.

Your testimony is powerful—share it with others and remind Satan daily how Jesus has changed your life.

5. A Love for God Greater Than the Desire to Live

Do you love your life? Do you continually try to preserve your reputation? Do you insist on claiming your rights?

The Bible tells you not to love your life. In fact, even if you are facing death for your faith, do not try to preserve your life. A unique spiritual power is activated when you do not love your life, even when you face death. Satan is overcome by this kind of courage. This demonstration of allegiance to Christ and denial of yourself can obliterate spiritual strongholds. The Bible declares boldly these words of defeat over Satan in Revelation 12:11: "They conquered him by the blood of the Lamb and by the word of their testimony; for they did not love their lives to the point of death" (CSB).

Closing Words

In closing, I want to share a few words from the living God that will bring Satan down and destroy all spiritual strongholds. Think upon them. Meditate upon them. Repeat them over and over again. Just as you have seen these words before, I am writing them again. Why? These are the words of life! The words of victory!

> For this reason also, God highly exalted Him, and bestowed on Him
> the name which is above every name, so that at the name of Jesus

EVERY KNEE WILL BOW, of those who are in heaven and on earth and under the earth, and that every tongue will confess that Jesus Christ is Lord, to the glory of God the Father. (Philippians 2:9–11)

For the word of God is living and active and sharper than any two-edged sword, and piercing as far as the division of soul and spirit, of both joints and marrow, and able to judge the thoughts and intentions of the heart. (Hebrews 4:12)

"They conquered him by the blood of the Lamb and by the word of their testimony; for they did not love their lives to the point of death. (Revelation 12:11 CSB)

Yes, these are words of life! Words of power! Words of victory!

CHAPTER 11

HOW TO EMPOWER
YOUR PRAYERS

E arly one February morning in 1995, I was in my study having
my personal time with God. While I was reading through *The
One Year Bible* and asking God to speak to me through His Word, I
was alarmed at what I sensed God was saying to me.

I observed in the book of Exodus how God called Moses to go up
on the mountain to spend forty days with Him in fasting and prayer.
The result of this extended time of fasting and prayer was that Moses
received the Ten Commandments. When Moses returned from his
time with God, he discovered the people of God abounding in idola-
try. Moses' heart was broken, and the Bible records that he returned
to the mountain to spend another extended time with God in fasting
and prayer. Although I have read that passage many times, on this
particular day I became frightened at what I sensed God was calling
me to do in my life.

As I was praying over this passage, I sensed God was calling me
to draw aside to be with Him for forty days of prayer and fasting.
Specifically, I sensed God wanted me to concentrate in prayer and
fasting for spiritual revival in America, in my church, and in my life.

This was the first time I had felt God nudging me to fast over
such an extended period. (This was before I felt called to fast in

connection with the Southern Baptist Convention in New Orleans.)
I knew such a fast would be a real challenge to complete, but I also
felt deeply that God was calling me to do it. Still, I told no one what
I was feeling, and I inwardly hoped that what I heard was not truly a
call from the Spirit of God.

During the next couple of days, I really struggled with God about
this calling. I had not heard of many people who had ever fasted and
prayed for that length of time. I had participated in fasting and prayer for
many years, but this was the longest fast I had ever planned to observe.
Previously, my longest was only over a three-day period of time. Three
days of fasting was one thing, but forty days seemed like an eternity.

After a few days of prayer over this issue, I was convinced that
this calling to fast forty days was from God. I began to study and
think through this time with God. I knew the timing was important
in relationship to my schedule. I had many questions, but I had no
one to ask.

On a Sunday morning in early March, I walked into my office and
discovered on my desk a book on fasting and prayer. A dear brother
named Rick Sparks, a man in my church who operated a Christian
radio station, had come across the book and just sensed that God
wanted him to give it to me. I was leaving town that day to preach a
revival for a few days. I began to read that book eagerly, wanting to
learn everything I could on the subject. It was another confirmation
that God was calling me to fast and pray.

I decided to tell my wife what I sensed God was calling me to do.
When I told her that I believed God wanted me to fast and pray for
forty days, she said, "If God is calling you, I will support you." Her
support was another confirmation that God was calling me to go on
a journey with Him.

Upon completion of our annual ski vacation over the spring break
season, I began to make serious and final preparations for this forty-
day journey with God. I really felt that I needed a plan to pray for this

time. I wanted a list of specific things that God wanted me to pray about during this time of fasting. I asked the Lord to make this plan and this list very clear to me. Within a day, the Lord had given me the plan of what I would do during these forty days.

As I've mentioned, I sensed that God wanted me to pray and fast for spiritual revival to occur in America, in my church, and in my life. The Lord gave me specific items for prayer concerning each one of those areas. I would spend most of the normal periods set aside for eating in prayer. As well, I would strive to spend two hours of uninterrupted time with Him every morning solely for this calling to fast and pray. I would interpret all hunger pangs as a call to prayer. I would attempt to draw aside several times a day just to be with God, so I needed to adjust my work schedule to accommodate this need. I would tell no one but my closest staff and my family, from whom I would need understanding and prayer. In addition to this, I would journal all activity that occurred between God and me during this forty days. I also sensed that God wanted me to conclude this journey with Him in a personal retreat so I could solidify what He was going to do in my life during this time. Finally, the dates were confirmed in my heart for the journey to begin.

Blastoff! The journey with God began for forty days. What happened? I wrote more than one hundred pages in my journal, documenting God's mighty activity in my life. I sensed oneness with Christ like I had never experienced. My spirit was very sensitive to the Spirit of God. I experienced the mighty anointing of God upon my life and ministry. I began to refer to these days as "forty days that changed my life."

What God chose to do in those forty days was remarkable. As I concluded that time in personal retreat with Him, I did not want to let go. I had been on a journey with God that was unprecedented. At the same time, I was involved with the details of life that seemed so mundane.

On that final day, I had to travel to Atlanta for an important meeting. As I was sitting on that plane, reflecting upon my experience, I began to write my final thoughts. The closing hour of the fast was coming upon me.

I did not want to leave the journey, but I knew it was time. That night, in an Atlanta hotel restaurant, I concluded my time of fasting and prayer. Very early the next morning, the Spirit of God woke me up. My heart was filled with celebration and praise. God came upon me in that room like I had never experienced before in my life. His grace fell upon me in a way that I cannot describe. Time seemed suspended. I do not know how long God and I dialogued that morning, but the oneness and fellowship with Him were incredible.

Blastoff! The journey with God began for forty days. What happened? . . . I sensed oneness with Christ like I had never experienced.

In case you decide to reach your own conclusions about my experience that early morning, I want you to know that I did not speak in tongues or any kind of prayer language. It was several days before I could even articulate what happened to me in that room. The power of God fell upon me with a new and fresh anointing, and my life and ministry have never been the same. Truly, it was one of the defining moments in my spiritual life.

I want you to also understand that I do not think the power of what happened that early morning is merely that one experience. I really believe that God graced me because of my humble obedience to Him. He loves a surrendered, broken, and weak life. In those final days of fasting, that is exactly what I was. God had everything in my life. I was totally surrendered. I was broken like never before. My body was weak, twenty-four pounds lighter, but my spirit was standing tall in oneness with Christ.

In that closing retreat with God, I really sensed that God was releasing me to tell my church about what God had done in my life. I wrote to the entire membership, encouraging them to be in our church on Sunday, June 4, 1995, because I believed that it would be one of the monumental days in our church's 125 years of existence. I told them that I was going to speak on forty days that changed my life.

On that Sunday morning, approximately ten days following the conclusion of my forty-day time of fasting and prayer, God showed up like never before in my ministry. Within moments of worship, I sensed the Holy Spirit usher Himself into that room like a tidal wave. The power was unbelievable! On that morning, I repented of my sins. I stood in complete transparency before my people. I appealed to them to get their lives right with God so that revival could come into our church.

On that morning, our service lasted two and a half hours. No one moved or left early. Time meant nothing because the Spirit of God was present among us. People were on their faces before God even before the public invitation began. Worship was powerful before the message and after the invitation. Incredible brokenness came upon the congregation. On that day revival came to Cross Church in Springdale, Arkansas.

I was in a place where I had never been as a pastor. Of course, that was not surprising because I was at a time in my life like I had never been. I asked the people to return that evening to see what God would choose to do among us as we sought Him.

Seventy percent of the Sunday morning crowd came back on Sunday evening. (I told you God moved!) When we assembled for the evening service, the Holy Spirit was again present among God's people. We whetted their appetites with stories of revival. I recounted some things God had shown me during my forty-day journey with Him. That evening, I saw openness and transparency in the church like I had never seen before. Many of God's people stood up before the church to repent of their sins, ask for forgiveness, and experience deep brokenness before God. Others who had been delivered from that sin joined them at the altar and covered them with prayer.

Yes, it was a profound evening in all of our lives. After four hours of true revival coming upon God's people, the Lord led us to close out the evening in unprecedented celebration. It was now past 10:00 p.m. on Sunday, but the people still wanted to sit around and talk about what God had done among us that day.

On June 4, 1995, God came to Cross Church. *On that day, the church got a new pastor without changing pastors. On that day, I got a new church without changing churches. When God comes, things are never the same again.* Audio and videotapes have been listened to and shown literally all over the world about what God did that day in our church. You can still receive copies.[1] It was a day that God was exalted!

As I told our people following that first forty-day fast: *God can do more in a moment than we could ever do in a lifetime.* I believe that! My life and my ministry are living proof of that spiritual reality. I am astounded at how God has chosen to use my obedience to Him. Complete surrender to God leads to boundless opportunities to experience His grace.

God will probably not call most people to fast and pray for forty days, but I guarantee you that He will call most people to experience specific days of prayer and fasting. This calling from God must come from Him. How do you know if it's from God? You'll know. God will make it clear that He wants you to respond to the burden you are feeling on a particular issue—and that He wants you to respond with prayer coupled with fasting. If God calls you, then you will have the power to do whatever He is calling you to do.

I want you to understand, though, that I do not believe that prayer and fasting are hoops that you jump through to get God's attention. God is not your puppet. He will not be manipulated. In addition, fasting and prayer are not something that others can call you to do. They may ask you to pray about whether God wants you to join them in fasting and prayer, but God is always the One who gives the calling to fast and pray.

As a pastor, I have often asked my people to join me in specific days set aside for fasting and prayer for specific needs in our church, for major events in our church, or for the purpose of evangelizing our region. Each of these has been connected to some specific needs in the body of Christ. Yet in each situation I have asked our people to pray about whether God would want them to join us in a day of prayer and fasting for the need that was upon my heart. I would encourage any pastor or spiritual leader to practice this with your people.

On June 4, 1995, God came to Cross Church. On that day, the church got a new pastor without changing pastors. On that day, I got a new church without changing churches.

Over the past few years, we have asked our people to join us each January in a twenty-one-day time of fasting and prayer. Each year there is great receptivity to it and many people participate at some level. This past year we even did a Facebook Live event each morning that was watched by many people. As a pastor, it is always a dynamic experience to have your people join you at some level of fasting and prayer.

I would encourage all Christians to join your pastor in these days if he is convinced that God is calling the body to fast and pray over a specific need. God honors people who will practice fasting and prayer. I believe that fasting and prayer are God's gateway to supernatural power. Prayer and fasting take your prayer life and church to a new level.

What Is Fasting?

Fasting is abstinence from food with a spiritual goal in mind. It is abstaining from the most *natural* thing your body desires—food—in order to entreat the God of heaven to do something *supernatural* in your life. Your entrance into God's supernatural power is fasting and prayer.

In a practical way, fasting can also be abstinence from other things in life. For example, just think what would happen in your life if you fasted from television for one week. Just think what would happen in your life if you fasted from time on the web or all social media for one week. *Whatever is important to you, fast from it for a time, and you will see God do something really great in your life.*

I believe fasting is powerful because you *humble* yourself before God. The Bible commands us to humble ourselves: "Humble yourselves, therefore, under the mighty hand of God, so that he may exalt you at the proper time" (1 Peter 5:6 csb). According to this scripture, *you are to take the initiative* to humble yourself before God.

The word *humble* means "to lie low, to make yourself flat, or to put yourself under." It indicates more of an action that you take rather than a position you hold. There is a continual correlation in the Scriptures between fasting and humbling yourself before God. This is why David said in Psalm 35:13, "I humbled my soul with fasting." If you study the Scriptures thoroughly, you will discover numerous commands to *humble yourself* before God. *You* are to take the initiative to humble yourself before God. I believe one of the most specific and direct ways to obey this command is to humble yourself through *fasting and prayer.*

When Ezra was leading the Jewish exiles back to Jerusalem, an amazing event occurred beside the Ahava Canal. Ezra halted the travelers in order to seek God's protection on their journey: "I proclaimed a fast . . . that we might humble ourselves before our God. . . . So we fasted and sought our God concerning this matter, and He listened to our entreaty" (Ezra 8:21, 23). Ezra and the people were in a moment of crisis, so he proclaimed a fast for the people. Why? *So that the people of God would humble themselves before God.* As they fasted and prayed about their need, God answered them. What a great spiritual truth! *Just as Ezra saw God's hand when the people humbled themselves through fasting and prayer, I have seen God's hand respond in my life in the same way.*

What Does the Bible Say about Fasting?

The practice of fasting occurs throughout the Scriptures. In addition to the stories I have already shared, I want to recount for you a few more accounts of fasting in Scripture.

In the Old Testament, the Jewish people would fast on the most important spiritual day of their year—the Day of Atonement. They understood that fasting *prepared and assisted* them in this spiritually significant day in their lives. As I have already stated, Ezra fasted and received *God's protection and power* for God's people. In 2 Chronicles 20:3, Jehoshaphat proclaimed a national fast to *seek the Lord for direction and protection.* As a response to their fasting, God delivered His people. When Nehemiah heard the condition of things in Jerusalem, *his great burden moved him to fast* (Nehemiah 1:4). In that time of fasting and prayer, God called him back to Jerusalem to rebuild the wall around the city. One of the greatest revivals in human history occurred in Nineveh as a result of fasting and prayer (Jonah 3:5).

In the New Testament, *John the Baptist fasted and prayed.* The apostle *Paul also practiced fasting and prayer.* The early church as recorded in Acts practiced seasons of fasting and prayer. In Matthew 6:17, Jesus taught, "When you fast . . .". He did not say *if* you fast or *if you want* to fast, but He said *when* you fast. Jesus placed fasting on the same level as praying and giving. When Jesus was returning from the Mount of Transfiguration with Peter, James, and John, they noticed that the disciples were trying to cast a demon out of someone. They could not understand why they could not cast out this demon. Jesus said that their unbelief was the obstacle that was keeping them from removing this demon from this person. But Jesus encouraged them and said that nothing is impossible with God (Matthew 17:20). He shared with them that if they wanted the faith to do these kinds of miracles they would only receive this kind of faith *through fasting and prayer.* Yes, even through Jesus' own recorded forty-day fast He overcame the devil and his temptations and was empowered by the Holy Spirit.

The Bible is full of illustrations of fasting and prayer. If this spiritual discipline was good enough for Jesus, it should be good enough for you and me. If Jesus saw the need to humble Himself before the Father, certainly we should sense the same need.

I believe that one of the reasons that fasting is so disregarded and ignored by Christians today is because of Satan. *Satan knows the power of fasting.* He has attempted to keep this truth from the church and does so quite effectively. He has also tried to keep the attention away from fasting by creating senseless concerns about it.

For example, should a person talk about their times of fasting? No, not while they are fasting (Matthew 6:16–18). However, Jesus does not forbid talking about the fast once it is over, if He directs you to do so in a God-glorifying way. Just think, if Moses had not talked about what God had said to him in his forty-day fast, you would not have the Ten Commandments. Enough said?

The Power of Fasting

In much of this chapter, I have written about the power of fasting. Fasting really does have the power to change your life. I believe it can even change your church. Yes, I believe it can even change our country.

Fasting is powerful because you neglect the flesh and its natural desire of eating in order to appeal to God to do something supernatural in your life. God always pours out His Spirit upon you when you neglect the natural in order to pursue God. Remember, you are to pursue God—not revival, not fasting, not His supernatural power. God is the source of those blessings, but those blessings should never be more important to you than God Himself.

I believe that fasting is so powerful that it can set a person free who has been enslaved in some kind of sin and bondage. Fasting breaks any bondage a person has in his or her life. Personally, I have become convinced that the bondage that is occurring in the lives of many people will never be broken only through countless sessions of counseling or only through hours of support-group assistance. I am not discounting the value of counseling and support-group ministry, but the problem is that a great amount of bondage exists as a result of demonic activity, especially in the areas of spiritual strongholds. This is why pastors and church leaders must teach people about the spiritual discipline of prayer and fasting as well as the reality of spiritual warfare in the life of each Christ-follower.

The Bible is full of illustrations of fasting and prayer. If this spiritual discipline was good enough for Jesus, it should be good enough for you and me.

In my days of extended fasting and prayer, God has set me free from sins that had plagued me for years. Extended times of fasting make you aware of the holiness of God and the exceeding sinfulness of yourself. God has used fasting to break the chain of sin in my life, and I know He will do the same in your life. Why? *Fasting empowers your prayers with real God power!*

When Should You Fast and Pray?

I believe there are some specific times when God wants you to fast and pray. Do you have a desire to have a new and fresh touch from

God? Do you have a desire to see God blow a fresh breeze of His Spirit upon your church? Would you like to see God bring a mighty spiritual revival and awakening to your country? If you would answer yes to any one of these questions, then it is time for you to fast and pray.

I also believe another time you should fast and pray is when you are desperate for God to do something supernatural in your life, your church, and your nation. Answer this question honestly: How desperate are you for God to do something supernatural in these areas? Along the way of life, God will create moments of desperation. The changes of life have a way of creating desperation. Illness, disaster, and tragedy have a way of creating desperation. These are desperate times in which we live.

You need to be desperate for God to move in you and through you in these days. Desperation accompanied by fasting is hazardous to Satan's health and will transform your spiritual life.

Helpful Hints When You Fast and Pray

I want to share four helpful hints that you need to adhere to when you fast and pray.

1. Discover God's Plan

Before you fast and pray, attempt to discover God's plan for you. He has a specific reason that He wants you to fast and pray. Attempt to define those reasons, regardless of the length of the fast. Remember: *fasting is abstinence with a spiritual goal in mind.* What are the specific goals for your time of fasting? Write down things that you sense God wants you to pray for during that time of fasting.

For example, if your fast is for one day, define three or four spiritual goals that you are praying for during this one-day fast. Write them on a card or make a note in your phone. Place them somewhere prominent such as in your Bible or somewhere you know you will see throughout the day. Look at the list through the day. Let it become your prayer list. Have a plan whenever you pray and fast. If your fast is extended in length, then pray over your plan to pray every day, even several times a day.

2. Determine the Length of Your Fast

Attempt to determine the length of the fast before you begin. There have only been a couple of times in all of my fasting experiences that I did not know the length of the fast before I began it. *I believe the magnitude of your need should determine the length of your fast.* Read the previous statement again. Digest it. Let it become your guide for determining the length for your times of fasting. Perhaps it may be helpful to see one more time: *I believe the magnitude of your need should determine the length of your fast.*

3. Withdraw

Fasting without withdrawing to some degree in some specific ways will only provide limited results. I am not talking about leaving your life for a number of days. But you should withdraw in some specific ways to create a few opportunities to be with God during your fast.

If your daily time with God is normally thirty minutes in length, then make it sixty minutes the day you fast. You can also turn the normal time allotments set aside for meals into times for prayer and communion with God. Withdraw with the Word of God in your hand, and talk to God without ceasing.

4. Journal

Whenever you fast, write down your thoughts in a journal, in your device, or in an online format. Every time you meet with God, record what God has said to you in His Word. There is a certain release that comes when you journal what God is saying to you. This record of your spiritual life will become a real treasure for you. God will use it to create greater faith in your life as you reflect upon your journal and remember God's activity in your life.

You Only Have Four Problems

I believe every Christian only has four problems in life. You might say, "Only four?" Yes, I believe you only have four problems in your life.

I believe when God comes to live in you, His Spirit resides in your spirit. In your spirit you are in complete oneness with Jesus Christ. When you fast, your spirit becomes very aware of the Spirit of God, who is united in oneness with your spirit. Your spirit also becomes sensitive to the needs around you. It also will stand up with a humble power unlike any other time in your spiritual life. So what are the four problems that interfere with this oneness with the Spirit of God?

The four problems you have in the Christian life are your mind, your will, your emotions, and your body. Your mind races away at times and thinks upon things that are not holy. Your will stands up periodically in opposition to God's will. Your emotions are like a roller coaster at times, measuring the ups and downs of your life. Your body is deteriorating every day regardless of your commitment to fitness.

Have you ever witnessed an orchestra conductor exercise his influence upon the orchestra? It is amazing! Whenever he lifts his arms in preparation to lead the music, the musicians raise their instruments in a single motion. Although the various members of the orchestra are each playing different notes and rhythms during the warm-up, when the conductor lifts his arms they are immediately prepared to follow his direction.

When you fast, your spirit becomes like an orchestra conductor. Your spirit is connected in supernatural oneness with God, and it calls to attention your mind, your will, your emotions, and your body. Through this experience, your mind becomes the mind of Christ. Your will is aligned with God's will. Your emotions reflect the emotions of Jesus—whatever He loves, you love, and whatever He feels, you feel. Your body, weak through fasting, is made strong through God's supernatural intervention.

When you fast, your spirit becomes very aware of the Spirit of God, who is united in oneness with your spirit.

Any one or all of those four problems can be restrained during times of fasting and prayer. *You do not have a single problem that God cannot solve.*

Fasting will definitely take your prayer life to a new level with God! Practice it and you will become a testimony of God's amazing supernatural power. Fasting will empower your life and your prayers with real God power! For more information, you can find my updated and revised resource on fasting and prayer available at booksellers.[2]

PART 4

BARRIERS TO PRAYER

CHAPTER 12

THE WALL OF STRAINED
RELATIONSHIPS

J ews and Gentiles have been at odds with one another for years. A wall existed between the two groups for centuries with little hope of its ever coming down. That wall was so deep you could not tunnel underneath it, so high that you could not climb over it. It was so thick you could not break through it. This wall indicated a definite and serious separation between the two groups.

In today's America, there are groups of people separated by bias, prejudice, or ideology. Sadly, even in our day, racial prejudice exists in some segments of America. Politically, the wall of separation has never been greater in our generation between the main two political parties; oftentimes people forget we are in the same nation and we are to be *"one nation under God."* Even in the church of Jesus Christ, there are divisions over secondary issues that create major tension within the body of Jesus Christ.

In the book of Ephesians, the apostle Paul described this wall or division that separated the Jews from the Gentiles, which can represent any wall or division occurring now. In this discussion, Paul revealed that this wall was finally broken down only by the work of Jesus Christ on the cross: "But now in Christ Jesus you who formerly were far off have been brought near by the blood of Christ. For He

Himself is our peace, who made both groups into one and broke down the barrier of the dividing wall" (Ephesians 2:13–14). This wall was brought down by the power of Jesus Christ on the cross. He died to make all people one.

This theological truth is also true for every barrier, wall, or obstacle that stands between any two persons, groups, or parties. Jesus' death on the cross tears down all the dividing walls, and His bodily resurrection grants us the power to experience unity with one another rather than division and disunity.

One of my major responsibilities as the president of the National Day of Prayer Task Force is to determine a theme for this special day across America. In 2018, I felt deeply the theme needed to be unity. Therefore, from the national observance held in Washington, DC, to the thousands of gatherings across America, these prayer observances were built on the theme of unity. For months leading up to the first Thursday in May 2018, we forwarded the call to *Pray for America: Unity.*

The scripture that we believed was God's heart for this experience was Ephesians 4:3: "Making every effort to keep the unity of the Spirit through the bond of peace" (csb). Each of us who follow Jesus need to do all we can to make every effort to live in unity and hold each other accountable to walk in unity. With great conviction I verbally stated and continually wrote these words, and still do today: *A divided church cannot call a divided nation to unity.* For those who are genuine followers of Jesus Christ, we must discover the only way to come together: through the supernatural power of God. Unity is supernatural!

In this section, I will share about barriers that have been raised up to lead you away from God, to disrupt your focus on God when you pray, or even to stand defiantly against God and His will. The goal you should have in your prayer life is for your prayers to be so effective that God hears them and answers them. This calls for us to address these barriers and seek the God of heaven to bring them down in the power of Jesus' name. Does this interest you? Is this needed? Read on!

What Must Come Down Before Your Prayers Go Up

The walls that are created by our sinful choices must come down before our prayers go up to God effectively. The great news is that the work of Christ on the cross has abolished all the walls. Therefore, the walls can come down and your prayers can go up to God.

Dr. Oscar Thompson was a very influential man in my life. He was my evangelism professor at Southwestern Baptist Theological Seminary. He is now with the Lord, as he died with cancer during my seminary years.

Dr. Thompson taught about the value of human relationships. He used to say the most important word in the English language is the word *relationship*. In his wonderful book *Concentric Circles of Concern*, Dr. Thompson wrote about the importance of developing relationships with people for the purpose of winning them to faith in Christ. As well, he taught about the value of relationships between believers in Christ. Dr. Thompson believed that love travels on the track of a relationship. Just as a train can run off the tracks if the tracks are not right, love will not operate effectively if the relationship is not right.[1]

One of the best examples of a pure relationship is the relationship of the Godhead: God the Father, God the Son, and God the Holy Spirit. The common belief among conservative evangelical Christians is that there is one God who is in three persons. Incredible harmony exists between the persons of the Godhead. There is no division. There is no strain or even a hint of disharmony. There is no part of God who wishes He were another part of God. The Godhead is an example of true unity and peace. This is the kind of relationship that should exist between people.

God's will for all relationships is harmony. He desires for all people to love one another. God wants unity to exist between all persons. His death on the cross obliterated the walls that have existed between all persons. This is why God can bring unity and harmony in all relationships. Only God can bring unity. Unity is supernatural!

This is why calling upon the Lord is so important. Prayer nurtures your relationship with God. Do you believe that your relationships with other people affect your prayer relationship with God? I believe the answer to this question is yes. In fact, there is something deeper involved . . .

A Spiritual Law You Cannot Break

There are many reasons why some of your prayers are not answered. I believe one of the main reasons is because of strained relationships. The spiritual law that you cannot break in your life as a Christian is this: God will not answer your prayers if your relationships with other people are strained. You cannot break this spiritual law if you expect your prayers to be answered. In this chapter, you will begin to see the reality of this spiritual law take place.

With this spiritual law fresh on your mind, take time to evaluate your relationships with other people. How is your relationship with each member of your family? What about your relationships with your relatives? Your relationships with your coworkers? Your relationships with your neighbors? Your relationships with the Christians who attend your local church? Your relationships with the leaders of your local church? What about your relationships with other Christians and followers of Christ? Are these relationships strained or unified?

Each Christian has the responsibility to be in a right relationship with other people. In Romans 12:18, Paul instructed, "If possible, so far as it depends on you, be at peace with all men." The burden is placed upon you. The burden is placed upon me. The blame game is unacceptable. Regardless of fault or problem, God places the burden on each of us to be at peace with all people.

The spiritual law that you cannot break in your life as a Christian is this: God will not answer your prayers if your relationships with other people are strained.

If you violate this spiritual law, your prayers will not be answered. Satan builds up this imaginary wall in relationships, making you think that there is no way you can relate properly to certain persons. When this occurs, a wall is created between you and God that hinders your prayers from being answered. God will not answer your prayers if your relationships with other people are strained.

Evaluate your relationships with other people more thoroughly. Begin this evaluation process by looking at your . . .

General Relationships

When Jesus preached what is known as His Sermon on the Mount, He dealt extensively with the subject of relationships. He gave powerful instruction about how we are to relate to others. In Matthew 5:21–24, Jesus shared:

> You have heard that the ancients were told, "YOU SHALL NOT COMMIT MURDER" and "Whoever commits murder shall be liable to the court." But I say to you that everyone who is angry with his brother shall be guilty before the court; and whoever says to his brother, "You good-for-nothing," shall be guilty before the supreme court;

and whoever says, "You fool," shall be guilty enough to go into the fiery hell. Therefore if you are presenting your offering at the altar, and there remember that your brother has something against you, leave your offering there before the altar and go; first be reconciled to your brother, and then come and present your offering.

These words from Jesus are penetrating words. Convicting words. Powerful words.

Jesus taught that murder was a sin and a violation of the court. Most of us would agree with this statement. But Jesus took it one step further and said that anger is as serious an offense as murder. *In relationships, anger must be dealt with or the relationship will be strained at best or terminated at worst.* The word *anger* in this passage refers to the kind of anger that is a settled condition of your mind without any intention of taking revenge. We tend to think of anger as an emotion that always explodes in outbursts. But this word for anger refers to the type of ongoing, suppressed anger that churns within you toward another person.

How does this anger ever come to the surface of your life? Jesus said it will surface in remarks such as, "That person is good for nothing" or, "That person is empty-headed." In these verses, Jesus said that if you are presenting your offering at the altar and remember that your brother has something against you, then you should be reconciled to your brother before you present your offering to God. If you have negative feelings in your heart toward someone else, then you cannot do serious business with God. Jesus instructed us to go and be reconciled to the people with whom we might have a strained relationship before we do our business with God.

If you want to do business with God in prayer, you must ensure as far as you can that the relationships in your life are right. There is no ground for you to get around the spiritual law concerning relationships. *If you have something against a person, go and make it right with him or her immediately.* If you know someone has something against you, go to that person now and attempt to make the relationship right. Drive to the person's house. Make a phone call. Write a card. Send a text or email. Do whatever it takes to get right with that person.

Communing with God is very serious business. It is holy business. Sin will not be tolerated in any form, even strained relationships. Here's a bold statement that you need to remember: *do not bother to pray until you are right with others.*

Do not think you can compromise or negotiate this spiritual truth. God wants your heart pure when you talk to Him. He wants things right between you and others before you attempt to carry on business with Him. Are you wanting to do business with God? If so, consider this checklist right now: Do you have anyone in your family today with whom you have a strained relationship? Do you have a friend with whom you lived in harmony, but now your relationship is strained? Do you have a strained relationship with someone in your church or your past church? Do not bother praying to God until your relationships are right. *Strained relationships must be healed before your prayers can go up to God with the greatest effectiveness.*

The most challenging place to live the Christian life is before your family. Would you enter into the privacy of your own life and in your own heart and evaluate your . . .

Family Relationships

One of the most spiritually convicting times for me is when I deal seriously with God about my relationship with my family. I believe this is true for all of us. I have been strongly committed to my family for years. The people in my church would give a strong testimony about my sincere and diligent commitment to family life. Even with that strong commitment, I still get under the Holy Spirit's conviction about my relationships with my family members. I hope you do as well.

I want to highlight a difficult passage of Scripture that concerns the importance of family relationships. In fact, this specific text is a challenge to every husband, but the spiritual principle also has deep meaning and challenge to each member of any family. The Bibles says,

> Husbands, in the same way, live with your wives in an understanding way, as with a weaker partner, showing them honor as coheirs of the grace of life, so that your prayers will not be hindered. (1 Peter 3:7 csb)

This passage is a deeply convicting passage of Scripture. Within the context of these words to and about husbands and wives, God gave a principle about relationships and prayer that must be adhered to by all persons. It is addressed primarily to the husband because men are not always known to be sensitive and considerate to their wives.

Never should any man be mean or abusive in any way toward his wife or any other woman. This is sinful, wrong, and inexcusable. The church of Jesus Christ must always call all men to honor all women at all times in the highest manner.

Obviously, this has to begin in the family because the family is the way most people are taught about relationships. No relationship in the family is more important nor more representative of the relationship between Christ and His church than a husband and his wife. The husband is to have a conscious sensitivity relating to God's will in the way he should treat his wife.

The reference to a wife being the weaker partner is only in relationship to a wife usually being weaker in the physical body. Therefore, the call from the Lord's Word is for husbands to always show honor and value to their wives, refusing to take any advantage of them due to the way God uniquely created men and women in a physical sense.

This is why the honor is taken to another level, telling the husband that his wife is a coheir of God's grace, discovered and experienced through Jesus Christ alone.

The Lord's Word is so strong about this relationship between the husband and his wife that He stated if any of this is ever violated, it will cut in or hinder their prayers offered to God. In other words, a husband cannot take advantage of, dishonor, demean, or abuse his wife in any way or his prayers to God will be hindered and ultimately go unanswered.

This phrase in this scripture is particularly important not just for the husband; the principle rises to be true for any Spirit-controlled believer, husband or wife, male or female. Remember what the Word says? If our relationships do not honor others, especially in marriage and family, the Bible says our prayers will be hindered or cut in their effectiveness. Therefore, the call to each of us, whoever we are, is to treat all relationships as important and value one another as joint partakers of God's grace so that "your prayers will not be hindered."

When husbands fulfill their unique role in marriage and wives fulfill their unique role in marriage as the Bible states we are each to do, harmony and oneness will occur. If either fails to fulfill their divine designed and assigned roles, the Bible states clearly that their prayers will be hindered. For clarity, this call is unquestionably to husbands, but as other principles in the Bible exist, it should also be followed for wives or any relationships within the family. Personally, I believe other passages in Scripture raise this principle so high, its truth is for all relationships in life.

The great Bible scholar and teacher Warren Wiersbe has a great insight about this word *hindered*. He wrote:

> The word *hindered* has an interesting meaning in the original. It means to break up a road so that the army can't get through. In ancient warfare, this method was often used. The soldiers would

block the road with rocks, trees and other barriers to prevent the opposing army from advancing. Thus, 1 Peter 3:7 is telling husbands and wives that if they are not getting along with each other, their prayers will be hindered. They will be putting up barricades and barriers along the road that will prevent God from answering their prayers.[2]

The most special human relationship on this earth is the relationship between a husband and his wife.

One of the main reasons that you may feel at times that your prayers never get above the ceiling is because of your relationship with your spouse or even your relationships with others in your life. But none illustrates this more than the husband and wife relationship, as well as other family relationships.

The principle rises to be true for any Spirit-controlled believer, husband or wife, male or female. Remember what the Word says? If our relationships do not honor others, especially in marriage and family, the Bible says our prayers will be hindered or cut in their effectiveness.

Notice the word picture of the word *hindered* described by Warren Wiersbe. *When a husband and a wife do not get along, they will put up a wall between themselves that will inevitably result in unanswered prayer.*

Every Christian needs to cease putting up barricades and barriers along the road of their relationships or it will prevent God from answering their prayers. Stop erecting walls between other people and you. These walls need to come down and each of the barriers be removed now!

These verses put forth a piercing, penetrating, and convicting principle for all persons who really want to be all that God has intended them to be in life: *the way you treat your spouse will determine the way God treats your prayers.* If you and your spouse are not enjoying intimacy in your relationship, then you will not see your prayers answered. Let me repeat: the way you treat your spouse will determine the way God treats your prayers. How are you treating your spouse? Is your relationship intimate every day or just when you have a need for your spouse to meet?

In my first pastorate, Jeana and I would leave our college setting and drive to our ministry on Sunday mornings. We had just been married, and the challenges were great as Jeana had just completed her degree and was working full-time. I was one year away from finishing my degree, so I was going to school full-time and pastoring this church on weekends.

One Sunday morning, Jeana and I had a disagreement that resulted in a fellowship problem between us. I went back to my "office" (actually, the janitor's closet) to pray before Sunday school as I always did, but I sensed that something wasn't right. I was convicted by the Holy Spirit that I needed to be reconciled with Jeana. God convicted me that He would not anoint me for the morning until I made things right with my wife.

I went to the auditorium where Jeana was sitting in preparation for worship. I took her aside and repented for my words spoken to her that morning. She repented of her part of the disagreement. Then the Lord was faithful to anoint us for the day.

I learned through that experience that Satan will do all he can to damage my relationship with my wife because that strained relationship would greatly affect my relationship with God and my effectiveness in serving Him. Therefore, Jeana and I made a covenant not to even come close to a disagreement on Sundays about anything ever again and later committed to try to live that way the entire week. God has truly honored this covenant between us during our years together.

While intimacy with your spouse will determine your intimacy with God, it is important to realize that intimacy with God will determine your intimacy with your spouse. Both must take place or else intimacy will not occur—in other words, your prayers will go unanswered.

Praying together with your family will create accountability for everyone in the family unit. It is difficult to hold a grudge with a person you are praying with regularly. Intimacy within the entire family will not occur without times of prayer with the family. The way you treat the members of your family will determine the way God treats your prayers.

For every Christian about every relationship you have in your life, you need to hear this: *the way you treat other people will determine the way God treats your prayers.*

Are things becoming clearer for you now? Are you understanding why you do not have intimacy in your family? Are you beginning to understand why you do not have intimacy with God? Are you seeing the value of making sure that all of your relationships operate in harmony and unity? Are you beginning to understand why many of your prayers go unanswered by the Lord? *The wall of strained relationships must come down before your prayers go up.*

Two Actions That Will Bring the Walls Down

If a wall is built up between you and God because of strained relationships, there are at least two actions you can take that will bring the wall down.

Action #1: The First Move Is Always Yours

If there is a strained or even broken relationship in your life, the first move is always yours. It does not matter who is at fault. It is never easy to make the first move. Periodically you may get into the "if only" game. You may say, "If only my wife would . . ." or "If only this guy in the church would . . ." or "If only my children would . . .".

These statements are senseless. It does not matter what anyone else does. What matters is what *you* are doing to bring the relationship into total purity and unity. Jesus does not want to do business with you until you have things right with other people. The first move is always yours.

There have been many times in relationships when I have sensed someone was being guarded with me. This usually comes because the person feels that I have offended him or her in some way. I used to wait for people to come to me, but that rarely happened. I decided to fulfill Scripture, so now when I sense this, I go to others, attempting to make sure all is well between us. This humble act of making the first move has proven to be effective, but has also become an example for them to follow.

Remember, the first move is always yours. You do as much as you can to make sure you are at peace with all people.

Action #2: Be a Bridge, Not a Barrier

Many Christians have become very discouraged through friendly fire. Some Christians are like guerrilla-warfare believers who blow up bridges with the intention of helping things but instead cause alienation. God is not in the business of alienating the world but reconciling the world unto Himself.

In your relationships with other people, be a bridge, not a barrier.[3] Do whatever it takes to build bridges with people. Try to keep things right with them. Go the extra mile so you can possibly experience unity with them. Your flesh may have to die in order to build a bridge with others. Periodically, your flesh may cause you to think you would rather blow up the bridge by walking away from the relationship and declaring that it is of no value. Do not do this unless you are 100 percent confident the relationship is toxic, even after you have tried to make peace in it. Remember this powerful challenge we must follow and try to live out with God's help: "If possible, as far as it depends on you, live at peace with everyone" (Romans 12:18 csb). It is on you to do all you can, but until God intervenes even after your attempts, it may not be possible at this time.

Regardless of how anyone responds to you in your life, always practice this: *never let anyone outside of your circle of love.* Always attempt to be a bridge builder with other people. This can serve as a way to win them to Christ or to win them over to walk in the ways of Christ.

> *Always attempt to be a bridge builder with other people. This can serve as a way to win them to Christ or to win them over to walk in the ways of Christ.*

This kind of humble spirit and these actions will bring down the walls between you and others, and the wall that may appear to be between you and God. Choose to make the first move. It is always your move! When possible, choose to build bridges with people. This is the way love can travel on the tracks of a relationship. It cannot travel apart from the tracks of a relationship. Do what you can to make each relationship successful.

A Major Sin in the Body of Christ

On a few occasions I have been asked, "Dr. Floyd, what do you see as the major sin in the body of Christ?" I believe that one of the major sins in the body of Christ is the sin of unforgiveness. It is amazing that the same people who have experienced God's amazing grace have the greatest struggle to forgive others when they are wronged. *Unforgiveness in your heart will quench the possibility for your prayers to be answered.*

In Jesus' Sermon on the Mount, He gave us the following instructions: "For if you forgive others their offenses, your heavenly Father will forgive you as well. But if you don't forgive others, your Father will not forgive your offenses" (Matthew 6:14–15 csb). Since Jesus readily forgives us when we repent, we should readily extend the grace of forgiveness toward others who may offend us. Since Jesus releases us from our offenses and sins against God and others, who are we to not release those who offend us? Doing so is imperative.

Therefore, it is important that you make the first move. Never let resentment or unforgiveness lodge in your heart for any length of time, or else you will hinder your prayer life and spiritual growth. It takes a committed person to build bridges with people. Anyone can blow them up!

The wall of strained relationships must come down before your prayers go up. Consider the following two statements as you deal with any strained relationships you have in your life:

1. Your vertical relationship with God will determine your horizontal relationships with people.
2. Your horizontal relationships with people will determine your vertical relationship with God.

The two relationships go hand in hand. Your relationships with people will be affected by your relationship with God. You do not treat people the right way when your relationship with God is not going well. In the same way, your relationships with other people will affect your relationship with God. If things are not going well with others, then do not expect to do any serious praying business with God. *Remember, the way you treat others will determine how God treats your prayers.*

What is God saying to you through this chapter? I hope you will meditate upon this chapter, and as you do, evalute your relationships thoroughly. This is one of the most pivotal walls that must come down if God is going to hear and answer your prayers.

Do whatever it takes to make things right with other people. Take actions now toward reconciliation. Not tomorrow, but today. *Do whatever it takes to make things right with God.* It is urgent to do business with God. He is waiting on you to do business with Him. *Whatever the cost, be right with God and with others so that your prayers will be answered.*

CHAPTER 13

THE WALL OF
IMPROPER MOTIVES

O ne of the great joys of my life has been serving as a pastor of a local church. I have seen many changes occur in my decades of pastoral ministry. Within the last five years, the changes have been rapid and frightening.

When I first began pastoring, people had a great love for the local church. The church was the source of strength for people. The church had great respect in the community. The pastor of the church was usually a highly respected leader in the community. People gave time to serve the Lord through their local church. The church was driven to help those who were truly in need, especially those who did not know Christ in a personal way.

Now, years later, the landscape of the local church has greatly changed. The church may be just one of many spiritual stops for a believer to gain strength. Few churches in our society today are respected by the community. It is highly unusual for the community even to know the pastor of a local church, much less respect him for the calling of God in his life. People give little time, if any, to serve the Lord through their local church. Today, the church is usually driven to meet the needs of its own members rather than the needs of unbelievers.

I believe one of the most distinct changes during my years of pastoral ministry has to do with the motives of people. No one truly knows the motives of another person. Yet, it is very obvious that, in a general way, the vast majority of Christians have experienced a major realignment of their motives. It is very rare to see Christians in today's culture motivated to serve others before they have their own needs met.

The church culture of today reflects the consumer-driven mentality of America. The number one priority of most church members is, "What are you doing to meet my needs?" Their goal is not to serve the Lord through serving others but to have their needs met by others. If a Christian does not have his or her needs met in a church, then he or she will just move on to greener pastures.

It is like the old service-station concept. Christians pull into the church. They sit in their car. They are waited on in every way. Then they drive away, only to return when they need help again. If the service does not meet their expectations, they change service stations.

This is the secular church in our day. Many Christians come to worship at a church out of personal need rather than personal conviction. Their goal is to have their needs met. The thought of others rarely enters their minds. If the church they have attended for years ceases to meet their needs, then they change the place where they receive service. The end result of this entire episode is that most Christians believe that the church exists solely for the purpose of meeting their personal needs.

The way Christians relate to the church today illustrates one of the most distinct hindrances to prayer. I am convinced that there are some walls that must come down before your prayers go up. One of the great barriers to prayer is the wall of improper motives. When you go to God in prayer with improper motives, your prayers will not be productive.

What is happening in today's church mirrors what is happening in the hearts of Christians. This "serve me" mentality is reflected in the way people pray. Their view of God is very limited. They see Him as a spiritual Santa Claus who exists only to meet their needs. The problem with that view of God is that people will tend to give up on God, just like they give up on their local church if their needs are not met according to their expectations.

Let me get something straight right now: God is sovereign. He is the supreme rank and rule in the entire universe. He has absolutely no need for us because He is God. God is holy. He cannot look upon sin. God is omnipotent. He can do anything at anytime and can do it anywhere He chooses. God is omnipresent. God is everywhere. God is omniscient. He knows everything about us, including our motives.

It would be helpful for you to think upon the omniscience of God. You cannot hide anything from Him. Remember, He knows everything about you, including your motives. You cannot pretend to pray in an unselfish way when your heart is filled with improper motives because God looks upon your heart. He is not impressed with the words you say to Him when your heart is not right. The bottom line is that you cannot play games with God. He is all. He has all. He knows all. What a God!

Is There a Word from the Lord about Improper Motives?

A motive expresses the reality of what is in your heart and who you really are in life. A motive shares why you do what you do in your life. No line of cosmetics can cover up the truth of why you do what you do in your life.

The American culture is extremely performance based. Our culture tends to judge just about everything on the basis of what is done and how it is done. Look at what happens on social media today. Opinions are shared about everything. Skepticism abounds. Cynicism roars. On the subject of performance-based leadership, we know that if the numbers are not there in regard to expected production, then you are regarded as a loser. If you do not have more wins than losses, people start to question your ability. These things, however, are not always a proper measurement of value.

God's primary concern is not *What have you done for Me lately?* The key question in the mind of God is, *Why do you do what you do for Me?* One day you will be judged not only for what you have done in your Christian life, but for why you have done what you have done. The *why* will usually determine the *what*. You need to be much more focused on why you do something than on what you have chosen to do.

The bottom line is that you cannot play games with God. He is all. He has all. He knows all. What a God!

Yes, there is a word from the Lord about improper motives. James 4:3 says, "You ask and do not receive, because you ask with wrong motives, so that you may spend it on your pleasures." The Bible says that the prayers of these believers were unanswered because their motives were improper.

When these Christians bowed to pray, they did not have the right heart. They never dealt with the critical question of, "Why am I praying for this?" They were probably so involved in expressing their requests to God that they never slowed down long enough to let Him talk to them about the condition of their hearts and the spirit of the requests.

The Bible calls these selfish motives evil. When you pray selfishly, you are praying in an evil manner. When you lift up yourself in prayer, you are praying in an evil manner.

The purpose of prayer is never getting your way or having your needs met. The purpose of prayer is always seeking God's will. One of the reasons you are commanded to pray is to get in on what God is doing around you. If you spend all your time asking God to meet your needs, then you will miss the real issue of prayer. You will see prayer as a frustrating spiritual exercise when God does not answer.

The problem in the lives of the Christians in James 4:3 is that they were asking for things with the wrong motives. God does not mind your making personal requests in prayer. After all, He wants to meet your needs. But He doesn't like for you to make your requests for the purpose of selfish gain. God is not pleased when your prayers are spent on your own pleasures.

Prayer is to be a holy time of communication with God. Prayer is a very special time with God. It is an act of true worship. All of your desires and pleasures need to be laid aside. Remember, praying is about God's will being done, not your will.

Some translations of James 4:3 use the word "pleasures," and others translate the word as "lusts." A great explanation of this text is as follows:

> Lust is anything for which we have a strong desire. James chose the word *hedone* in Greek for this idea. You don't have to be a rocket scientist to see a close English derivative: *hedonism,* the belief that pleasure or happiness is the sole goal of life. . . . Praying for God to give you something for no purpose other than your hedonistic pleasure is a sure way to have your prayers fall on deaf ears.[1]

This is a sobering commentary.

American culture is committed to the god of hedonism. At times, the church even commits adultery with this god. When you understand James 4:3, you begin to realize how far off base we are in our prayers. We have squandered many of our prayers on a belief system that says pleasure or happiness is the sole goal of life. This is hedonism, not biblical Christianity.

Hedonism declares that the goal of your life should be making sure your own pleasures are met, with the ultimate outcome being your own personal happiness. Christianity declares that the goal of your life is bringing glory to God by pleasing Him in everything you do. Many times this has nothing to do with your needs being met or your pleasures being experienced.

When you pray for selfish motives in your heart so that your life can be more filled with pleasure or happiness, you have missed God's heart for prayer. When you choose to spend your prayers on your own pleasures, then you are disregarding God's will.

America is a country that is consumed with self-gratification. This hedonistic mentality has invaded the church of Jesus Christ. Christians have been so deceived by Satan that they have adopted the philosophy and practice of hedonism and brought it into the church. This is why the main agenda of most Christians is their personal happiness, which they think is possible only when their needs are met. This is tragic, and it breaks the heart of God.

This wall in prayer is why the church is so powerless today. When Christians and their churches buy into this vain pagan philosophy, they exchange the truth for a lie. Since God knows everything, He is aware of the intents and the motives of each person. When God sees that a person's motives for prayer have been polluted by this unbiblical mentality, then He does not answer that person's prayer.

It is time to check your motives in prayer. One day in the future God will reveal all of your motives in life: "For God will bring every act to judgment, everything which is hidden, whether it is good or evil" (Ecclesiastes 12:14).

Jesus reaffirmed that everything you do will be made known: "But you, when you pray, go into your inner room, close your door and pray to your Father who is in secret, and your Father who sees what is done in secret will reward you" (Matthew 6:6).

This emphasis on your motives being revealed is affirmed again in Hebrews 4:13: "There is no creature hidden from His sight, but all things are open and laid bare to the eyes of Him with whom we have to do."

Nothing and no one in creation is hidden from God. One day everything and everyone will be laid bare before the Lord. *All will give an account to Him.* You will not one day stand before a jury of men concerning your motives; you will one day stand before God Himself. In this setting you will give an account of your life to Him. Juries of men make mistakes, but God never makes a mistake. You could hide your motives from a jury of men, but you will not be able to hide any motives from the all-knowing, holy God.

God always knows your motives when you pray. God always knows what you are up to in your life. When your motives are not right, then God will not answer your prayer. This wall of improper motives must come down before your prayers go up.

Does this mean that it is wrong to pray for your needs to be met? Absolutely not! It is only wrong when you pray with the improper motive that disregards the will of God in order to accomplish your own will. This sovereign and holy God is not your puppet who stands ready to respond to you when you choose to pray some cute prayer. The Father cannot be manipulated. Your will is not the issue. The will of the Father is always the highest concern in prayer.

> *You could hide your motives from a jury of men, but you will not be able to hide any motives from the all-knowing, holy God.*

There is a word from the Lord about having improper motives in prayer. The word about this subject is not gentle but firm. If we pray the way God wants us to pray, the walls will come down and our prayer lives will be effective. Productive praying will happen when you check your motives in prayer.

Three Questions to Ask Yourself in Order to Check Your Motives in Prayer

Since your goal is to be an effective prayer warrior, then you must make sure your motives are right. I want to give you three questions to ask yourself when you pray that will check your motives in prayer. The first question is . . .

1. Why Am I Asking God for This?

For the next several days, present your requests to God in prayer. Then ask, "Why am I asking God for this?" The heart of the issue in prayer is not *what* you are asking for as much as it is *why* you are asking.

Are you asking God for something in prayer so that your will can be accomplished in the situation? Are you asking God for something in prayer so that your needs will be met? Are you asking God for something in prayer because you think you will be happier if you receive it? Could it be that you are asking God for something in prayer because you know if He answers that prayer you will receive all the glory for it?

I guarantee you that the issue of why you are asking God for something in prayer will be one of the biggest struggles you will face in your prayer life. Regardless of whether you are a veteran in prayer or a rookie in prayer, the challenge before you will always be "why."

This question of "Why am I asking God for this?" cuts to the quick. If you ask yourself this question when you pray, you will be more likely to have pure motives in prayer. The ultimate result will be that your prayers will be answered.

2. Am I Willing to Lay Aside My Will so That God's Will Can Be Done?

This question has the power to show you how much of a problem your prayer life may be experiencing today. When you ask yourself this question, you may discover how some of your views of God have blurred; therefore, your prayer life may not be as effective as needed. In addition, you may discover some things about yourself that you do not want to talk about with anyone except God.

The next time you are really baring your heart to God in prayer about something, stop for a moment and give yourself a motive check. After you ask, "Why am I praying this prayer?" go another step and ask, "Am I willing to lay aside my will so that God's will can be done?" Jesus was clear that prayer should always be not my will but God's will being done. Personally, I am very pleased that God does not let my will determine my prayers. If He did, my life would probably be in chaos, heading for destruction.

Your goal in prayer should not be for the Lord to meet your needs so that you can have a better life. Your goal in prayer should be, *God, I only want it done if it will please You.* Sometimes God may give you what you want, then you wake up and realize it really was not important at all. Are you willing to set aside your agenda in prayer and exchange it for God's agenda for your life?

There are times in your prayer life when you need to set aside your plan for prayer. You need to get on your knees before God, with your Bible open, and tell God you want to pray according to His will about everything. Lean on Him to help you pray in the Spirit as you were taught to do in chapter 6. Do you know what will happen when you do this? God will dictate the next few minutes of your prayer life, rather than it being dictated by you and your selfish desires. The end result is that you will pray according to His will and your prayers will be productive.

God makes His will known to you through His Word. God energizes His Word. He does not energize your words. This is why you must be willing to lay aside your will so that God's will may be done. I can assure you that, even as a veteran of prayer, I still struggle in this area. As much as I want God's will in my life and do not want to live away from His will in prayer, I still struggle with laying aside my own will.

Personally, I am very pleased that God does not let my will determine my prayers. If He did, my life would probably be in chaos, heading for destruction.

Sometimes it is just hard to discern your own will from God's will. Hopefully, most of the time they are one. In prayer they had better be one, or else your prayers will go unanswered.

3. Is My Main Concern That God Will Get the Glory for It?

Is your concern in prayer that you get this prayer answered because you really need it answered, or is it because you want God to get the glory for answering it? God is a waymaker when you get desperate enough that you want Him to get the glory for what is done. God does not respond with great favor to proud, self-sufficient, and pleasure-driven Christians; He does give favor when people come to Him with a pure heart and pure motives.

Your heart should be that if your request pleases the Father, then you want God to do it. After all, if it does not please the Father, why in the world would you want God to do it? You see, God wants the glory for your life. He will not share His glory with anyone. The number one competitor to the glory of God is your glory.

The number one goal in your prayers must be that God would receive the glory for the requests you make and for the answers He provides. Your heart needs to be like this: *Lord, if it will bring You glory to do what I have asked You, then I pray that You will do it. If the request does not bring You glory, then, Lord, please disregard it.*

When you have completed your prayer requests the next time you pray, conclude your prayer time with the following prayer:

Lord, with the requests I have made of You today, only give me what brings glory to You. I have laid all of this stuff before You. I need You to get involved in these matters and for You to operate in my life. You know at times I am selfish and proud. At times, I do not even know the difference between what is right and what is wrong. Therefore, protect me from myself so that You alone would receive glory. Give to me today only what will bring You glory, God.

This is an important prayer. If you will bare your heart to God like that, He will be your waymaker. He will take away all the walls of prayer so that perfect peace will be set upon your heart in all things.

When you pray in this manner, your desires will become the desires of God. As the psalmist said, "Delight yourself in the LORD; and He will give you the desires of your heart" (Psalm 37:4). One of the ways you can delight in the Lord is to delight in His will for your life. When this occurs, the result will be that your desire will become God's desire for your life. At this point, God will energize your will to become His will. This is what brings God glory.

Ask yourself these three questions when you pray and you will develop motives that are pure. The result will be answered prayer that brings God great glory!

A Final Word

I want to close this chapter by presenting to you a passage of Scripture:

According to the grace of God which was given to me, like a wise master builder I laid a foundation, and another is building on it. But each man must be careful how he builds on it. For no man can lay a foundation other than the one which is laid, which is Jesus Christ. Now if any man builds on the foundation with gold, silver, precious stones, wood, hay, straw, each man's work will become evident; for the day will show it because it is to be revealed with fire, and the fire itself will test the quality of each man's work. If any man's work which he has built on it remains, he will receive a reward. If any man's work is burned up, he will suffer loss; but he himself will be saved, yet so as through fire. (1 Corinthians 3:10–15)

This is a passage about the judgment seat of Jesus Christ, when all Christians will stand before the Lord and answer to God for their lives. This judgment is not to determine eternal salvation; as a Christian, all your sins were once and for all judged at the cross and wiped away forever. The judgment seat of Christ will determine the amount of rewards in heaven that each Christian will receive.

Everything that you have done in your Christian life will be judged by fire. Every work you have built for the Lord will be judged. This time of judgment will judge the quality of your work for the Lord while you are here on earth. What does this mean?

This means that what you have done for the Lord and why you have done what you have done for the Lord will be judged. *Please understand that why you have done what you have done will have as much value as what you have done for the Lord.* Rewards will be given in heaven not for what you do but for what you do with the right motive.

The wall of improper motives must come down before your prayers go up. Check your motives. Just as an experienced airline pilot goes through his detailed checklist before takeoff, you need to go through the three questions on the checklist I have given you in this chapter each time you pray. Even though the pilot is experienced in flying, he does not negate the need to go through the checklist prior to his departure. Likewise, even though you may have years of experience in prayer, you need to check your motives daily. God energizes your prayers when you pray with a heart overflowing with pure motives. The ultimate result of such purehearted praying is answered prayer.

CHAPTER 14

THE WALL OF AN
UNREPENTANT HEART

Many years ago, home architecture created the wave of building shotgun houses. This simple structure acquired its name because you could open the front door of the house and see all the way through the house, peering even through the back door. If you took a shotgun and shot at the front door, nothing would stand in the way as the blast traveled all the way through the back door of the house.

Some of the houses built many years ago had a similar design. When you walked into the front door you would walk through the hallway toward the back of the house, seeing numerous doors off of the hallway, opening into several rooms, such as a kitchen, living room, bedrooms, and a bathroom. The doors to these rooms would all be open—except one door. If you happened to be a guest in that house, you might be tempted to open the one door that was shut. But if you placed your hand on that door to open it, the owner of the house would say, "Do not dare go into that room. That is my junk room." Each room of the house would be clean except for the junk room. Therefore, this room was off-limits to all guests.

Is your heart in the same condition as what is described in these shotgun houses? Perhaps most of the rooms of your heart are clean and presentable, but is there a junk room in your heart? Are you afraid to let anyone enter that room and see its condition? Most likely, you would be embarrassed for others to know what is inside the junk room in your heart. That room may contain some passions, desires, vain imaginations, speculations, and secret sins that you have lived with so long that you are not sure you are willing to live without.

Just as keeping the door closed to the junk room of the house does not eliminate the junk, not dealing with the junk in your heart does not eliminate it either. This chapter is about the secret sins of your life— the kind of sins you would be ashamed of if others knew about them. These secret sins in your heart are like bricks that are used to build a wall—a wall that keeps your prayer life from being effective. This wall built by the secret sins of your heart must come down for your prayers to go up.

The Bible teaches that sin should never be cherished in the life of those who follow God. Psalm 66:18 says, "If I regard wickedness in my heart, the Lord will not hear." The word "regard" in this verse can also be translated as "cherish." So it could read, "If I *cherish* wickedness in my heart . . .". This is the Hebrew word *rasah*, which means "to approve of, to enjoy, and to show respect for something."

I really like what Woodrow Kroll wrote about this:

> If we are enjoying sin and praying to God at the same time, we are showing more respect to sin than to God. God is under no obligation to listen to prayers that come from disrespectful hearts. If we approve of something we know is wrong and attempt to talk with God at the same time, we might as well save our breath.[1]

This is a strong word based on the Word of God.

The Scriptures say that if you cherish or approve of sin in your life, the Lord will not answer your prayers in a manner you desire. I mentioned in chapter 12 that I once tried to pray for God's anointing on my ministry while I was holding on to the sin of an unrepentant heart toward my wife. At first, I didn't want to apologize to her for the brief disagreement we had on the way to church. Because of my unrepentant heart, God did not hear my prayer. I knew I needed to repent or God would not anoint me with His Holy Spirit as I preached that day. It was not until I confessed my unforgiveness to God and then truly repented to Jeana that God prepared us for ministry that day.

Is there something in your heart that you really love but know it is not right? Is there something in your junk room that you know needs to be thrown out of your life, but at this time you have simply not dealt with the problem? This sin may be something that is private. It may be something that you do not want others to know. According to the Scriptures, God will not hear the prayer of a Christian who is willingly holding on to sin in his or her life.

This chapter is about the secret sins of your life—the kind of sins you would be ashamed of if others knew about them.

When you choose to hang on to your sin, your heart is unrepentant. The word *repent* means to have a change of mind about your sin. Therefore, if you are unrepentant, you have not changed your mind about your sin. Instead, you accommodate your sin. You cherish your sin. You are hospitable to the sin in your heart. The result is that your unrepentant heart becomes a wall between you and God.

The Connection Principle

I believe there is a principle that is aligned with the teaching of Psalm 66:18. I am calling this principle the connection principle. Stated simply: **prayer that is acceptable to God must be connected with a purpose to forsake all sin.** Prayer connects you to God and gives you the joy of talking to God. You connect with God for the purpose of keeping your life on the right path. But if you truly desire to be on the right path in your life, you must forsake all sin.

If you are going to connect with God, you must forsake all sin in your life. This divine connection does not permit evil to interrupt the connection. *It is important to remember that God is very concerned about your attitude toward your sin.* For you to pray without forsaking sin in your heart is like attempting spiritual exercise without getting any results.

Repentance involves abandoning sin in your heart when you pray. *Repentance is forsaking all sin, including the secret sins, for the purpose of connecting with God and communicating with Him.* Do you want God to speak to you when you pray? Do you want God to empower you when you pray? These things will only happen as you forsake all sin by connecting with God.

Secret sin has a way of settling into your heart. Would you be embarrassed if all the rooms of your heart were exposed to everyone? Let me remind you that God knows the content of every room in your heart. What is the secret sin of your life?

- Is there any degree of pornography in your life? Perhaps pornography began to invade your life as a child. Through the years, a stronghold of sensuality and sexuality has turned into a fatal attraction in your life.
- Is there any level of unforgiveness in your life? Perhaps you hold a grudge toward someone that has now lodged itself deep into the junk room of your life. You know that you should not live with this, but you are having a hard time letting it go because it gratifies you to resent the person.
- Are you stealing from God with the resources God has entrusted to you? God has asked you to honor Him by giving at least the first tenth of all your resources to the Lord through your local

church. Your greed and personal drive for satisfaction have kept this from occurring regularly, as the Bible states it should.

- Are you struggling with lusts in your life? Your workplace may serve as a field for lusting after persons of the opposite sex. Perhaps a few might be reading this book who struggle with lusting after a person of the same gender. Yet a desire to cherish sin will result in your prayers not going up to God.

If your prayers are going to be acceptable to God, then you need to forsake all sin in your life.

Would you let the Holy Spirit clean out the junk room of your heart? He will ensure that you no longer tolerate these sins. In addition to allowing the Holy Spirit to be involved in your life, submit yourself to another person who can make you accountable for what has been piled up in your heart's junk room. This person must be willing to speak the truth to you in love.

You see, the connection principle teaches you that the secret sins of your life must be forsaken for your prayers to be acceptable to God. You can pray, shout, clap your hands, raise your hands, witness, sing, and even preach. But if you do any of these things while cherishing sin in your heart, God will neither hear your prayers nor accept your worship. *The wall of an unrepentant heart must come down before God will answer your prayers.*

Is your heart unrepentant?

Four Symptoms of an Unrepentant Heart

There are certain physical symptoms that may tell you when you have heart trouble. These symptoms are not the main problem, though you may initially think so. These symptoms reveal that you have a problem with your heart. A proper medical diagnosis will determine what needs to be done in order for your heart problem to be solved.

Just as this is true for the human heart in relation to physical health, it is also true for the spiritual heart in relationship to your spiritual condition. I want to share with you four symptoms that indicate that you may have a problem with an unrepentant heart.

Symptom #1: Keeps On Sinning

When your heart is unrepentant, you just keep on sinning. You continue to give in to your sinful nature and desires. Your life is ruled more by sin than by righteousness. You have a passion to fulfill the sinful desires of your flesh, not a serious desire to neglect them. As a result, you just keep on sinning.

For example, consider a man who claims to be a Christian but has a real problem with extreme lusts. In spite of the fact that his lusts have resulted in several adulterous relationships, he attends church on a weekly basis. His involvement in small group has turned into an opportunity to pursue other women. When confronted, he always denies his sinful behavior. Yet he continues committing adultery.

This man's problem is that his heart is unrepentant. He just keeps on sinning. If he never repents from his sin, he is probably lost spiritually. If he knows Christ, he will be under severe judgment in his life. The sad commentary on this man's life is that he has never gotten over this problem.

Lusts and adultery are not his problems; they are merely the symptoms of his problem. His problem is that he has an unrepentant heart. This is evidenced because he keeps on sinning.

Do you keep on sinning in your life? If so, you have an unrepentant heart. God wants you to repent. He wants you to forsake sin, not embrace it. A person with an unrepentant heart keeps on sinning.

Symptom #2: Ignores God's Convicting Spirit About the Sin

Every true follower of Jesus Christ is indwelt by the Holy Spirit of God. He is there to assist and empower you, but He is also there to convict you of sin in your life. Therefore, whenever you sin, the Holy Spirit will show you that you have sinned and convict you that you have done wrong.

If your heart is unrepentant, then you will choose to ignore the conviction of God's Spirit in your life when you sin. This unrepentant heart chooses to take life into its own hands. It is a dangerous place to be in life.

My wife, Jeana, has the gift of mercy. I remember one time when she decided to take up an offense for me and confronted a person about something. This needed to be done, but she was not the person to do it. After the confrontation, the Lord kept her up all night. When I awakened that morning, she was under major conviction from God for this action, which I interpreted as being a minor issue. As soon as she could call that person that morning to make things right through repentance, she did so.

Do you keep on sinning in your life? If so, you have an unrepentant heart. God wants you to repent.

You see, Jeana had a repentant heart. I commend her for her extreme sensitivity to the Holy Spirit. She responded to His conviction as every Christian should respond to the Holy Spirit. She recognized her sin. She dealt with her sin. She repented of her sin. She made restitution for her sin. This story has always been a great model to me of how each Christian should respond to the Holy Spirit when He convicts us of our sin. Jeana's response in this situation was an example of a repentant heart.

Do you have a repentant heart? An unrepentant heart ignores God's convicting Spirit toward sin. When God convicts you of sin in your life, repent of it. Do not ignore the Holy Spirit's conviction.

A person who has an unrepentant heart continues to sin and ignores God's Spirit when He convicts him or her of sin he or she has committed.

Symptom #3: Turns into a Hard Heart

You enter a danger zone in your spiritual life when you let your heart become unrepentant. *Repentance does not end at salvation; repentance begins at salvation.*

When you ignore the conviction of the Holy Spirit toward the sin in your life, you will develop a hard heart. When your heart becomes hard, your personality changes. Your countenance changes. Everything about you changes. You do not see things the way you need to see them. Your life becomes somewhat blurred.

Remember this: *once you reject the Holy Spirit's conviction upon your life, it will become easier to say no to Him again.* Why? Because your heart is being hardened. *Saying no to God's conviction in your life is dangerous.* Once your heart is hardened, sinning will become more of a way of life for you.

An unrepentant heart keeps on sinning, ignores God's convicting Spirit about the sin, turns into a hard heart, and . . .

Symptom #4: Is More Interested in Learning How to Manage Sin Effectively Than Learning How to Overcome Sin Victoriously

For many years, I have had the opportunity to meet many Christians from many theological persuasions. I have also preached in several different settings. In these travels I have been able to learn so much. Along with these opportunities and others, I have discerned something disturbing that is taking place in Christianity—that is this symptom of an unrepentant heart.

Most of the Christians I have met seem to be more interested in learning how to manage their sin effectively than they are in learning how to overcome their sin victoriously. Most Christians just want to make sure they do not get caught in their sin. They want to make sure that they can enjoy their sin and not have to pay too heavy a price for it. Therefore, their goal is to manage their sin, not to overcome it.

This symptom is dangerous and deceitful. I want to warn you not to let your spiritual life get that twisted. Do not become deceived. Your goal as a growing Christian should be to overcome your sin, not just manage it more effectively.

Remember that an unrepentant heart will keep your prayers from being answered. I know you want to have a repentant heart. Therefore it is time to . . .

Clean the Junk from Your Heart

Can you pray in the Spirit if you cherish sin? Can you pray in faith if you cherish sin? Can you pray with passion, fire, and conviction if you cherish sin? Can you do serious warfare praying and cherish sin? The answer to these questions is the same: no!

If you cherish sin, your spiritual life will eventually become dull and heavy. The things that used to bother you will no longer bother you because your heart will have hardened. This hard heart will grease the slide for Satan to take you deeper into sin. When you cherish sin, you stop expecting God to work in your life.

Would you take some time right now and look into the junk room of your life? Do not keep it off-limits from the Holy Spirit. Do not let things pile up to such a point that you do not even know what is in there. Deal with the secret sins of your life. Now is the time to clean the junk out of your heart.

In just a moment would you take the time to investigate seriously what is in that private room of your heart? Would you let the Lord show you what is in there that does not please Him? Would you

Would you take some time right now and look into the junk room of your life? Do not keep it off-limits from the Holy Spirit.

respond to His Spirit when He shows you that there are some things that you have held on to for years that do not need to be in your life? It is time to clean out the junk.

During these next few moments, take the time to evaluate what might be in the junk room of your heart. This inventory calls you into being honest with God and with yourself.

Evaluate your junk room with the following scriptures and questions:

1. In everything give thanks; for this is the will of God in Christ Jesus for you (1 Thessalonians 5:18 NKJV).

Do you worry about anything? Have you forgotten to thank God for all things, the seemingly bad as well as the good? Do you neglect to give Him thanks for your breath, your health, and for life itself?

2. Now to Him who is able to do exceedingly abundantly above all that we ask or think, according to the power that works in us (Ephesians 3:20 NKJV).

Do you shy away from attempting to do things in the name of your heavenly Father because you fear you are not talented enough? Do feelings of inferiority keep you from your desire to serve God? When you do accomplish something of merit, do you choose to give the glory to yourself rather than to God?

3. You shall receive power when the Holy Spirit has come upon you; and you shall be witnesses to Me in Jerusalem, and in all Judea and Samaria, and to the end of the earth (Acts 1:8 NKJV).

Have you been hesitant to thank God for the miracles He has performed in your life? Have you been satisfied to live your Christianity in a casual manner and to think that it's not all that important to share the good news of your deliverance with others?

4. I say . . . to everyone who is among you, not to think of himself more highly than he ought to think (Romans 12:3 NKJV).

Are you overly proud of your accomplishments, your talents, or your family? Do you have difficulty putting the concerns of others first? Do you have a rebellious spirit at the thought that God may want to change you and rearrange your thinking?

5. *Let all bitterness, wrath, anger, clamor, and evil speaking be put away from you, with all malice (Ephesians 4:31 NKJV).*

Do you complain, find fault, or argue? Do you nurse and delight in a critical spirit? Do you carry a grudge against believers of another group, denomination, or theological persuasion because they don't see the truth as you see it? Do you speak unkindly about people when they are not present? Do you find that you're often angry with yourself? With others? With God?

6. *Do you not know that your body is the temple of the Holy Spirit who is in you, whom you have from God, and you are not your own? (1 Corinthians 6:19 NKJV).*

Are you careless with your body? Do you defile your body with unholy sexual acts?

7. *Let no corrupt word proceed out of your mouth (Ephesians 4:29 NKJV).*

Do you use language that fails to edify others or tell off-color jokes or stories that demean another person's race, habits, or culture? Do you condone these comments when guests are in your home or when your colleagues share them with you at work?

8. *Do not . . . give place to the devil (Ephesians 4:26–27 NKJV).*

Do you close your eyes to the possibility that you may be a landing strip for Satan by opening your mind to him through ungodly practices, psychic predictions, occult literature, and violent or sex-driven movies and videos? Do you seek counsel for daily living from horoscopes, on television, or on the internet rather than from God, your true and ultimate source for living? Do you let Satan use you to set up barriers that inhibit the cause of Christ in your church and in your home through criticism and gossip?

9. Not slothful in business (Romans 12:11 KJV).

Are you chronically late in paying your debts, sometimes choosing not to pay them at all? Do you charge more on your credit cards than you can honestly afford to pay? Do you neglect to keep honest income tax records? Do you engage in shady business deals?

10. Beloved . . . abstain from fleshly lusts which war against the soul (1 Peter 2:11 NKJV).

Are you guilty of a lustful eye toward the opposite sex? Do you fill your mind with sexually oriented television programs, lewd movies, or unsavory books and magazines? Their covers? Centerfolds? Especially when you sense no one is watching? Do you indulge in lustful activities that God's Word condemns, such as fornication, adultery, or perversion?

11. Bearing with one another, and forgiving one another, if anyone has a complaint against another; even as Christ forgave you, so you also must do (Colossians 3:13 NKJV).

Have you failed to forgive those who may have said or done something to hurt you? Have you written off certain people as not worthy of your friendship?

12. You also outwardly appear righteous to men, but inside you are full of hypocrisy and lawlessness (Matthew 23:28 NKJV).

Do you know in your heart that you are often not what people see? Are you hiding behind being active in your church as a cover for your activities away from the body of Christ? Are you mimicking the Christian faith for social status or acceptance in your church or your community? Are you real?

13. Finally, brethren, whatever things are true, whatever things are noble, whatever things are just, whatever things are pure, whatever things are lovely, whatever things are of good report, if there is any virtue and if there is anything praiseworthy—meditate on these things (Philippians 4:8 NKJV).

Do you enjoy listening to conversation that hurts others? Do you pass it on? Do you believe rumors or partial truths, especially about an enemy or a competitor? Do you choose to spend little or no time each day allowing God to speak to you through His Word?[2]

I want to challenge you to implement this chapter immediately. Find a quiet place right now. Get on your knees if you are physically able. If not, just make sure you settle in however you can with a humble posture and let the Holy Spirit do spiritual surgery on your heart. Ask the Holy Spirit to evaluate your heart as you go through this inventory point by point. Let the Lord use this spiritual inventory to clean the junk out of your life. The result will be that God will remove the wall that keeps your prayers from going up to Him. *The wall of an unrepentant heart must be abolished in order for your prayers to go up.*

PRAYING FOR OTHERS

CHAPTER 15

HOW TO PRAY
FOR THE SICK

A decade ago, Pastor Matt Chandler was diagnosed with brain cancer and given a short time to live. With his wife, younger children, and growing church walking with him through this journey, prevailing in prayer as well as receiving great medical attention, Pastor Matt is still alive today. He is a noted author and a gifted leader, preaching God's Word to thousands of people weekly.

Back in 2009 when Chandler was diagnosed, he stated in an interview that when he was meeting with doctors in those initial days, he felt like he was being punched in the soul. He said when it felt like things were spinning out of control, his theology and the Holy Spirit were there to remind him of the following: "'He is good and He does good'—to remind me that God has a plan for His glory and my joy that He is working. I was reminded that this cancer wasn't punitive but somehow redemptive."

Pastor Matt had to come to the holy place of realizing that God was not punishing him, but was going to use this disease to bring Himself glory.[1]

I remember during our own experience of Jeana fighting cancer, one day a godly saint called and wanted to speak to both of us.

His name was Manley Beasley Sr., and he had an ongoing bout with several diseases in his own life. For years and years he was diagnosed again and again with a hopeless death sentence. In 1971, he was diagnosed with seven diseases, three of which were deemed to be terminal. He lived by God's grace to the glory of God until God called him home to heaven in 1990.

Jeana was a young mom of two boys at the time. Josh was nine and Nick was six. Jeana and I were walking through a very fearful time in our lives. When we got on the phone that day with Manley, after words of encouragement and prayer were extended, he told Jeana the following: "Jeana, this is not about living or dying; but about what will bring God the most glory." At that time and in that moment, neither of us wanted to hear those words. She wanted to live to raise her boys, which was also my desire.

But we needed to hear those words from this man of God. We had to come to a clear reality that this sickness had far more to do with God's glory than whether Jeana would live or die. Thankfully, through the course of surgery, radiation, aggressive chemotherapy treatments, as well as years of follow-up medical attention, God has blessed Jeana with health and wellness.

Whether someone gets as sick as Pastor Matt or Jeana with the serious disease of cancer or whether they have never dealt with serious illness, there is not one person in this world who knows all there is to know about why anyone gets sick. Certainly you have probably wondered before, "Why do Christians get sick?" I can assure you there are people in hospitals, emergency rooms, hospice centers, recovery units, rehabilitation centers, oncology clinics, homes, and churches today wondering questions like:

- "Why do I have this disease?"
- "Why me?"
- "What did I do wrong?"

- "Where do I go from here?"
- "Will God heal me?"

Each of these questions is legitimate, but please know that ultimately, only God knows how to answer them.

Why Christians Get Sick

I want to mention four reasons I believe Christians get sick.

1. Our Imperfect World

After Adam and Eve disobeyed God in the garden of Eden, sinning against Him, God cursed Satan for eternity. I believe God crushed Satan's head through the cross of Jesus Christ and Satan is sentenced to eternal hell forever. Additionally, God told Adam and Eve that their sin would cost them—they would one day die and return to the dust. Their choice to sin was a choice to die.

Romans 8 affirms that since all of creation has been corrupted by sin, the whole world has been groaning and aching due to this sin. Yes, in this imperfect world, we will suffer, we will get sick, and we will die. We can improve the quality of our days while on this earth through practicing principles of health and wellness, but we must also understand the reality that God has our days numbered. Unless the Lord comes back in our generation, we will each suffer death.

2. Poor Choices

Kings and paupers alike make poor choices. For example, King Uzziah made a choice as recorded in 2 Chronicles 26 that led to his own destruction. He decided he would take on the role of a priest. He disregarded the counsel of others and as a result developed a skin disease that led him to live the rest of his days alone. His sickness followed a poor, sinful choice.

King Nebuchadnezzar was filled with arrogance and pride. He ignored the warnings. God struck him with a mental breakdown, resulting in him acting and living like a cow. Until he repented, he remained sick.

Even the apostle Paul warned the Christians in Corinth to examine their lives before they took the Lord's Supper or, as some refer to it, Communion. He said if they took of it unworthily, disregarding sin in their lives, they would bring judgment on themselves. He even stated these words of warning in 1 Corinthians 11:30: "This is why many are sick and ill among you, and many have fallen asleep" (CSB).

Poor choices can lead to sickness and even death.

3. Satanic Attack

As we've seen throughout this book, the Bible is clear that we have an enemy, Satan, who is bent on our destruction. And there are times when he is allowed to attack specific people—even people who have been saved through the blood of Jesus, shed on the cross. For example, remember how Satan appealed to God to let him loose on Job, telling God that Job would be unfaithful to Him. Job refused to curse God and did live faithful to God.

It is also recorded in Acts 10 how God anointed Jesus with the Holy Spirit and power, "healing all who were oppressed by the devil, for God was with Him" (v. 38). Satan uses his tools of sickness, suffering, abuse, addiction, and more to turn people from God and the power of Jesus Christ.

This word for "healing" is the Greek word *iaomai*, which means Jesus healed them instantaneously and supernaturally. It is important to remember this because Jesus does have the ability, power, and anointing to heal all diseases and sicknesses instantly and supernaturally.

Jesus' reversal of the sin and satanic curse through His death on the cross for the sins of the world gives us spiritual authority over all the attacks of Satan on our lives.

4. To Demonstrate God's Glory

One day Jesus noticed a man who had been blind since birth. His disciples asked Jesus whose sin it was that caused this man's blindness. Jesus absolutely stunned them with his answer. He stated in John 9:3, "Neither this man nor his parents sinned. . . . This came about so that God's works might be displayed in him" (CSB).

What did Jesus do next? He spat on the ground, made some mud, and then put it on the man's eyes. He told the man to go wash in the pool of Siloam. The man did and came back to Jesus, healed miraculously. God used the healing of this blind man to show His glory and power to the world.

For all Christ-followers, whether God chooses to heal us on this side of heaven or in heaven itself, God can bring glory through sickness in our lives.

Christians do get sick, and each of us gets sick for all kinds of reasons. Thankfully, when we are sick, we do not walk alone.

God Alone Is Our Healer

I believe that doctors, nurses, medical professionals, medical technology, and hospitals are tools in the hands of God. He created each of them to administer His will in the ministry of healing. Therefore, whether healing occurs instantaneously or therapeutically, God alone is our healer.

God declared these words in Exodus 15:26: "For I am the LORD who heals you" (CSB). Additionally, David declared about God in Psalm 103:3, "He forgives all your iniquity; he heals all your diseases" (CSB). The prophet Isaiah declared about the coming Messiah in Isaiah

53:4, "Yet he himself bore our sicknesses, and he carried our pains" (CSB). Therefore, whether our sickness is through disease, afflictions, addictions, abuses, depression, or other problems, it is Jesus alone who lifts them from us and carries them away.

Furthermore, Isaiah declared in Isaiah 53:5, "we are healed by his wounds" (CSB). Jesus died for all sins. As stated earlier, sickness entered the world due to sin. Since heaven will be where we are freed from sin forever and permanently, this is where we will be completely healthy and all sickness will be healed.

One of the words that describes healing in the Old Testament is the Hebrew word *Rapha* or *rophe*, which means "to heal, to make healthy, physician." This word meant so much to Jeana and me during her sickness and bout with cancer because we believe firmly that God alone is the One who makes us healthy. He is the God who heals.

Malachi 4:2 states, "But for you who fear my name, the sun of righteousness will rise with healing in its wings, and you will go out and playfully jump like calves from the stall" (CSB). This is a prophetic word about what will happen when the Messiah comes, the Sun of Righteousness! He will drive all darkness away, becoming the medicine that cures the darkness of disease, pulling people from their sickness, and giving them great energy to spring about physically like a calf released from the stall. This word for healing is the Hebrew word *marpe*, which means to "bring healing, a cure, to restore, and to bring health." This is such a strong, encouraging word.

The story from Acts 28 is one of great insights into the subject of healing. Publius's father was in bed suffering from fever and an infection in the intestines, resulting in severe diarrhea. In Acts 28:8–9, the Scripture states, "It happened that the father of Publius was lying in bed afflicted with recurrent fever and dysentery; and Paul went in to see him and after he had prayed, he laid his hands on him and healed him. After this had happened, the rest of the people on the island who had diseases were coming to him and getting cured."

Please notice two words in these verses: "healed" and "cured."

The word "healed" is the word *iaomai*, which means "to cure, to heal, or to make whole." It is the same word used in Acts 3 for the lame man who was healed instantaneously. Luke, who traveled with Paul, was a physician. He authored the book of Acts and recorded these stories. His use of the word *iaomai* indicated that God healed the people instantaneously, supernaturally, through God's power. Even in Luke's gospel account, this same word was used when Jesus stated He had come to heal the brokenhearted and hurting. In Luke 4, this kind of healing was instantaneous.

Now, this same Dr. Luke said that while some people were healed instantaneously, God healed other people over the course of time through medicine or therapy. In Acts 28:9, the word was "cured," which is the Greek word *therapeuo*, meaning "to serve, to do service, to care for, to treat, or to restore to health." This word indicates someone is ministering medicinal care of some kind, restoring people to health. Therefore, Luke, the physician, believed some were healed supernaturally and instantaneously, while others were healed medicinally or therapeutically, through ongoing care. Both were restored to health.

Ultimately, here is what must not be missed: *God alone is our healer! God can heal miraculously or medicinally or through a combination of the two.*

Do not underestimate what our God can do: God is our Healer. He can choose to heal instantaneously or through ongoing care. He can heal this side of heaven or He will heal all in heaven.

When Christians Get Sick

Paul could not heal whomever he wanted. Trophimus, who was Paul's partner in ministry, was left sick in Miletus. This is important to remember because people came from all around for Paul to heal them, yet according to 2 Timothy 4:20, he had to leave one of his partners in Miletus because he was sick.

That's an important insight: *Paul could only heal people according to the will of God; he could not heal whomever he wanted.*

Nor can we. We are all subject to God's will and purpose.

In a moment, I am going to lead us to understand some actions we need to take when Christians get sick. But before I do that, I want to take you into a final quick study on sickness and healing throughout God's Word.

Hezekiah

In Isaiah 38, when Hezekiah found out he was going to die, the first thing he did was pray. Remember what I said earlier: prayer needs to be your first choice, not your last choice! Prayer was Hezekiah's first choice. He knew God alone was able to heal him.

Isaiah told him his life would be extended for fifteen years. They were to take a lump of figs, which had a healing influence due to nutrients, and mix them with olive oil. They applied the mixture to the infected and inflamed areas on Hezekiah's body. Then Isaiah told him to go to the temple and worship God. In time, Hezekiah was healed.

Publius and Others

Remember what I stated earlier in this chapter? Publius's father was healed instantaneously and miraculously. Others were cured over the course of time therapeutically or medicinally. Both resulted in healing: while some were healed through treatment and over time, others were healed instantaneously and miraculously.

James and His Counsel

In James 5, James mentions there are all kinds of people who need to be prayed for relating to being healed. These are people who are:

- Suffering: not physical illness, but a burden one carries, such as depression, an emotional sickness, an addiction, or a problem
- Sick: weak, feeble, diseased, and needy physically

While each of these are unique, prayer and worship need to become part of where they are spiritually, emotionally, and physically as a part of seeking healing.

James counsels the people who are ill to call upon the elders of the church to pray for their healing. The elders are those who are more mature and advanced in the faith. We would say it this way: "Let the sick person call upon the pastors of our church to pray for them."

Here is a major insight that cannot be overlooked: the sick person takes the initiative here, not anyone else, including the elders of the church.

In our church, I interpret this literally and teach our people the value of them calling upon the elders of our church to pray over them. A friend or family member cannot make this request for them. It must be something they do personally. Then, the next movement is prayer. *Pray* is the main verb, and is absolutely primary. This word for *pray* and *prayer* means "to intercede, to make supplication on behalf of the sick person."

Therefore, after anointing the sick with olive oil, which was believed to have medicinal value in the ancient world, the elders were to pray over the sick person. In New Testament days, they would apply the olive oil on the place of pain or use it to massage the pain. Prayer coupled with the oil would strengthen and build faith. To be clear, this practice of anointing was and is secondary to prayer. Meaning, the power was in the prayer, not in the oil.

This prayer was to be offered in the powerful name of Jesus as the elders prayed with faith over the sick. This is not a reference to some magical prayer, but the emphasis is that prayer is an act of faith—the faith of the sick person to call upon the elders to pray with faith for

God to heal and restore him or her. The elders pray with faith, believing God will rescue the person from sickness, and the Lord will raise the person up and restore him or her to health.

If a sin has existed that may have brought on the sickness, then the call is to confess it to God and the elders, believing God will cancel out and forgive the sin. This is a strong call to prepare yourself to be prayed over for healing. Even confessing to one another and praying for one another is spiritual healing!

This is a fantastic truth for the church to implement: *spiritual healing should take priority over physical healing.* Never should the physical receive more attention than the spiritual.

Then we see another encouragement. When a person is right with God and prays with great intensity and urgency, the outcome is powerful in its operation. The elders or pastors of the church who pray over the sick should be godly spiritual leaders who pray with intensity and urgency, resulting in seeing a powerful God move extraordinarily.

Three Actions to Take When Christians Get Sick

Based on these truths, I believe there are three key actions that need to be taken whenever a member of God's kingdom becomes sick.

Action #1: Prioritize Prayer

From Hezekiah to Paul to the account in the book of James, it's clear from God's Word that prayer needs to carry the highest priority. Prayer is not inaction, but rather your greatest action. Prayer is to be your first and highest priority when you get sick.

The Bible declares loudly that prayer is the most significant factor in healing. When you get sick, will you ask people to pray for you? When you have a need now and it does not have to do with illness, do you ask for people to pray for you? Self-centeredness, independence, and human arrogance often prevent us from asking others to pray on our behalf. Prayerlessness indicates you are trusting in yourself.

Prayer is the most significant factor in healing. When you get sick, ask for others to pray for you, summon the church to pray for you, and ask the pastors of the church to pray over you for healing.

Action #2: Practice Faith

Again, all the biblical passages we have highlighted in this chapter teach us that we should prioritize prayer and practice faith when we get sick. Faith is acting on the Word of God. Remember the story when the paralyzed man was carried with faith by his friends, who even removed part of the roof to lower him down to Jesus? When this happened, the Scripture says something so clear and compelling in Mark 2:5: "Seeing their faith." When Jesus saw their faith, the man's sins were forgiven, he was healed, and this unprecedented move became powerful for all who watched.

The Bible declares loudly that prayer is the most significant factor in healing.

The hallways, classrooms, and worship centers of the churches across our nation and beyond need to be like those four men who carried the paralytic man to Jesus Christ, letting nothing stop them. They found a way and made a way to get this paralyzed man to Jesus. We each need to be like these four men: do all we can to carry people to Jesus when they get sick and have need for freedom, deliverance, restoration, and healing.

Action #3: Pursue Medical Care

When a Christian gets sick, this person should:

- Prioritize prayer
- Practice faith
- Pursue medical care

After Hezekiah prayed with faith, the figs and olive oil were placed upon his infection for healing. Paul and Luke administered treatments, cared for others, and restored people to health using medicine and treatment of some kind. James insisted that when Christians get sick, we should take several steps: pray, summon the elders of the church, be anointed with oil (symbolizing the value of medicine), doing all of this in the name of the Lord Jesus Christ who is our Healer!

Don't miss the spiritual principle here: *prayer is primary and medicine is secondary.*

Obviously, in emergency situations, prayer and pursuing medical care should happen simultaneously. But please understand this clearly: *Scripture does not minimize pursuing medical care; it maximizes praying with faith.*

This should call each of us into account. Neither a doctor nor a therapist is a god. Medicine is not a god. Jesus is the only ultimate Healer. People, medicine, technology, and hospitals are tools in Jesus' hands. *We must have the proper perspective so we will not try to elevate therapy above theology, medicine above prayer, and humans above God.*

Do not make the mistake of King Asa when he became ill. This king had many great years leading Judah, was commended continually by the Lord, and was given favor. But then King Asa went into a treaty with the king of Aram and ceased his dependence upon the Lord alone. From that point on, after thirty-five years of peace, King Asa experienced wars and began personally mistreating many people.

Here is what I do not want you to miss: King Asa did not finish as well as he started.

In his thirty-ninth year of leading Judah, he developed a foot disease, which became very severe. It's interesting that this man who had sought God throughout his life in public leadership for at least the first thirty-five years still got sick. It's also interesting that, as severe as the illness became, "Yet even in his disease he didn't seek the Lord but only the physicians" (2 Chronicles 16:12 csb). Two years later, he died.

Asa lost perspective when he got sick and only sought physicians, not the Lord. This is *not* the Lord's will for any of us. *Never elevate therapy above theology, medicine above prayer, and humans above God.*

Your life is a gift from God. He holds your life and future in His hands.

A Personal Word

My theology related to healing—what I believe God wants us to do as Christians when we get sick—is the very thing our family practiced when Jeana had cancer and when my son, Josh, was diagnosed six years ago with multiple sclerosis. This is exactly what we did and what I would encourage everyone to do:

- Know Jesus is the only Healer.
- Pray with faith.
- Summon the church and leaders of the church to enter the journey with you and for you.
- Pursue the best medicine possible.

Thankfully, we have seen the hand of God's power evident through both Jeana and Josh.

My final reminder for each of us is that we are not humanists, but Christians. We are not alone in sickness because we have the church. When we are praying with faith and receiving the best medical care possible, we are acting in the biblical combination necessary for healing. Both lead to the One and only Healer, Jesus Christ, the Son of the living God.

HOW TO PRAY FOR YOUR FAMILY

The greatest thing you can do for your family is to take up the role of praying for them daily.

I've committed this entire chapter to sharing some thoughts and ideas on how to pray for your family. As a parent or even as a young adult, you can leave a legacy of praying for your family daily.

I've been praying for my family since before I got married. I even prayed for Jeana before I ever met her or knew who she was. When I met Jeana and fell in love with her, I knew she was the woman God had for me. When we were married, my journey of praying for family took on a new meaning.

When our two boys came into our lives, it eventually led to two daughters-in-law entering our family. Then with the blessed addition of our seven grandchildren, let me be clear that prayer for my family is not optional. As a husband, father, and grandfather, it is my responsibility to pray with great intentionality and intensity for my family.

I have filled this book with verse after verse, biblical reference after biblical reference, hopefully leading you to know and act upon building your life on the value of prayer. With this biblical and personal conviction on prayer, I want to share specifically how you can pray for your family.

Before I enter this conversation, understand that I come to you not as an authority, but in humility. I promise you, we can each learn from one another. As I share my heart about ways you can pray for your family, I hope God will plant some seeds so deep into your life that you will see a great harvest in your family for generations to come.

With that in mind, I want to challenge you toward four ways you can pray for your family.

General Daily Needs

I believe there are some general needs that we need to pray for each day for the members of our immediate family. When I use the term *general*, I am referencing something each member of the family needs in prayer daily.

Spiritual Protection

I feel a deep sense of responsibility to pray for each member of our family in relationship to the spiritual and even physical protection of their lives. I will not repeat what I wrote about in chapter 10 on "How to Do Warfare Praying," but a great deal of space was given in that chapter to praying the armor of God on each member of my family. By name. Daily.

You can do the same.

I have also begun praying daily for the physical protection of our family in two additional ways. In the beginning of 2018, I began praying for each of my family members and their protection as they drive and ride all over the respective regions in which they live. The Bible says that God is our shield. It says these words in Psalm 28:7: "The LORD is my strength and my shield; my heart trusts in him, and I am helped" (CSB).

Therefore, I pray something like this to the Lord about the physical protection of our family members:

Dear Lord, I pray for Josh, Kate, Peyton, Parker, and Jack as they drive and ride all over the Birmingham region, as well as for Nick, Meredith, Reese, Beck, Norah, and Maya as they drive and ride all over the Northwest Arkansas region, and for Jeana and I as we do the same here; O God, You are our Shield! As we drive and ride today, be our shield behind us, in front of us, to the left of us and to the right of us, underneath us and even over the top of us. Surround us as our Shield and protect us.

Obviously, if any of us are flying that day, we always pray for safe and timely flights.

Shortly after I began praying like this, Josh, Kate, and their boys came to see us over their spring break. As they left the morning they were returning home, their vehicle hydroplaned on Interstate 49, just miles south of Fayetteville, where we live. When Kate called us, it gave us the scare of our lives. While their vehicle was completely totaled as they bounced against both guardrails on each side of the interstate in a horrible storm, they all walked away with only bumps and bruises. To this day, their lives have been altered by this experience.

On that day, while we were racing in a horrible rainstorm to the scene of the accident, I thought again and again how I had felt led to start praying for protection during travel just three months earlier. I am thankful that in this situation, God was the Shield for our family.

Another area of deep concern for us now, and another area in which I pray for daily for our family members, has to do with the security of the schools each of them attend or are connected to. In a recent trip to metro Birmingham, as I drove with three of my grandchildren past the school they attend, I asked God for their protection. We must pray for the security of our children and grandchildren in the schools of our nation.

Personal Walk with God

I try to be attentive to where I sense each member of our family is with God spiritually. Therefore, I pray for each of them based on where I sense they may be with God, always asking God to move them forward with Him. I have seen many of them come to Jesus already and increase their walk with Christ in both intentionality and intensity.

These pages would not provide enough space to record several decisions I have seen them make, some of which I had prayed for seriously. Thank God for answered prayer!

Future Opportunities

In my recent book *Living Fit*, I wrote an entire chapter called "Live Dreaming," which is based upon the prayer of a man named Jabez recorded in 1 Chronicles 4:10. In fact, I mentioned this prayer earlier in this book. I mention it again because I pray this daily for the members of our family.

Why? I do so because this prayer asks God to bless and intervene in their lives, to extend the borders of their influence in the future; it pleads with God for His hand to be upon them as they live, and for His protection to be upon them so they will not be harmed. This simple, clear, profound, and compelling prayer covers so much of what needs to happen in each of our lives. But it also covers what we can pray for our family daily.

I would challenge you to pray this prayer not just for your family, but also for your own life.

Specific Needs Individually

If one of the members of my family mentions something casually or even offers a serious request for me to pray about, I write it down and then pray for it daily. I will not share with you their specific needs, but I will tell you I have seen God answer prayer. Many prayers!

Yes, God does answer our prayers for our family members, prayers related to:

- Health and healing
- Salvation and walking with Christ
- Houses being sold and purchased
- Decisions related to career and future
- Godly friends given and provided
- Personal choices toward godliness

Pray for the specific needs of each of your family members.

Together Each Day

There are two practices relating to prayer that we have done with our family daily. When my children were growing up, we prayed with them daily. Quite honestly, I do not know if there was one day from kindergarten through their graduation from high school that we did not pray for them before they walked out of the house to go to school. Most days it was all of us, but if Jeana or I was unable, the other would carry on.

Parents, do not let your children leave home in the morning without praying over them. It does not have to be the longest prayer of your life. One to three minutes in length is sufficient. This prayer needs to be focused and to the point because it teaches them how to pray in their own lives.

At other times, at the dinner table or before the children go to bed, this can be another time to pray for them or to let them pray about various things. How will your children learn how to pray if you do not teach them? It is your responsibility to disciple your children in how to pray and how to walk with God. Again, if you do not, who will? Who should, other than you? You are their parent, their spiritual leader. Teach them how to pray.

Another practice relating to prayer is critical for the husband and wife. Jeana and I pray with each other every night before we go to sleep. It is usually nothing long, but it focuses on our evening of rest, our schedule before us the next day, our children and grandchildren, Jeana's mom, any major needs of friends or people within our church, as well as something in our nation we are facing or perhaps even some major national or international tragedy or need.

There have been times we have done this on our knees, but the vast majority of time we do this lying down in bed, holding hands, and I usually lead in this time of prayer while Jeana agrees with me in prayer.

How will your children learn how to pray if you do not teach them?

Listen, go, and grow forward together. Is there a "right way" to do it? I don't know, but what I do know is this: do what works for you, but just make sure what you do involves praying together as a couple and as a family.

Don't put pressure on each other about this, or even compare yourself to other families. You are not living in their family but in yours. Everyone has a different journey. Start your journey or continue forward in the one you are in, but prioritize prayer in your family. Do not require a tragedy or diagnosis to ignite you to prioritize prayer in your family.

Seasonally with Fasting

In my book *The Power of Prayer and Fasting*, I wrote about the seasons of prayer and fasting that will come into the life of a Christian and even for a church. Annually, I enter seasons of fasting. Annually, my church enters into seasons of fasting.

In these seasons, some of my major focus is matters on my heart about the members of our family. As my boys grew up, there were times I fasted for them a day each week over successive weeks, or even long-term seasons of fasting for them. I did the same for Jeana.

When Jeana was diagnosed with cancer in 1990, I fasted at least one day a week for over a year, asking God to heal my wife. God answers prayer given with a day or even a series of days joined with fasting.

Our family has seen miracle upon miracle, answered prayer upon prayer, because of our commitment to praying for seasons of our lives joined with fasting.

Find Your Way, but Pray!

I close this chapter with this personal challenge for you and your family. Find your way, but pray!

To be honest, I hesitated writing this chapter because I do not want to heap any guilt upon anyone or try to make you think that what our family has done should be done by everyone. Absolutely not!

Honestly, here is my appeal to you: *find your way, but pray!*

You can do something. You can do better than you are doing right now in praying for your family, just like I can do better than what I am doing in praying for my family. The key to your family's future together is to prioritize the importance of prayer in your family.

Do you remember the old adage that states: "The family that prays together stays together"? I remember it and I still believe it! I am sure there are a few exceptions where this has been violated, but I still believe in the power of praying as a family.

I cannot promise the fulfillment of that adage, but what I can promise you is this: *The family that prays together has a far greater chance of staying together over the long-term.* Yes, a far greater chance than any family that minimizes or even eliminates prayer together.

In your family, pray together and pray for one another.

CHAPTER 17

HOW TO PRAY FOR YOUR PASTOR AND CHURCH

Every church member has a pastor and a church.

Every pastor needs prayer.

Every church needs prayer.

Every Christ-follower should pray for his or her pastor and church. That's the conversation I want us to engage in throughout this chapter.

How to Pray for Your Pastor

Your pastor may appear as though he is so strong he does not need you to pray for him. But I can assure you that your God-called pastor knows he needs prayer—earnest, passionate, and effective prayer.

"Pray for me" should be the number one personal request from a pastor of the church he serves.

With that in mind, here are seven specific areas in which you should pray for your pastor.

1. Pray for Your Pastor to Love God with His All

Pastors are not exempt from fulfilling Deuteronomy 6:5, which says, "Love the LORD your God with all your heart and with all your soul and with all your might."

God wants your pastor to love Him above anyone and anything in his life. He wants your pastor to love Him more than his family, his church, and his calling.

God wants your pastor to love Him with all of his heart, with all of his soul, and with all of his strength. In other words, with everything he is and with everything he has, God wants your pastor's complete focus and his full person—to love Him with his full energy.

The competition for the heart of a pastor is fierce. Talk to God about your pastor and appeal to God to guard his heart, to let absolutely nothing compete with God in his heart. Pray for your pastor to love God with his all.

2. Pray for Your Pastor to Walk with God Daily

I really do believe that one of the greatest statements in the Bible is a testimonial about the man of God named Enoch. The Bible says in Genesis 5:24, "Enoch walked with God."

Your pastor will have everything in the world and everyone in the church drawing him away from his personal walk with God. You want your pastor to be a great preacher. But more importantly, you want your pastor to be a man who walks with God.

Therefore, pray for your pastor's personal walk with the Lord. Pray for his personal time in the Word daily to nourish him personally and his personal time in prayer daily to flourish his life fully. Your pastor will never be stronger than his own personal, daily walk with God.

3. Pray for Your Pastor's Marriage and Family

When I was a young pastor in Texas, the Lord surprised me by calling me to pastor a church in Arkansas. The greatest surprise is how the Lord has blessed my life and ministry in this phenomenal church. And I would be remiss not to mention how surprised I am that the Lord has left me here to pastor this church for over thirty years. However, those who are the most surprised are the people who are shocked I made it! I was *so* young and *so* helpless at times! Thank God they loved us through!

Last summer, Jeana and I realized one of our greatest benefits of being in this long-tenured pastorate. We conducted our thirty-first consecutive summer staff advance for our ministry team members and their spouses. This three-and-a-half-day investment is something we have done for thirty-one years in a row.

In my presentation this past summer, I made the following statement that sets the stage for how important it is that you pray for your pastor and his family: *God-called leaders will never rise above their marital relationship with their spouse, nor will they ever rise above the engagement of their spouse in their own local church ministry.*

That is why Jeana and I have spent these days each summer investing in our team of pastors and wives. That is why you must pray for your pastor and his family.

Specifically, pray for your pastor and his family about the following things:

- His wife and her walk with Christ
- His wife and their marriage
- Their children and their walk with God
- Their children and their love for the church
- The daily protection and security of their family

Listen, my friend: if I were sitting with you having a conversation, I would do all I could to impart to you the dire need for the pastor and his family to be prayed for by name daily. And when you do this, let your pastor and his family know in all kinds of ways that you are praying for them.

4. Pray for Your Pastor to Be Laser Focused on the Great Commission of Jesus Christ

Jesus was clear with each of us about our mission on this earth. Just before His ascension into heaven, He shared what the utmost assignment is for each of us. In fact, a pastor must lead his church in continually fulfilling this assignment. The Bible gives us the Great Commission of Jesus Christ in Matthew 28:19–20: "Go, therefore, and make disciples of all nations, baptizing them in the name of the Father and of the Son and of the Holy Spirit, teaching them to observe everything I have commanded you. And remember, I am with you always, to the end of the age" (CSB).

The pastor is to focus on leading the church into the main business of making disciples of all people groups in the region, in the country, and across the world. In other words, he is called by God to lead the church in reaching the world for Jesus Christ. This great advancement of the gospel leads toward going, baptizing, and teaching every new and present follower of Jesus Christ all that Jesus has commanded us to do.

Keeping this main thing the main thing is one of the most difficult tasks a pastor must accomplish. So pray for your pastor to keep his focus on leading his church to be a Great Commission church regionally, nationally, and internationally.

5. Pray for Your Pastor to Preach the Word with Power from on High

Your pastor is called to lead, feed, and intercede for your church. As he leads the church to fulfill the Great Commission, he must do so through his high calling to teach and proclaim the Word of God faithfully. Your pastor needs the mighty anointing of the Holy Spirit upon him when he stands before your church weekly.

Call upon the Lord with great intensity that your pastor will proclaim God's Word each Sunday in the power of the Holy Spirit and

His anointing upon him. As Elisha wanted a double portion of the Spirit of God, every pastor should desire for a double portion of the Holy Spirit to be upon him as he stands faithfully before God's people each week.

One of the final things I do each Sunday on my knees on my prayer altar in my back office at our Cross Church Springdale campus is take the Bible that is always open to 1 Corinthians 2:4–5, read it to God, and pray for Him to do this in and through me while I preach the Word. The passage reads, "My speech and my preaching were not with persuasive words of wisdom but with a demonstration of the Spirit's power, so that your faith might not be based on human wisdom but on God's power" (csb). This is what I plead with God passionately each week to happen in me.

I want the power of God and His anointing of the Holy Spirit to be upon me any time I preach the Word of God to the people of God. I will not settle to ever preach the Word and to lead the people of God without the power of God upon my life and ministry. I really believe even as I want God's power from on high upon me, your pastor desires the same. Pray him there!

Call upon the Lord with great intensity that your pastor will proclaim God's Word each Sunday in the power of the Holy Spirit and His anointing upon him.

6. Pray for Your Pastor's Decision Making

Earlier in the book, I elevated the powerful text of Colossians 1:9–12. It says:

> For this reason also, since the day we heard this, we haven't stopped praying for you. We are asking that you may be filled with the knowledge of his will in all wisdom and spiritual understanding, so that you may walk worthy of the Lord, fully pleasing to him:

bearing fruit in every good work and growing in the knowledge of God, being strengthened with all power, according to his glorious might, so that you may have great endurance and patience, joyfully giving thanks to the Father, who has enabled you to share in the saints' inheritance in the light. (CSB)

This is a tremendous text to pray for anyone, but especially for your pastor.

Most pastors do not lose their ministries because of moral failure, but they lose their ministries due to unwise decision making in their leadership.

That is why Colossians 1:9–12 needs to be prayed into the life and ministry of pastors. Since I have dealt with the text earlier in the book, I will keep my focus on these basic things. Pray for your pastor to:

- Be filled with the knowledge of God's will
- Be filled with all spiritual wisdom
- Be filled with spiritual understanding, which is the experience of seeing the facts and hearing information, but also be able to put these things together biblically, spiritually, and practically
- Be able to walk worthy of the Lord
- Be strengthened with God's power

I emphasized the specific need of spiritual understanding because this is the key for decision making. A pastor must be able to see what God sees biblically, but then make God's Word walk in every situation in a practical way through the power of God's Spirit leading him. Decision making is at the heart of leadership. Pray for your pastor and his decision making.

7. Pray for Your Pastor to Finish Well

Whether your pastor is in his twenties or in his seventies, he needs to finish well. Not only in the long-term of his ministry calling, but in his present God-assigned calling in your church. We need pastors to finish their present calling and their ultimate calling in a steadfast and immovable way, always excelling in the Lord's work, knowing that their work is not in vain.

These are the words found in 1 Corinthians 15:58: "Therefore, my dear brothers and sisters, be steadfast, immovable, always excelling in the Lord's work, because you know that your labor in the Lord is not in vain" (CEB).

Pray for your pastor to finish well.

How to Pray for Your Church

Most of this chapter has been given intentionally to challenging you to pray for your pastor. There are two reasons I have done this. First, as your pastor goes, so goes your church. Pray him through and you will take your church up in many great ways. Secondly, I have done this because, generally, people know how to pray for their churches more than they know how to pray for their pastors.

Yet, I am deeply convicted of the need for people to pray for their churches. That is why I have led massive movements of prayer for years in my church as well as around the country.

So, here are five specific ways to pray for your church.

1. Pray for Your Church to Experience a Spiritual Revival, the Manifest Presence of God

Psalm 85:6 asks this compelling question to God: "Will You not Yourself revive us again, that Your people may rejoice in You?" Experiencing spiritual revival is not an event, but being in the manifest presence of God. The manifest presence of God is the presence of the Lord revealed through ways you can see and feel—moments in which the culture of the room or the actions of people change in a Christ-honoring manner. As God's glory is revealed, the actions of God's people change. Everything changes.

A church in revival is a church that is living in a season of experiencing the special, powerful manifest presence of God. The hearts of people are being warmed and set on fire for God in a new way. The worship of God's people explodes as they experience seasons of prayer on their faces before God all the way to seasons of great joy before the Lord. Such a season of genuine revival among God's people always results in new lives entering God's kingdom through people coming to Christ.

Prayer always precedes great movements of God. Prayer always sustains great movements of God. Therefore, pray for your church to experience a genuine spiritual revival. Pray for your church to experience a season of the manifest presence of God. Pray for your church to never settle for doing church without the power of God. Plead with God and fast before God for your church to experience a mighty spiritual revival. We need God's manifest presence upon our lives!

We need to have the heart and desire of Moses, who did not want to go anywhere without the presence of God. The presence of God is the revealed glory of God. Feel the passion and look into the heart of Moses when he prayed these words in Exodus 33:18: "Please, let me see your glory" (csb). Moses pleaded with God to experience the glory of God, His manifest presence.

This is what we need! My church needs this revival! Your church needs this revival! The churches across America and the world need this revival!

For far too long the world has seen only what *we* can do. Now is the time the world needs to see what *God* can do through His church living in revival.

Would it not be so powerful if God would make our generation known in church history as the revival generation?

2. Pray for Your Church to Be a House of Prayer for the Nations

Jesus was very clear with His words as recorded in Mark 11:17: "Is it not written, *My house will be called a house of prayer for all nations?*" (CSB, emphasis in translation). He rebuked the people of His day for making God's house something completely opposite, but do not miss the question of Jesus to the people of God. Jesus was clear: *his house will be called a house of prayer for all nations.*

Is prayer happening in your church on Sunday mornings? Real prayer? Engaging, conversational, passionate prayer? The kind of prayer that is beyond a few churchy words or a group of empty phrases that are vacant of emotion before God?

Worship services today are filled with singing, teaching, talking, and promoting. Why are they not filled with prayer?

The schools in America are in desperate need to have prayer return to them. When prayer was taken out of the schools, it was one of the worst decisions ever made in the history of America. Christians and Christian leaders need to call for prayer to be unleashed in the schools of America!

But this is where we need to begin, and I would like to extend this challenge: *we need to bring prayer back into the church!* Jesus wants His church to be a house of prayer for the nations to experience His glory and redemptive power.

This is one reason our church has at least one Sunday a year when every worship service is turned into a prayer service. We also try to have focused times for prayer and opportunities to respond to God in prayer every Sunday.

When you lead your church to turn one Sunday a year into prayer services, follow these guidelines:

- Biblically based: Each prayer time needs to be based on a teaching time from God's Word, probably not longer than five minutes. We stand on His Word, not on our words or passions.

- Prayer-focused: Each prayer time should be focused on principles like repentance, revival, surrender to the lordship of Christ, the filling of the Holy Spirit, spiritual awakening, and reaching the world for Christ beginning in your own community.
- Spirit-led: Worship and prayer moments should be led as God's Spirit leads, not necessarily the order of worship.
- Worship-expressed: Hymns and worship songs are given to us to express our worship of Jesus Christ as our Lord. These can be powerful expressions as transition moments, moving from one prayer time to the next.

Just imagine what God would do in America if the three hundred thousand–plus churches turned one Sunday morning a year into worship services focused on prayer.

Perhaps the events of Acts 4:31 would occur again: "When they had prayed, the place where they had gathered together was shaken, and they were all filled with the Holy Spirit and began to speak the word of God with boldness."

Do it again, Lord!

3. Pray for Your Church to Be a Great Commission Church

Earlier, I appealed to you to pray for your pastor to be focused on fulfilling the Great Commission of our Lord as given in Matthew 28:19–20. This section is for you.

Now, you are ready to pray for your church to be a Great Commission church! Yes, each church should be focused on completing this commission by our Lord as directed to us before He left this earth. Acts 1:8 calls us to complete this commission regionally, nationally, and internationally.

Here at Cross Church, our missional vision is: *Reaching Northwest Arkansas, Southwest Missouri, America, and the world for Jesus Christ.* We are focused on completing this mission. This is our strategy.

Prayer is the power that mobilizes the church to this strategy of reaching the world for Christ.

Therefore, pray for your church to be a Great Commission church.

4. Pray for the Needs of Your Church

Every church has needs, and every church needs to call upon their people to pray for those needs. Here are a few examples of the needs people and families experience in our churches today—needs that we should pray for unashamedly:

- Pray for the sick.
- Pray for the grieved.
- Pray for those who are homebound and unable to attend worship services.
- Pray for special projects the church may be embracing, like building projects or purchasing properties.
- Pray for the needs of the ministry budget to be met and even surpassed.
- Pray for special ministry projects like student camp, vacation Bible school, mission trips, neighborhood block parties, and more.

Here is my point: whatever the church needs, call upon the church to pray for these needs.

5. Pray for the Pastoral Prayer to Return to Your Church

One of the great traditions of most churches was a time when the pastors would lead in what was deemed the pastoral prayer. Rushed worship services have replaced this holy time with more songs or boring announcements.

The pastoral prayer is when the pastor of the fellowship prays for the people in the room and for the time of worship they are experiencing. He can lead in prayer about anything on his heart, but the pastoral prayer is the pastor praying publicly before the people.

The pastoral prayer in worship needs to return. The pastors in America from all denominations need a time when they call out to God before their people for the needs of the people and the needs of America, rather than offering an empty prayer. We need to replace the predictable with the unpredictable, the power of man with the power of God.

Prayer will return to the church when pastors lead the way by returning to leading their church in a strong pastoral prayer during each worship service—a pastoral prayer that is clear, concrete, compelling, and compassionate, expressed by a passionate pastor who prays with great conviction in the power of God.

Final Word

Please know there are all kinds of ways you can pray for your pastor and your church. This is not a comprehensive study on either one. I do hope this chapter has launched within you a fresh desire to pray for your pastor and church, and even given you a few ways each of them can be done.

I am appealing to you in this chapter to become the kind of passionate Christ-follower who is committed to praying for your pastor and your church consistently. Will you respond to that call?

CHAPTER 18

HOW TO PRAY FOR AMERICA

America needs prayer today more than ever before. While we are facing many crises, our greatest crisis continues to be spiritual. In fact, our spiritual crisis is the foundational cause at most, if not all, of the other ongoing crises confronting our nation.

How do we pray for America? I hear this question frequently. In fact, with the ongoing divisiveness present in our nation, it seems to be asked continually.

With that in mind, here are some specific ways we can celebrate the liberty we have been given in America by choosing to intentionally and deliberately pray for our country.

Look What God Has Given Us

Do you realize the treasure the Lord afforded us back in the year 1952? This spiritual treasure was taken to a new and definitive level in 1988.

On Thursday, May 5, 1988, President Ronald Reagan signed into law an amended law that began in 1952 with President Harry Truman. Imagine this miracle: In 1988, both the United States House of Representatives and the United States Senate unanimously recommended to the president of the United States that the first Thursday in May each year would become the National Day of Prayer. This special day would be set aside to call upon all Americans to pray for their nation.

As the president of the National Day of Prayer Task Force that mobilizes unified public prayer for America, I stand amazed we live in a nation where our leaders felt so strongly about the importance of prayer for our country. Each year since 1988, the first Thursday in May has been designated the National Day of Prayer.

On that day every year, thousands upon thousands of prayer observances are held from sunrise in Maine to sunset in Hawaii, from small towns to state capitals to Washington, DC. Additionally, people stop their activities to pray for America in schools, businesses, churches, homes, county courthouses, and on the steps of city halls. The National Day of Prayer is even observed across most countries of the world. Millions participate in some way in the National Day of Prayer each year.

Some would pridefully boast that we should not need a day of prayer and a law to encourage us to pray. I agree, but I am so glad we have one! I would rather live in a nation with this day than a nation not afforded the opportunity.

Others would say arrogantly that we should not mix God into our public life as a country. I say that when God is the center of our lives, He is not compartmentalized away from the rest of our lives, but is integrated into each area of our lives—including life in America.

Let me ask you now to mark your personal, church, business, and denominational or church network calendar for the National Day of Prayer, always on the first Thursday of May every year. Our goal should be for every town, every city, and every county in America to have a prayer observance on the National Day of Prayer. Lead it. Help others lead it. Forward it. Advance it. America needs prayer!

The National Day of Prayer is becoming a multichurch,

multidenominational, multiministry, multigenerational, multiethnic, and multilingual movement of prayer for America. We need to infiltrate this entire nation with prayer.

To whom much is given, much is required. Therefore, this spiritual treasure of the National Day of Prayer in America needs to be celebrated and observed. *Mobilizing united public prayer for America may be the most important thing we can do for our nation.*

America is broken. Division is undeniable. Racial tension is alarming. Lawlessness abounds. Reconciliation appears impossible. The government cannot fix us. Politics will not heal us. America needs God now more than it has at any other time in our generation.

It is prayer that precedes and forwards the advancement of the gospel. It is prayer that precedes any great movement of God. It is prayer that will precede the revival of the church and the next Great Spiritual Awakening.

In this desperate and urgent time, when turmoil and division are evident in America and security threats are very real, it is imperative that we do all we can to mobilize unified public prayer for America. Will you answer the call?

Ten Ways to Pray for America

Just think what could happen if—once a month, or in a time of crisis or need in our nation—our churches prayed for our country in their Sunday worship service. This is not political, but biblical. Christians in every country should pray for their country and the leaders of their nation. Because I'm a citizen of the United States of America, I have tailored the following list for my specific nation.

Imagine what would happen if once a week or once each day you personally prayed for America. Our nation needs the prayer of every Christ-follower, including you. Pray for America!

Here are ten ways you can do just that in your personal prayer life each day.

1. Pray for America to Experience a Nationwide Great Spiritual Awakening, Resulting in Millions Coming to Faith in Christ Alone for Salvation

America has had some major movements of God in her history. The First Great Awakening occurred during the 1730s and 1740s in what was then the thirteen colonies of America. Jonathan Edwards and George Whitfield were the two men God used powerfully in that nationwide revival. The Second Great Awakening began in 1790 and went into the 1820s, having lasting effects into 1850. Charles Finney, Timothy Dwight, and many others had a major influence in this awakening.

In each of the great moves of God upon our nation, churches were revived by the Holy Spirit's presence, resulting in great spiritual vitality. But these awakenings were also known to be great movements of people coming to Jesus Christ as Savior and Lord, leading to even greater evangelism.

These Great Spiritual Awakenings have shaped our nation's spiritual heritage in the past. We need a fresh and new Great Spiritual Awakening that will shape America's spiritual future.

2. Pray for the Church in America to Wake Up and Be Revived

In the previous chapter, I shared the deep burden I feel to see churches in America experience a mighty spiritual revival, the manifest presence of God. The church in America as a whole needs to wake up and be revived spiritually. We need pastors and churches to lead the way toward the next great movement of God in America.

The churches of America need to rise up to agree clearly, unite visibly, and pray extraordinarily for the next Great Spiritual Awakening in America to occur in our generation.

3. Pray for the Leaders of Our Nation

Regardless of who the president or vice president, the speaker of the house, or the majority leader of the Senate may be, we need to pray for our nation's leaders. Regardless of the political party in power, they are subject to God's power and we need to pray for them. Praying for your president, governor, or mayor has nothing to do with their party of affiliation, but it does have everything to do with your personal responsibility as a Christian.

We need our leaders to be filled with wisdom. We need our leaders to be filled with the courage to lead our nation and continually protect our nation.

Whether we are praying for the executive branch, legislative branch, or judicial branch of our government, we need to pray seriously and consistently for these leaders in our nation. We are ultimately depending on God, but we are also depending on them to make the needed decisions that lead our nation to safety and blessing, flourishing in every segment of our country.

Generations in America can be influenced by the decisions of justices and judges in America. We need to boldly pray for God to raise up justices for our Supreme Court as well as judges at all levels of influence throughout our judicial system who believe in:

- Personal accountability to God
- Rule by the law, not by preference
- Administration of justice impartially and fairly
- Security of the dignity of every human life
- Protection of religious liberty given by God and additional liberties extended to Americans by our constitution

One of the great scriptures to pray for America is found in the Old Testament book of Micah. It says in Micah 6:8, "Mankind, he has told each of you what is good and what it is the LORD requires of you: to act justly, to love faithfulness, and to walk humbly with your God" (csb).

We need to pray for all of our leaders in the executive branch, legislative branch, and judicial branch to live and lead like Micah 6:8 instructs each of us to do.

4. Pray for America's Military

Thank God for the members of our nation's military. Whether they are serving in the homeland or overseas, they put their lives on the line daily to provide protection for our nation and others. They are a major center of influence in this nation, and we need to pray for them continually.

Additionally, we need to pray for their families as well. Their sacrifices are just as real, and just as worthy of God's blessing.

5. Pray for Our Media in America

The media in our nation often determines the tone and spirit for the debate in our democracy. We need to pray for the members of the media to lead, write, broadcast, and amplify news that is objective and truthful through their venues for communication.

6. Pray for Businesses in America

The businesses of America have one of the greatest platforms for influence in our nation. Pray for businesses to have leaders who operate with integrity so that these businesses can create economic blessings for families. As these businesses prosper, they can also become a source of light and blessing to the communities in which they are located.

7. Pray for Education in America

Education is a powerhouse of influence today and for the future of our nation. These centers of enormous influence may be private or public, from grade school to grad school, but we need to pray for them to be education centers that are truth-centered, excellence-driven, and opportunity-afforded.

This also reminds us to pray for the security of these centers of education—specifically for the protection and security of teachers, faculty, administration, and students.

8. Pray for Families in America

There is not a greater influence in American life than the family. It is in the family where we learn how to relate to God and one another. The family is the teacher of community.

While dysfunctional relationships can occur within families, we need to pray for families to function as godly units and operate according to the biblical model. The family is the first community where we need reconciliation to occur in broken relationships and the restoration of all to love and unity.

Families need prayer. The families of America will affect our nation's future in every way.

9. Pray for Unity in America

We are not the divided states of America, but we are one nation under God. America needs to live in unity.

A divided church cannot call a divided nation to unity. The church needs to live in unity together in Christ and His gospel so we can call our nation to live in unity. Ephesians 4:3 states, "Making every effort to keep the unity of the Spirit through the bond of peace" (csb). This is a daring call to unity. It means we need to take every action necessary to operate and live in unity, and it is why we need to pray.

Unity is supernatural; only God can give it. As the church operates in unity, the church can call the nation to come together in unity.

Pray for unity in America. Pray for God to empower us to make every effort to live in unity, call for unity, and forward unity in America continually.

Specifically, we need to pray for unity to occur in these areas in America:

- Unity in the churches of America
- Unity in the families of America
- Unity in the workplaces of America
- Unity in the communities of America
- Unity in the cities in America
- Unity among all ethnicities and people in America

One of the greatest needs for prayer in America is prayer for unity.

10. Pray for the Security of Our Nation, Schools, Churches, and All Public Venues

Our nation is in major need of security and protection. As a nation, we need to be a people who live in the shadow of the Almighty. The Bible states in Psalm 91:1, "The one who lives under the protection of the Most High dwells in the shadow of the Almighty" (CSB).

Daily, we need to ask God to protect our schools, our churches, and all public venues. We need to plead with God in prayer to restrain all evil and secure our nation from all external enemies. We need to ask God to move upon the president and cabinet, Congress, governors, state legislators, and local leaders to work together to secure our schools, our churches, and all public venues.

How Important Is Prayer to You?

Dependence on God is essential. When we pray, we are depending on God. When we do not pray, we are depending on ourselves.

Prayer is an act of faith because when you pray, you are declaring absolute dependence on God. When you pray, you are trusting in the Lord completely. Prayer builds faith in our lives. Prayer creates expectancy!

That is why we need to pray for America daily and consistently. Many times in our nation, we do not know what to do. But we can pray! When you pray any time, anywhere, about anything in our nation, you are taking action.

Impulse and impatience should not rule our response to what is happening in our nation. Prayer needs to be our first response!

For these reasons and more, pray for America. Pray like you believe in prayer. Pray for America like you believe it will make a difference.

Prayer *will* make a difference in America.

Prayer *will* influence the future of America.

Many times in our nation, we do not know what to do. But we can pray!

2018 National Prayer for America

Speaking of prayer being an influence, I wrote this prayer for the 2018 National Day of Prayer. It was used in thousands of gatherings, including the national observance of the National Day of Prayer in Washington, DC. This would be a great prayer to lead your church in praying for America.

Our dear heavenly Father, while we come to You in complete humility, we also come to You with boldness in the authoritative name of Your one and only Son, Jesus Christ, who is the Lamb of God who takes away the sin of the world. In Jesus' name, fill us now with Your Holy Spirit and lead us as we pray in Jesus' name for America.

Oh God, we are burdened for our nation today. We turn from the sins that we have committed against Your Word and

Your Name. We turn away from our contentious words and ways toward one another that have led us to division and polarization. We turn away from our disrespect and lack of dignity toward each other, and we turn away from our continual devaluation of all human life from the womb until death in this world. We also turn away from and refuse to participate in skepticism, criticism, and cynicism in our nation. We turn away from anything that divides us, and we run toward the gospel of Jesus Christ that is the only thing that has the power to unite us together.

Lord, in this critical hour in our nation, we pray for unity in America. Only You can bring unity, harmony, and oneness in America. As Your Word calls us in Ephesians 4:3, "Making every effort to keep the unity of the Spirit through the bond of peace" [CSB], we ask You to empower us to make every effort to live in unity, to call for unity, and to forward unity in America continually.

We pray for the churches in America to unify in Jesus Christ and to pray as one unified spiritual family for America. May Your church pray for America passionately, perpetually, privately, and publicly.

We pray for God's power to unify families, workplaces, communities, and cities in America. By Your Spirit, lead us to forgiveness, reconciliation, healing, and unity.

We pray for people of all ethnicities and races in America to come together as one, living in peace and unity together. Oh Lord, because each of us is created in Your image, please give us the courage to stand against all racial and ethnic division, denouncing it as evil and sinful, while simultaneously coming together in unity with all persons knowing this is God's will for us.

We pray in unity for the security of our nation. We ask You to preserve the United States of America from the forces of evil that are threatening our lives and our future. God, please guard all persons in public and private settings from anyone or anything that desires to harm us or take our lives. Our future is in Your hands.

We agree clearly, unite visibly, and pray extraordinarily for the next Great Spiritual Awakening in America. Oh Lord, wake up Your church spiritually and convict Your people to agree clearly, unite visibly, and pray extraordinarily until the next Great Spiritual Awakening occurs in our generation.

Oh God, we stand together upon Your words in Psalm 133:1, "How good and pleasant it is when brothers live together in harmony" [CSB]. Through Jesus' name and by the Holy Spirit's power, we pray for all Americans to unify and to live together in unity.

In the mighty and majestic name of Jesus Christ who is the Only Savior and the Only Hope in this world, we pray, amen.

CHAPTER 19

HOW PRAYER
INFLUENCES OTHERS

P rayer changes me. Prayer changes you. Prayer changes everything. Not one thing is prohibited from being influenced or changed when we pray. Whether we are praying for one another, for the sick, for your family, for your pastor and church, or even for America, prayer influences every person and every thing.

Prayer invokes the presence of God. And when the presence of God enters into anyone or any place, God's presence brings change.

What kind of influence does prayer have in your life? Is God using prayer to change you at all? When prayer changes you, then God will use you to influence other people in powerful ways.

That's what I've experienced personally. When God really began to deeply bring change into my life through prayer, He then began to use me in a greater way across the nation and the world. Additionally, my church began to be influenced dramatically.

When Jesus makes a difference in us, He will make a difference through us. The greater His impact is on us, the greater our impact will be upon others.

Remember what we learned earlier in this book: *effective prayer occurs when you talk to God and listen to what God is saying to you.* The main thing in your life is that you meet with God the first thing every day. When you pray, it demonstrates that you depend on God in your life. When you do not pray, it demonstrates that you are depending upon yourself. *God wants to use prayer to influence your life.*

When prayer is prominent in your life, you will be able to influence other people in a significant way. One of the biblical passages that shows the value of influencing others through prayer is found in Acts 16:25–34:

> But about midnight Paul and Silas were praying and singing hymns of praise to God, and the prisoners were listening to them; and suddenly there came a great earthquake, so that the foundations of the prison house were shaken; and immediately all the doors were opened and everyone's chains were unfastened. When the jailer awoke and saw the prison doors opened, he drew his sword and was about to kill himself, supposing that the prisoners had escaped. But Paul cried out with a loud voice, saying, "Do not harm yourself, for we are all here!" And he called for lights and rushed in, and trembling with fear he fell down before Paul and Silas, and after he brought them out, he said, "Sirs, what must I do to be saved?" They said, "Believe in the Lord Jesus, and you will be saved, you and your household." And they spoke the word of the Lord to him together with all who were in his house. And he took them that very hour of the night and washed their wounds, and immediately he was baptized, he and all his household. And he brought them into his house and set food before them, and rejoiced greatly, having believed in God with his whole household.

These two men of God in this passage are Paul and Silas. Before Paul's conversion, he killed Christians as an occupation. After his conversion to Christianity, Paul surrendered his life to fulfill God's calling to preach the gospel to the world.

Paul and Silas were ministering in the city of Philippi. On their way to pray, they had the joy of winning Lydia and her entire family to Jesus Christ. After leading Lydia to Christ, they came across a young girl who was controlled by Satan. They stood against this demonic spirit in Jesus' name, and through warfare praying, the girl was delivered. Again, while they were on their way to pray, God used them significantly.

Once Paul and Silas had cleansed this girl, the enemies of God became angry with them. The leaders of the city arrested them, stripped them, and beat them with a rod many times. Then they threw them into prison and placed them under tight security. They took them into an inner dungeon and fastened their feet into stocks connected to the walls of the prison. All of this happened while Paul and Silas were on their way to pray. God used them in a great way, but they paid a high price.

Paul and Silas were influential men because they were men of prayer. They modeled a deep commitment to prayer, even in the midst of experiencing persecution. These men influenced their environment everywhere they went, including even this jail.

The American culture needs to witness men, women, teenagers, and children who are people of great influence. Just as prayer made Paul and Silas influential, prayer will make you a person of great influence. Yes, the price is high, but the reward is great. Whether you are a corporate leader, manual laborer, university student, politician, lawyer, medical doctor, or stay-at-home mom, God wants you to be a person of great influence.

Your influence upon others will never be any greater than your prayer life. Anyone can follow the crowd. But you need to be willing to stand for God. Your stand for God is usually determined by the power of your prayer life. You can greatly influence the lives of other people through your prayers.

This is the reason why you need a plan of action in your prayer life. As I have said before, if you do not have a plan to pray, you usually will not pray. God wants to raise up millions of Christians to be great prayer intercessors and warriors who can influence others.

Let's pursue other ways in which prayer can be influential.

Prayer Influences People

Paul and Silas were beaten because they loved Christ. They were placed in stocks in the inner dungeon of the prison. The Bible says that they were under tight security. I am confident that Paul and Silas would have preferred not to have been in prison. Like most people, I am sure they preferred not to experience pain. Yet at midnight, Paul and Silas began to pray and sing praises to God. Others in the prison were influenced by Paul and Silas's ability to worship God even in dire circumstances—especially the jailer, who later came to Christ. In fact, not only did the jailer come to Christ, but his entire family also.

One of the greatest preachers ever to have lived was a man named Charles Haddon Spurgeon. When he pastored in London in the latter part of the 1800s, he would speak to crowds of ten thousand people. Spurgeon was a great man of prayer. His sermon on this passage about Paul and Silas was called "Songs of the Night." He said the praise and prayer of Paul and Silas were songs in the night that can only come from God, not from men.

This is so true. Nothing within Paul and Silas would have desired to be in prison, and certainly nothing in them would have desired to sing and to pray at midnight. They could have griped to God, *Lord, here we are trying to serve You, and look at us—we cannot even move. They are beating us and trying to kill us. If You loved us, You would not have us go through this persecution.* Yet Paul and Silas did not pray like that. Their prayers were from the divine energy within them, the Holy Spirit. As they prayed, the Spirit of God fell all over that prison. Their prayers influenced people.

How could they pray like that under such adverse circumstances? Paul and Silas were men who loved Jesus Christ more than they loved themselves. They experienced the transforming power of God in their lives. They knew what it was like to have once been spiritually lost but now found by the grace of God. They knew what it was like to have their sins forgiven and to experience the promise of heaven. They counted it as joy to suffer for Christ. This happened because they were men of prayer.

When people pray, God influences their lives. Even more, these men of prayer impacted the lives of others.

When you face adversity in your life, do you pray? How do you respond? Is prayer your first response or your last response when all else seems lost? When others ridicule you for your faith, do you pray? Prayer can make you stand strong for God. *The power of your stand will be determined by the power of your prayers.* Take prayer seriously and influence other people. God wants to use you for His maximum impact, so become a person who is committed to prayer. Prayer influences people!

Prayer Influences Circumstances

When Paul and Silas prayed, God began to move in their circumstances. We do not know what they were praying about, but we do know God moved when they prayed. The Bible says the prison was shaken by God. An earthquake shook the ground and opened the prison doors. In fact, even their chains were loosened by the power of God. The jailer awakened at these supernatural events and naturally assumed that the prisoners would leave. Since he knew that he would be killed if the prisoners left under his guard, the jailer began to take actions to take his own life. When Paul observed what the jailer was about to do, he shouted at him to stop because no one had left the prison.

It is important for you to remember that God is in charge of everything. He is in charge of all circumstances. Nothing happens in your life without a purpose. When you pray, you position yourself to see what God is doing in your midst. *When you pray, God will change you. He may even choose to change your circumstances.* He can move miraculously and providentially.

Is there anything too hard for God? Absolutely not! Prayer can change your marriage even if your marriage seems hopeless. Prayer can change what is occurring in your workplace even if your boss conducts himself wrongly. Prayer can change your child even if she is running away from God and living in rebellion toward you. Prayer can change the doctor's diagnosis even if it is terminal. Yes, God responds to someone who depends on Him through prayer. *God has the power to change your circumstances through prayer.*

> It is important for you to remember that God is in charge of everything. He is in charge of all circumstances. Nothing happens in your life without a purpose.

Have you ever looked back and wished you had changed some things in your life? Looking back, it is easy to have 20/20 vision. Yet only God can see with 20/20 vision when looking into the future. Prayer enables you to see what He sees in the midst of circumstances.

You are not hopeless. Your circumstances are not hopeless. God can change you and your circumstances through prayer.

Prayer Changes Eternity

In the midst of the prison turmoil, the jailer rushed into Paul and Silas's cell and asked them how he could be saved. Evidently their lives had been an outstanding testimony to him. Perhaps they had witnessed to him before he fell asleep. No doubt he had heard them praying and praising God in the midst of unjust torture. When he saw that Paul and Silas could have left the cell but chose not to do so, he was astonished by this commitment.

I believe the testimony of believers would be greatly enhanced if we would respond with a positive witness for Christ through difficult circumstances. Rather than whining, we need to testify of God's greatness even in the midst of trouble. *Effective praying will result in an effective witness.*

This lost jailer wanted to know the Jesus that Paul and Silas knew. Paul told him that if he wanted to be saved he would have to believe in the Lord Jesus Christ only for his salvation. Paul did not tell him to go to church. Paul did not tell him to live a good life. Paul did not tell him to go and be baptized. Paul told him one simple thing: *believe in the Lord Jesus Christ and you will be saved.*

In order to believe in Jesus Christ, you have to place your confidence and trust only in the Lord. You have to deny yourself by putting away your dependence upon yourself. Only Jesus has the power to forgive your sins. Only Jesus has the power to give you eternal life. You cannot save yourself. Only Jesus can save you from your sins and give you the gift of eternal life.

This jailer gave his life to Jesus Christ. God used him to win his family to Jesus Christ. All of them were baptized to symbolize the new life they received in Jesus Christ. The jailer's life and the lives of his family members were transformed by God's grace.

Prayer changed the eternity of these people. The prayers of Paul and Silas caught their attention. God's power fell upon them. Their trust in Jesus Christ and Him alone for their salvation saved the jailer and his family. Their calling upon God was life-changing and eternal.

If you have come to a point in your life where you are not certain about your eternal destiny, please know that prayer can change your eternity. If you would like to settle your eternal destiny right now, would you place your faith in Jesus Christ and Him alone for your salvation and call out to Him right now in prayer? Look at the prayer below. Talk to God right now and place your faith in Christ alone for your salvation. Mean these words you say to God. I believe God will respond to you and Jesus Christ will come into your life, take away your sin, and give you heaven when you die.

Pray these words right now:

Dear Lord Jesus, I know that I am a sinner. I know that I do wrong every day of my life. I believe that You died for my sins. I believe You died in my place. I believe that You were raised from the dead for me. I turn from my sins right now and turn to You. By faith right now, I place my faith in Jesus Christ and Him alone. I open the door of my heart and I ask You to come into my life right now. I commit my entire life to You. Save me now. Take away my sin. Give me heaven when I die. Oh God, thank You for saving me. Thank You, Jesus, for coming into my life right now. Thank You for taking away my sins. Thank You for giving me eternal life, amen.

Did you take the time to pray this prayer and place all of your faith and trust in Jesus Christ and Him alone for your salvation? Please do now if you have not!

When I was fifteen years old, Jesus Christ came into my life. I was in that small church that I told you about earlier. You see, in that small church, God did a big work in me initially, but He also began a great work that night and He is still working in me. He is still changing me to this day. Let Jesus come into your life right now.

Prayer changes people. Prayer changes circumstances. Prayer changes eternity. Prayer is very influential.

Just Do It!

No longer can you say, "I do not know how to pray." This book has taught you the basic principles about how to pray. Again, regardless of your level of prayer, if you are teachable, you have surely learned something that can add to your prayer life. No longer can you use the excuse that you just do not know what to do in a time with God. The appendix describes in detail how you can develop a personal prayer notebook that is easy to use every day.

Listen, just do it!

Don't make any more excuses in regard to prayer. Now is the time to do what you know you need to do.

A PERSONAL PRAYER
PLAN FOR YOUR LIFE

The most effective prayer plan is the one you will use.

If you do not plan to pray, you will fail to pray. The key is to have a plan to pray daily. You can do this, and I want to show you how.

I really hope that many people will read *How to Pray*. But if they only read it as an intellectual exercise or to simply check it off of their reading list, then they have not engaged the God I want them to have a personal, intimate relationship with each day. God is ready to meet with you anytime, anywhere, about anything.

As your prayer life goes, so goes your spiritual life. As your spiritual life goes, so goes the rest of your life. This is why it is incumbent upon each of us to develop a plan to pray.

Prayer is a spiritual journey. Just as a journey from your present location to the other side of the country requires that you have a plan to reach your destination, you need a plan to assist you in your spiritual journey of prayer. Prayer is your personal communication with God. Since connecting with God should be your goal daily, you need a plan to help you reach your spiritual destination more effectively and consistently.

I want to share a couple of plans you can use or build from to create your own plan to pray daily. A prayer plan is critical to praying effectively and consistently.

Since I became a Christian, I have had seasons in which I have followed a plan to pray on a consistent basis. Conversely, for whatever reason, there have been other times when I chose not to follow a particular plan for prayer. I have observed that the greatest times in my prayer life have been those in which I followed a specific plan of action for prayer. In these seasons I have been consistently and effectively in the presence of the Father.

You see, prayer is a journey. If I am going to reach my destination of communicating with God regularly, I need a plan that will help me get there. Most people do, probably even you.

You should not feel that you are following someone else's plan for prayer. You should not feel bound to rules, regulations, and expectations. The ideas I will give will present a structure upon which you can customize your own prayer plan. Customizing your own prayer plan will meet your spiritual needs and desires.

Four Reasons That You Need to Consider Using a Prayer Plan

There are four characteristics of having an effective prayer plan daily. These characteristics will create consistency as well as effectiveness in your prayer life. Make sure the prayer plan you use in your life is marked by these characteristics.

Simple

Keep the plan simple. Make it so simple you will know how to use it daily. It needs to be so simple you could teach someone else how to use it. Having a simple prayer plan will inspire you to pray consistently and help you pray effectively.

The simplicity of this plan makes it perfect for everyone. I do not like complex or complicated things. I like to keep things simple. I promise you that the two plans described in this chapter will be easy for you to use in your journey of prayer. I believe if you will use either of them for a number of weeks, your prayer life will never be the same.

Sequential

There needs to be a sense of order to any prayer plan. It is a plan that is so orderly that it just makes sense. It is a plan that anyone can follow.

Many of you may consider yourselves rookies in the ministry of prayer. This may be your first attempt to establish a plan of prayer. Many of you may consider yourselves veterans of prayer, but have never really developed a prayer plan. If you did, perhaps you got burned out on it! Whether you are a rookie or a seasoned veteran of prayer, I believe one of these plans or the ideas from them will inspire you to go forward. Why?

Simplicity combined with sequence produces relevance and productivity in prayer.

Specific

One of the reasons why one of these plans can become so dynamic in your life is that it will lead you to pray for others as well as your own life.

It can become easy to generalize your prayers. An effective prayer plan helps you to pray more specifically.

Spiritual

These plans incorporate the Bible, the Word of God. These plans encourage the dynamic of the Holy Spirit in the ministry of prayer. Any time the Word of God is used and the Holy Spirit is present, something very spiritual will take place.

Therefore, you need to consider using one of these plans or developing your own prayer plan. Always remember, these prayer plans are only tools, hopefully useful tools that will make a real difference in your life. The most effective prayer plan is the one you will use.

Option #1: Using an Electronic Device to Create Your Personal Prayer Plan

If you do not have a plan that helps you stay current, remain on task, and be specific, then I suggest you consider trying this one.

Right now, I am using an iPad and iPhone, which came with an app called Notes. I have turned my iPad into an intercessory prayer list through the Notes app. If you have an iPhone, it will sync with your iPad, providing you accessibility on either device. If you have an Android or other device, it has something similar, or you can even download an app that works for you. The brand of the product is not what is important—it is the functionality it provides.

There are three practical reasons why I use my iPad for prayer:

1. Simplicity: The Notes app is very simple to use. Access to my iPad and saving my prayer list on the Notes app is very simple. *Simplicity usually increases usability.*

2. Change: It is simple to change this kind of electronic prayer list. It is simple to adjust any part of the list or all of it.

3. Relevance: In the past, a challenge of using a prayer list in a notebook has been keeping it current and relevant. With the Notes app, I can easily keep my list current. I can add to my list upon hearing a need, wherever I happen to be at the time. A current, relevant prayer list increases the usability of such a list.

What Is on My Daily Prayer List?

I have used all kinds of prayer plans through the years. Nothing keeps me more focused, on task, and effective in prayer than a current, relevant prayer list.

As I stated earlier, for decades, I have begun each day with a personal time with God. God uses the mornings with me to transform my personal life through the Word and prayer because I am connecting with God daily. Because of this, I have grown spiritually over the years, and my desire is that the Holy Spirit will navigate me through this list each day as He so desires.

As with any plan for prayer, it always needs to be led and empowered by the Holy Spirit. My daily prayer list is lengthy; therefore, I will only share a few of the commitments I have in daily prayer. Each of the elements below has a separate category in my Notes app.

Personal preparation: Daily, I make myself available for God to prepare me to pray. I spend moments praising God, followed by moments thanking God for what He has done for me. I then move into a time of spiritual evaluation, confession of sin, and acknowledging His finished work on the cross for forgiveness of my sins. From this point, I approach God for protection, asking for His spiritual covering and armor upon my family and me. I call out the names of my family, asking God to put on His armor of protection upon each of us.

Filling and anointing of the Holy Spirit: I believe in the filling of the Holy Spirit daily and even in specific moments. While I do not understand fully the anointing of the Holy Spirit, I know I need God's anointing upon my life and in everything I do. I ask God to anoint me for preaching, teaching, leadership, decision making, vision, writing, relationships, and with His gladness.

Empowerment to walk in the authority of the Great Commission: I believe in the Great Commission and committing the rest of my life to do everything I can so that each person in the world is told about Jesus Christ. Therefore, I pray for God to give me the authority to personally fulfill it; pastorally, in leading my church; nationally, leading the National Day of Prayer Task Force; and globally, through writing, sending, speaking, and influencing others to reach the nations with the gospel of Jesus Christ.

Asking God for a mighty spiritual revival in my church and in America: I believe God wants to send a mighty revival upon His church and ignite a spiritual awakening in America. I plead with the Lord, asking Him to pour out His Spirit upon us powerfully.

Asking God's leadership upon the leaders of our nation: I believe in praying for the leaders in our nation. Daily, I call out the names of our president, vice president, our state's governor, senators, congressmen, and the mayors of the major cities in our region of Northwest Arkansas.

Asking God for wisdom and favor upon the leadership of our region: When the economy really turned sour years ago, I began to pray for forty to fifty leaders who help shape the financial future of our region, even our state, some in America, and a few globally. Therefore, I keep this list current, and for several years have prayed for some of the prominent leaders of Northwest Arkansas by name.

Asking God to provide healing and restoration upon people who are ill and those who have lost loved ones: Prayer is powerful, and we need to believe in God to heal people. Some need it physically, others emotionally or mentally; however, no one can bring healing like God. This list is current and keeps me accountable to pray for people with major needs. As soon as I hear about them, I place them on this list, with 90 percent of these people never knowing I am praying for them unless I tell them.

There is much more, but that's enough for now. There are many more things I work through in prayer daily. However, this gives you some ideas about how to transform your iPad or other device into an intercessory prayer list.

Option #2: Creating a Prayer Notebook

A second option is for you to design your own personal prayer notebook suited to your specific needs. I am going to give you three major steps in having a time with God daily, the second of which focuses on a prayer plan—one that you can easily customize to your life and desires, mostly to the Holy Spirit's leadership.

Step #1: Read God's Word

As I have stated in previous chapters, I believe it is important to listen to God speak to you daily through His Word. What He says to you in His Word will prepare you to talk to Him and will influence what you say to Him in prayer.

Before you begin to read God's Word, bow your head and be quiet for a few moments. After this brief time of meditation, pray the following prayer: *Lord, speak to me through Your Word now.*

Now take your time. Let God speak to you through His Word. You may write in your notebook the verses that are meaningful to you so that you can remember them throughout the day.

Always keep in mind that the Word of God and prayer go hand in hand. As you continue through the prayer outline, keep your Bible open near you.

Step #2: Pray Using Your Prayer Plan

The five talking principles of prayer I described in chapter 1 need to be followed each day after the reading of God's Word.

The first principle is Confession. It is important that you are prepared spiritually before you attempt to have a serious conversation with God. Effective prayer occurs when you talk to God and listen to what God is saying to you. Better communication will result when the lines of communication are clear.

Sin clogs the lines of communication between you and God. Therefore, you need to confess your sin and your helplessness to God. Confession and repentance are very important in the life of the growing Christian. Claim the promise of 1 John 1:9 as you confess your sins. Remember: God hears and answers your prayers when your heart yearns to be clean and right with Him.

The second principle of prayer is Praise. Praise is the expression of your love and adoration for who God is. In this time of praise, focus on three attributes of God's character. You may even take the time to pray through portions of the Scriptures that are filled with praise to God. Make this a rich time of worship between you and your Creator.

The third principle is Thanksgiving. This is the expression of gratefulness to God for all the things He has done for you. Spend some time offering your thanks to Him for all He has done for you. Thank Him for provisional, physical, and spiritual blessings. Thank Him for people who have blessed you. Take the time to say, *Thanks, God.*

The fourth principle is one that comes easily to most of us. It is Petition. At this time, focus your prayer on personal needs that you want to present to God. Do not pray for others yet; pray for the things you believe to be within God's will for your own life. Record your requests in the space provided in your notebook. As you use your personal prayer notebook, remember to record God's answers to the prayers you lift up to Him both for yourself and for others.

Always keep in mind that the Word of God and prayer go hand in hand. As you continue through the prayer outline, keep your Bible open near you.

The final principle of prayer is Intercession. Intercession is the privilege of standing in the gap between the God of heaven and the person you are praying for at the time. Concentrate on praying for the needs of others whom God brings to your mind. Write down each request as you bring it before the Lord. Consider praying for the needs of your family members, your friends, your pastor and his family, and your fellow church members. Remember: God is attracted to the *specific* prayers you pray for yourself and others.

Urgent Requests

During your prayer time, you will also want to list urgent requests that you will pray for every day. An urgent prayer request is so critical that it requires daily attention from you for a specific time or until the crisis has passed. When God places an urgent need in someone else's life upon your heart, commit yourself to pray for that person daily.

Focus-Day Requests

As you become familiar with the basic principles of this plan, you may choose to add an additional layer of intercession that involves focusing your prayer on a special area each day. You may customize your own plan or implement the following schedule:

1. *Sunday: Local Church.* Jesus loves the church. He gave His life for the church. He empowers the church with the Holy Spirit. He entrusts His mission to the church. He prays for the church. Since the church is so important to Jesus, it should be as important to you. Pray for the power of the Holy Spirit to be upon your local church. Pray for your church to be involved in reaching your region, your country, and the world for Jesus. Pray for God's protection to be upon your pastor, your pastor's family, and your local church family. Pray for the worship services and Bible studies that will take place at your church this week. Pray for the Spirit and burden of prayer to come upon your church. Pray for the lay leaders. As you pray, you will begin to see some of these very things take place. Give God the glory and witness to others about the power of prayer.

2. *Monday: Lost and Unchurched.* God wants people to experience life in His Son, Jesus Christ. His desire is not for anyone to perish, but for people across the world to repent of sin and receive Jesus Christ into their lives. On this day, pray for lost and unchurched people by name. Pray for God's direction about whom He wants you to pray for, and write their names and need for salvation in your notebook. Pray for an opportunity to share the gospel of Jesus Christ with these individuals. Pray for an opportunity to invite them

When God places an urgent need in someone else's life upon your heart, commit yourself to pray for that person daily.

to your local church. Also pray for the lost and unchurched people in your area. Ask to see what Jesus sees and to feel what Jesus feels. May the Lord move you to His compassion toward the lost.

3. *Tuesday: United States of America.* Our country is a nation that is in trouble spiritually and morally. Christians need to be committed to praying weekly for their nation. Pray for the gospel to be presented to each person in this country. Pray for spiritual revival and spiritual awakening to happen. Pray for various leaders in America, both nationally and locally (the president, congressmen, the governor of your state, the mayor of your city, your school board officials, and so forth). God will empower you as you pray, and He will give you great insight as you pray for your nation.

4. *Wednesday: Friends.* Jesus was a real friend to His disciples. He loved them and met their needs. Most important, He prayed for them. You can show your love for your friends by praying for them weekly. Pray for God to guide you as you pray for your friends. Ask Him to show you how to pray specifically for each one. Pray for God to show you how you can minister to these friends by meeting their needs.

5. *Thursday: Christian Leaders.* In recent years, the world has witnessed the moral failure of many Christian leaders. Perhaps much of this has occurred because these people were not covered in prayer by all of God's people. Prayer gives a covering of protection. Prayer gives an empowerment for daily living. Pray for the Lord to put the key Christian leaders on your heart whom He wants you to pray for each week. These may be authors, pastors, evangelists, or influential laypersons. Pray for their continued spiritual success and sphere of influence. Ask God to protect them from moral indiscretion and failure. Pray for their spiritual growth. Your prayers for these leaders

will enable them to remain spiritually strong, morally faithful, and totally protected from the missiles of Satan.

6. *Friday: World Missions and Missionaries.* While many of us are not called to full-time missionary work as a career, we are all called by Jesus Christ to make sure the gospel is heard throughout the world. The ministry of prayer can be your involvement in world missions. Pray for the gospel to be taken to the entire world. Many doors need to be opened by the Holy Spirit, and we need to pray for these doors to be opened. Pray that missionaries, evangelists, and pastors will effectively take the gospel throughout the world.

7. *Saturday: Relatives.* You need to have a legitimate concern for your relatives. You should pray for them, even though you may be separated by great distances or your past experience was negative with some of them. Ask for God's direction as to which relatives to pray for each Saturday. Ask Him to show you their needs so that you can pray for them specifically. If they are unbelievers, pray for their salvation. Pray for God to lead you in how you should minister to them through phone calls, notes, or personal visits. Always close this time of prayer by asking God, *Is there anything You want me to do to nurture any of these relationships?*

When you add focus-day requests to your times of intercession, you will have a healthy balance of prayer. This also will eliminate the selfish tendency to concentrate solely upon yourself, even in prayer.

One of the great features of this plan is what happens when it is followed. Not only will you experience quantum leaps in your prayer life, you will also develop a global perspective of the ministry of prayer. As you commit yourself to this personal plan for prayer, I believe that you will develop Jesus' heart for prayer, and your focus in praying for others will become very much like His.

This plan can be customized to fit your specific needs and desires because you write in your own daily prayer requests for yourself and for others. Be careful not to overload this section, because too many requests on your prayer list may overwhelm you and even squelch your desire to pray. But remember: prayer is work!

Step #3: Journal

I believe in the life-changing power of closing your time with God by writing a one-page letter to God. On this one page, you will be recapturing your main burdens as well as the joy of answered prayers. Journaling provides a means of concrete communication with God. It also provides a sense of relief from your burdens. As you document your walk with God in this way, your faith in the power of prayer will increase. Journaling can become one of the greatest dynamics in your prayer life.

Journaling provides a means of concrete communication with God. It also provides a sense of relief from your burdens.

This is a suggested plan intended to help you, not bind you. Feel free to customize it according to your desires. The Holy Spirit will work through this plan, granting you spiritual liberty as you communicate with God. In time, these steps will become natural for you. You can also exchange one step with another. Do not make the plan itself holy. What is holy is when you meet with God in a personal and intimate way every day of your life.

NOTES

Chapter 1: What Prayer Is All About

1. John F. MacArthur, *The Freedom and Power of Forgiveness* (Wheaton, IL: Crossway Books, 1998), 71.
2. Oswald Chambers, "The Key of the Greater Work," My Utmost for His Highest (website), October 17, 2018, https://utmost.org/the-key -of-the-greater-work/.

Chapter 2: Why Christians Do Not Pray

1. Ronnie Floyd, *Living Fit: Make Your Life Count by Pursuing a Healthy You* (Nashville, TN: B&H, 2018), 39.

Chapter 7: How to Call Upon the Lord

1. Jim Cymbala, *Fresh Wind, Fresh Fire* (Grand Rapids, MI: Zondervan, 1997), 71–72.
2. J. Paul Reno, *Daniel Nash: Prevailing Prince of Prayer* (Asheville, NC: Revival Literature, n.d.), 1–26.

Chapter 8: How to Pray It Through

1. Woodrow Kroll, *When God Doesn't Answer* (Grand Rapids, MI: Baker Books, 1997), 157.
2. Kroll, 157.
3. Kroll, 157.

Chapter 11: How to Empower Your Prayers

1. CDs or video links of the June 4, 1995, service and other services at Cross Church are available by calling our communications ministry at (479) 751-4523 or emailing your request to info@crosschurch.com.

2. For more information about fasting, see the author's book *The Power of Prayer and Fasting* (Nashville, TN: B&H, 1997).

Chapter 12: The Wall of Strained Relationships

1. Oscar Thompson, *Concentric Circles of Concern* (Nashville, TN: Broadman, 1981).
2. Warren W. Wiersbe, *Famous Unanswered Prayers* (Lincoln, NE: Back to the Bible, 1986), 11, 13.
3. Kroll, *When God Doesn't Answer*, 65.

Chapter 13: The Wall of Improper Motives

1. Kroll, *When God Doesn't Answer*, 102.

Chapter 14: The Wall of an Unrepentant Heart

1. Kroll, *When God Doesn't Answer*, 32.
2. Adapted from Floyd, *The Power of Prayer and Fasting*, 104–7.

Chapter 15: How to Pray for the Sick

1. Justin Taylor, "One Year Later: An Interview with Matt Chandler," The Gospel Coalition, November 1, 2010, https://www.thegospel coalition.org/blogs/justin-taylor/one-year-later-an-interview-with -matt-chandler/.

ABOUT THE AUTHOR

D R. RONNIE FLOYD, senior pastor of Cross Church located in Northwest Arkansas, is the author of twenty-three books. He is also the president of the National Day of Prayer Task Force, which mobilizes millions of Americans to pray for America annually, and a past president of the Southern Baptist Convention. Dr. Floyd's writing, speaking with messages broadcast live across the world via the Internet, and leadership have opened doors through major news media outlets. Dr. Floyd and his wife, Jeana, have two sons and seven grandchildren.